Accounting for Income Taxes

ANALYSIS AND COMMENTARY

Arthur Siegel, CPA

James O. Stepp, CPA

Robert P. Roche, CPA

Jacqueline M. Tomlin, CPA

PRICE WATERHOUSE

WARREN, GORHAM & LAMONT

Boston • New York

WG
&L

ISBN 0-7913-0115-X

Library of Congress Catalog Card No. 88-50677

PRINTED IN THE UNITED STATES OF AMERICA

Preface

The long-debated, long-awaited new Statement on accounting for income taxes has at last been issued. As is usually the case when the Financial Accounting Standards Board (FASB) releases a new pronouncement, some will like it, some will not—but all affected entities will have to accept it.

The effects of FASB Statement No. 96 will be pervasive, as it applies to all taxable entities (and some nontaxable ones). In the new Statement, the FASB adopted the liability method for accounting for income taxes, and this choice, in tandem with the newly lowered corporate tax rate under the Tax Reform Act of 1986, will require substantial adjustments of many balance sheet deferred tax accounts.

Recognizing that significant changes are often hard to grapple with, we have prepared this implementation guide to assist you. It is a practical guide to implementation, structured to take you step by step through the computation of a FAS 96 income tax provision. The guide discusses implementation strategies, tax-planning strategies, business combinations, and several other topics. In addition, some of the more common implementation issues have been summarized in a question and answer format in Chapter 13.

The theoretical basis for the FASB's conclusions is discussed in the Statement itself, parts of which have been excerpted following Appendix B. The Statement's Glossary is a helpful reference to understanding new terms introduced by FAS 96 and other more familiar terms that have been redefined by it.

As with any attempt to translate complex theory into practice, potential conflicts and unforeseen problems are inevitable. The FASB has appointed an Implementation Group to consider implementation issues as they arise and to act in an advisory capacity to the FASB staff. The Implementation Group met for the first time on January 29, 1988 and again March 31, 1988. The implementation issues addressed at those meetings and the tentative views expressed by the FASB staff have been incorporated into this guide.

We have identified other problem areas, not yet addressed by the Implementation Group, and have given guidance in accordance with our understanding of the spirit of the Statement. It is possible that the FASB staff's conclusions on certain issues will differ from our interpretations. It is also likely, of course, that additional questions will surface as companies implement the Statement.

The positions already taken by the FASB staff are still considered to be tentative at this time. After all indentified questions concerning FAS 96 have been considered, their tentative views will be reviewed for consistency. Until FASB staff conclusions are finalized, there will be uncertainty as to what the ultimate resolution will be on various issues, even those issues for which the FASB staff has provided tentative conclusions with which the Implementation Group concurs. The FASB staff views, when finalized, will be published, probably as a "questions and answers" book. The answers would presumably have the support of the Board itself. The staff of the SEC generally ascribe to such publications the standing of an SEC Staff Accounting Bulletin.

Accordingly, a company may adopt FAS 96 following, in good faith, a particular interpretation and may later have to change its accounting to comply with a different conclusion reached by the FASB staff. At the March 10, 1988 meeting of the FASB Emerging Issues Task Force, the Chief Accountant of the SEC addressed the situation where a registrant follows a position on an issue that differs from a later FASB staff interpretation. As long as the registrant's position represents a reasonable interpretation of FAS 96, the Chief Accountant indicated that the SEC staff would not require restatement of the prior financial statements.

Even so, a number of transition questions could be raised in these circumstances. First, there is the question whether a position is a reasonable interpretation of FAS 96. Second, companies that originally adopted FAS 96 by restatement may wish to change to the FASB staff interpretation retroactively but without suggestion that an error was involved in prior financials. Third, application only to new transactions is generally used for adoption of consensuses of the Emerging Issues Task Force. Would that transition be appropriate for the FASB staff interpretations? Or would a cumulative-effect adjustment be required? It is possible that the FASB staff or the SEC staff will itself address transition questions.

A word about the exhibits: The exhibits in this guide are based on current U.S. tax law enacted through December 31, 1987. For simplicity, most examples assume that the incremental tax effect of additional taxable income or loss will be at 46 percent in pre-1987 years, 40 percent for 1987, and 34 percent in subsequent years. In performing actual calculations, the actual incremental tax effects of (for example) carrybacks for refund claims or inclusion of additional taxable income would be used.

ARTHUR SIEGEL
JAMES O. STEPP
ROBERT P. ROCHE
JACQUELINE M. TOMLIN

PRICE WATERHOUSE
April 4, 1988

Summary of Contents

Contents

CHAPTER 3 _____
Scheduling

CONTENTS

CHAPTER 4
Carrybacks and Carryforwards

CHAPTER 5
Tax-Planning Strategies

CHAPTER **6** _____
The Tax Computation

CHAPTER **7** _____
Making the Adjustment

CONTENTS

CHAPTER 8 _____
Business Combinations

CONTENTS

CHAPTER 11
Implementation Strategies

CHAPTER 12
Financial Statement Disclosures

CHAPTER 13
Questions and Answers

APPENDIX
Corporate Alternative Minimum Tax—Why All Corporations Will Be Affected

CONTENTS

An Overview of FAS 96

The Financial Accounting Standards Board (FASB) issued Statement No. 96, *Accounting for Income Taxes,* in December 1987. The new Statement represents the culmination of almost six years of work by the FASB to revise the income tax accounting model contained in Accounting Principles Board (APB) Opinion No. 11.

FAS 96 profoundly alters the accounting for income taxes used during the past 20 years. It supersedes not only APB 11 but also 18 other pronouncements of the APB and the FASB. It also amends, in some cases significantly, 28 other pronouncements. The methodology adopted by the FASB is extremely complex and

EXHIBIT 1-1
Implementation: Step by Step

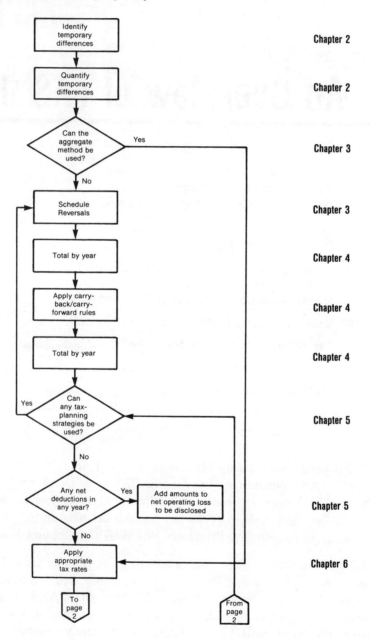

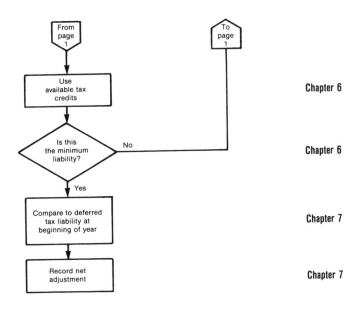

companies will be required to expend considerable effort to implement it.

¶ 1.01 PLANNING FOR IMPLEMENTATION

This publication is a step-by-step guide through the process of implementing FAS 96 (see Exhibit 1-1). It also discusses the effects of FAS 96 on a company's financial statements (currently *and* in future years) and what actions might be taken to plan its implementation.

Various alternatives available for the adoption of FAS 96 are discussed in detail in Chapter 11. Companies should keep in mind that the Statement must be adopted no later than the first quarter of fiscal years beginning after December 15, 1988.

The new Statement is applicable to all financial statements prepared in conformity with U.S. generally accepted accounting principles. Therefore, all public and nonpublic taxable entities will be affected by it. In addition, all public enterprises that are not subject to income taxes because their income is taxed directly to their owners (e.g., S corporations and partnerships) will be affected by certain FAS 96 disclosure requirements.

FAS 96 is applicable to all tax jurisdictions. Accordingly, city, state, and foreign income taxes need to be considered. In addition, the amounts reported for foreign subsidiaries or equity investments in the financial statements of U.S. companies may need to be adjusted. This will require an understanding of FAS 96 as well as the tax laws in each applicable country. Companies with foreign operations will need to train their financial people on a worldwide basis on the intricacies of FAS 96 or obtain sufficient information from the foreign locations to permit head-office personnel to make the appropriate adjustments.

¶ 1.02 THE LIABILITY METHOD

Statement 96 mandates the liability method for computing deferred income taxes. The deferred tax balance in the pre-FAS 96 era was an accumulation of annual adjustments that defied simple explanation. The new Statement transforms it into a calculable liability or asset. While the calculated liability or asset could be payable or collectible at various future dates, discounting is specifically precluded by FAS 96.

For decades, accountants have debated the merits of the liability method. This concept holds that future tax effects, rather than past or current tax effects, should be the basis of the deferred tax computation. In FAS 96, the FASB has converted that generalized concept into a rigid methodology that leaves limited discretion in application.

The rationale that FAS 96 adopts is that the deferred tax liability (or asset) should be a measurement of what is implicit in the balance sheet. The FASB starts with the premise that it is an inherent assumption of financial statements that assets will be realized and that liabilities will be settled at their carrying amounts (book bases). When tax bases differ from these carrying amounts, there are implicit future tax effects. These effects result from reversals of the book/tax basis differences as a consequence of the enacted tax laws. Future events other than realization of assets and settlement of liabilities at their carrying amounts obviously are not implicit in the balance sheet. Thus, the deferred tax balance will represent what would be paid to or received from various taxing agencies assuming break-even operations (for book purposes) in future years.

[1] An Example: Depreciation

To appreciate fully the ramifications of this concept, consider differences in book and tax depreciation of fixed assets. The financial statements presume future realization of the carrying amount of the fixed assets; that translates, under the liability method, to taxable income in each future year equal to scheduled book depreciation for that year. The future tax deductions are those that are available based on the remaining tax basis and the depreciation pattern used for tax purposes. The liability method recognizes the future tax consequences of the future taxable income equal to future book depreciation and the future tax deductions for tax depreciation. While it may be a counterintuitive concept, under FAS 96 future book depreciation means future taxable income.

¶ 1.03 A CHANGE IN FOCUS: FROM INCOME STATEMENT TO BALANCE SHEET

Under APB 11 (which opted for the time-honored but now-superseded deferred method), the focus was on the income statement. Generally, it assumed a current year's tax return based on pretax accounting income adjusted for permanent differences. The tax provision was computed on that income, and the deferred tax charge or credit was the difference between the total provision and the taxes actually payable for the current year.

In contrast, FAS 96 focuses on the balance sheet. Taxes payable for the current year and the deferred provision are separate computations. If an item has been treated differently for financial reporting and for tax purposes, a deferred tax asset or liability is computed based on the difference between the book basis for financial reporting purposes and the tax basis of the asset or liability.

A hypothetical tax return is prepared for each future year reflecting as taxable income or deductions only the reversal of those book/tax bases differences. Enacted tax laws are applied to compute the deferred tax liability or asset. For example, net deductions scheduled to occur in a specific future year would be treated in the computation as a net operating loss (NOL) subject to enacted carryback/carryforward rules.

Exhibit 1-2 summarizes the major differences between APB 11 and FAS 96.

¶ 1.04 VOLATILE EFFECTIVE RATES

Concentration on the balance sheet usually will have no appreciable effect on the relationship between the tax provision and income before taxes. Under certain circumstances, however, the effective tax rate can become volatile.

Major causes of volatility are new tax laws or legislated changes in tax rates. Such changes in any jurisdiction in which a company operates will cause an immediate, cumulative effect on the tax provision. The deferred tax previously provided on items that will become taxable or deductible in any future year will be adjusted downward or upward to reflect the new laws or rates. This effect will be a charge or credit to ordinary operations, *not* an extraordinary item. By contrast, under APB 11, tax rate changes were recognized prospectively.

A reduction in tax rates could cause volatility in another way. Future tax deductions may be used in the deferred tax computation through carryback to a prior high-rate year. Actual realization of the deduction on a subsequent year's tax return at a lower rate would require write-off in that year of the effect of the rate differential (see ¶ 4.05).

EXHIBIT 1-2 _____
A Comparison of APB 11 and FAS 96

APB 11	**FAS 96**

———————————— Periodic tax expense (benefit) ————————————

Tax effects of revenue and expense transactions included in the determination of pretax accounting income. *Income statement emphasized.*	The sum of current tax expense (benefit) and deferred tax expense (benefit). *Balance sheet emphasized.*

Differences between recognition for tax purposes
———————————— and financial statement purposes ————————————

Timing differences. Transactions that enter into the determination of taxable income and pretax accounting income in different periods.	*Temporary differences.* Differences between the tax basis of assets and liabilities and their basis as reported in the financial statements that will result in taxable or deductible amounts in future years.

———————————— Calculation basis ————————————

Tax computation based on (under the net change method) pretax accounting income (adjusted for permanent differences) for the current year. Measures income tax expense. Deferred tax expense is the difference between income tax expense and taxes currently payable.	Deferred tax liability or asset at year-end is measured by tax computation for all future years assuming temporary difference reversals are the only items entering into the tax returns. Deferred tax expense is computed as the change in the deferred tax liability or asset (i.e., difference between the beginning and end of year amounts). Current tax provision is computed separately.

———— Rates used to tax-effect timing/temporary differences ————

Tax consequences of timing differences are recognized at the rates in effect when the difference	Tax consequences of temporary differences are computed based on rates enacted for periods of

(continued)

EXHIBIT 1-2 *(cont'd)*

APB 11	FAS 96

originates. Calculation focuses on timing differences as the *last* items in the tax computation for the current year, yielding a tax effect at the marginal tax rate in effect for that year.

reversal. Temporary differences are considered the only items attracting tax in the years they are scheduled to reverse, thus they are the *first* items to enter into future years' tax computations. As a result, the scheduling and tax-effecting of temporary differences considers all availble rate-bracket adjustments. Scheduling also affects the carryback rates used.

—————————— Enacted change in tax law or rates ——————————

A change in the tax law or rates does not give rise to an adjustment of deferred tax balances.

A change in the tax law or rates is recognized in deferred tax balances when enacted.

—————————— Deferred tax liability ——————————

Net credit representing the cumulative effect (i.e., tax benefits) of unreversed timing differences, deferred for allocation to future periods.

Taxes payable in future years as a result of deferred tax consequences of events recognized in financial statements in the current or prior years.

—————————— Deferred tax asset ——————————

Net debit representing the cumulative effect (i.e., taxes paid exceeding tax expense) of unreversed timing differences, deferred for allocation to future periods. Subject to test of reasonable assurance of realization.

Limited to tax benefit of *net* deductible amounts that could be realized by loss carryback to reduce (1) taxes currently payable, (2) taxes paid in prior years, or (3) a deferred tax liability classified as current.

—————————— Loss carryforward ——————————

Book loss carryforwards can be recognized in loss period if realization (i.e., through future pretax accounting income) is assured beyond any reasonable doubt.

Tax loss carryforwards are deducted from net taxable amounts resulting from temporary difference reversals scheduled to occur in future years (in the carry-

APB 11	**FAS 96**
Otherwise, recognized in year of realization as an extraordinary item.	forward period). Expected future book income is not considered in recognizing loss carryforward benefits. If not recognized when generated, reported in the year of recognition in the same manner as the source of income giving rise to its recognition.

————— Presentation and classification of deferred taxes —————

Net current and net noncurrent amounts are determined and presented based on the classification of the underlying asset or liability that gives rise to the deferred tax.	Classification determined by the timing of the tax consequences of temporary differences. That is, a current *deferred* tax liability represents the amount of taxes payable attributable to temporary differences that will result in net taxable amounts in the following year. Also, for assets and liabilities classified as current on the basis of the operating cycle, related deferred tax amounts are also classified as current.

————————— Purchase business combinations —————————

The net-of-tax approach, with discounting of the tax effects permitted, is used for allocating the aggregate purchase price to identifiable assets and liabilities acquired. Deferred taxes are not provided.	Each identified asset and liability is assigned its respective fair value (assuming an equal tax basis). Temporary differences resulting from the purchase price allocation are considered in establishing the deferred tax balance of the combined entity at the acquisition date. Discounting is not permitted. If the temporary differences of the acquired company permit, under applicable tax laws, use of an NOL of the acquiror not previously recognized, the NOL benefit is considered an acquired asset in the purchase price allocation.

(continued)

EXHIBIT 1-2 *(cont'd)*

APB 11   FAS 96

———————————— Acquired NOLS ————————————

Purchase business combination:
Benefit cannot usually be recognized at the date of acquisition.
Any benefit subsequently realized
is used first to reduce goodwill,
then any other noncurrent assets
of the purchased company and
finally to establish negative
goodwill, all on a retroactive
basis.

Purchase business combination:
Benefit may be recorded at the
acquisition date if, under the laws
of the applicable tax jurisdiction,
it can reduce the acquiror's deferred tax liability. If not recorded
at the acquisition date, the benefit
first reduces goodwill and any
other intangible assets (prospectively, not retroactively). Once
those assets are reduced to zero,
the benefit is included in income
as a reduction of income tax
expense.

Pooling:
Benefit of an NOL of a constituent company, existing at the consummation date, is not recognized until it can be used in post-
combination operations.

Pooling:
Benefit of an NOL (or unused future deductions) of a constituent
company, existing at the consummation date, may be used against
the deferred tax liability of the
other company if permitted under
the laws of the applicable tax
jurisdiction and the temporary
differences of the other company
reverse in a period after the
combination but before the NOL
carryforward expires. The benefit
would be reflected in the pooled
statements not in the period of
the pooling but retroactively in
the loss period or a subsequent
period.

Other factors will also cause volatility in the effective tax rate. Tax benefits may be recognized for future tax deductions only if they can be used in the liability method computation. A change from one year to the next in the amount of unused future deductions will increase or decrease the effective tax rate. For example, new temporary differences may arise in the subsequent year that, absent the unused net deductions, would require a deferred tax liability. The previously unused deductions would offset the taxable income arising in the subsequent year, eliminate the need for the deferred tax liability and thus reduce the effective tax rate. The use of the net deductions would be reported as the benefit of an NOL carryforward.

A list of "rate differentials" that can be expected in income tax expense is given in ¶ 6.08. The first six of the eight listed result from application of the FAS 96 liability method.

¶ 1.05 TAX REFORM AND THE NEW STATEMENT

It is interesting to note that FASB's income tax accounting project started in 1982, but the push for lower tax rates that were enacted by the Tax Reform Act of 1986 (TRA 1986) did not gain significant momentum until 1985. If there had not been a dramatic change in tax rates, FAS 96 might have been, for many companies, largely a nonevent. But now adoption will require adjustment of deferred tax liabilities to reflect the change in corporate income tax rates from 46 percent to 34 percent.

TRA 1986 also contains other changes that will affect the tax provision:

- The investment tax credit has been eliminated (again). Any unused credits may be carried forward but can be applied to any tax otherwise due only at a reduced amount.
- One of the more significant changes is perhaps the least understood: the alternative minimum tax (AMT). A discussion of how AMT affects the computations under the liability method follows. The subject is explored in depth in Chapter 9.

- The law mandates that certain tax accounting practices must change, among them increased capitalization of inventory costs, a significant reduction in the number of companies permitted tax bad debt reserves and the cash basis of accounting, restrictions on installment sales accounting, and limitations on the completed-contract method of accounting. (Further limitations on installment sales accounting and on the completed-contract method were enacted by the Revenue Act of 1987.)

These changes, as well as changes resulting from the Revenue Act of 1987, are discussed in the chapters that follow.

¶ 1.06 ALTERNATIVE MINIMUM TAX

To facilitate understanding of FAS 96, only a few references are made to AMT and the examples compute the tax liability considering only the U.S. "regular" tax. Clearly, however, this new provision in the Internal Revenue Code must be carefully considered by all U.S. companies when they perform the computations under the liability method. It is also clear that AMT will sometimes make the computations exceedingly complex. In addition, AMT may have to be provided in the deferred tax calculation even if the company never anticipates actually paying AMT. Chapter 9 contains an example of a deferred tax computation including AMT.

¶ 1.07 PRECISION COUNTS

FAS 96 will require much more precision in the computation of the provision for income taxes. Under APB 11, most permanent differences were easily identifiable; there was no need to refine the estimates of timing differences until the tax return was filed. The proper identification and quantification of timing differences generally had *no* effect on the total tax provision. It affected only the split between the current and the deferred amounts. Most companies made adjustments in the following fiscal year to correct any differences between the estimated taxable income and that reported on the actual return.

Unlike APB 11, FAS 96 does *not* compute a total provision that must then be allocated between the current and the deferred amounts. As noted, FAS 96 computes the current and the deferred amounts independently; the sum of the two is the total provision.

Whether or not particular temporary differences are included in the deferred tax calculation can affect recognition of potential tax benefits (deductions or credits). Their inclusion can also affect what tax rates are applied when there are graduated rates or when rate changes have occurred in the past or are enacted for future years. Accordingly, it is important, when computing the tax provision, to estimate as carefully as possible the amounts to be reported on the current year's tax return and the corresponding temporary differences. It is also important to include in the computation of the deferred tax liability any changes in temporary differences taken into account in estimating taxes currently payable.

Temporary Differences

Of the many concepts FAS 96 introduces, that of "temporary differences" may well be the linchpin. In fact, temporary differences are the basis of the deferred tax calculation. APB 11 was oriented toward the income statement, and its focus was on timing differences between pretax accounting income and taxable income. Consistent with its balance sheet approach, FAS 96 instead measures temporary differences—any difference between the book

EXHIBIT 2-1
Types of Temporary Differences

Temporary differences, as defined in paragraph 10 of FAS 96, are as follows:

A. Revenues or gains that are taxable after they are recognized in financial income:
   - Profit from installment sales
   - Earnings of investees
   - Subsidiary's earnings not "indefinitely reinvested"
   - Increases in equity in subsidiary's net assets resulting from its capital transactions

B. Expenses or losses that are deductible after they are recognized in financial income:
   - Accrued warranty costs
   - Additions to bad debt reserves
   - Inventory or other valuation reserves
   - Accrued losses from discontinued operations
   - Other accrued losses (e.g., from litigation)
   - Accrued pension expense in excess of the amount deductible
   - Organization costs

C. Revenues or gains that are taxable before they are recognized in financial income:
   - Rental and certain other income received in advance
   - Intercompany profits on transactions between affiliates in different tax jurisdictions

D. Expenses or losses that are deductible before they are recognized in financial income:
   - Higher depreciation deducted for tax than for books
   - Certain software development costs
   - Deductible pension funding exceeding expense

E. A reduction in the tax basis of depreciable assets because of tax credits:
   - Property qualifying for the investment tax credit, placed in service after 1984, if an election was made to claim the higher allowable investment credit rate

F. ITC accounted for by the deferral method.

G. Foreign operations for which the reporting currency is the functional currency.

H. An increase in the tax basis of assets because of indexing for inflation:
- Certain plant and equipment in countries with hyperinflationary economies is subject to indexing

I. Business combinations accounted for by the purchase method:
- All purchase business combinations in which different amounts are assigned to assets and liabilities for book and for tax purposes

---

basis and the tax basis of an asset or a liability that at some future date will reverse, thereby resulting in taxable income or deductions.

Exhibit 2-1 lists nine types of temporary differences; the first four are recognizable as APB 11 timing differences.

¶ 2.01 IDENTIFY AND MEASURE

Determining a company's temporary differences may prove to be exceptionally difficult. Ideally, the company could pull out its current tax balance sheet and compare it to the financial statement balance sheet; in most cases any differences would be temporary differences. Unfortunately, many companies do not have current tax balance sheets. Alternatively, a review of Schedule M items in prior-year tax returns is a practical first step.

Schedule M, included with every corporate U.S. federal income tax return (Form 1120), reconciles not only book and taxable income but also beginning and ending retained earnings. If all tax returns, including amendments and IRS audit adjustments, back to the date of the company's incorporation are reviewed, each temporary difference will be identified. Clearly, many companies would find this task difficult, if not impossible.

A practical approach is to begin with the latest tax return and sequentially review each prior year until the company is reasonably sure that virtually all of the temporary differences have been identified. The financial statement balance sheet should also be examined—for example, the balance of warranty reserves would represent a temporary difference.

This discussion has confined itself to the requirements for a single U.S. tax return. Conceptually, however, the Statement requires that temporary differences be identified for each taxing jurisdiction—that is, each city, state, or foreign country where the company files a tax return. There may even be a tax return consolidating certain operations for which a comparable consolidated financial statement has not been previously prepared.

¶ 2.02 EXCEPTIONS TO THE RULE

Under APB 11 and APB Opinion 23, *Accounting for Income Taxes—Special Areas*, deferred taxes were not required for certain items if there was sufficient evidence that the items would not reverse for an indefinite period. The same exceptions continue even though these items meet the definition of a temporary difference (see the list in Exhibit 2-2). It should be pointed out, however, that it may be necessary to measure these temporary differences to meet disclosure requirements (see ¶ 12.01).

¶ 2.03 PURCHASE BUSINESS COMBINATIONS

Before the advent of FAS 96, recording deferred taxes in a purchase business combination was specifically precluded. The future tax effects of the differences between the book and the tax bases of net assets acquired were considered when establishing their carrying values. Now, however, FAS 96 mandates that deferred taxes be provided when accounting for purchase business combinations consummated after initial application of the Statement.

Assets and liabilities related to a *prior* purchase business combination will call for close scrutiny, for there is more than one

---

EXHIBIT 2-2 _____

Temporary Differences Not Requiring Deferred Taxes

As stated in paragraph 8 of FAS 96, deferred taxes are not required for the following temporary differences.

1. Indefinite reversal criteria must be met:
   - Undistributed earnings of subsidiaries and corporate joint ventures
   - Bad debt reserves of stock or mutual savings and loan associations or mutual savings banks
   - Policyholders' surplus of life insurance companies

2. Indefinite reversal criteria inapplicable:
   - Statutory reserve funds of U.S. steamship companies

In addition, deferred taxes should not be provided for temporary differences arising from goodwill and unallocated negative goodwill. (It might be appropriate to provide deferred taxes for goodwill that has tax basis—see ¶ 3.03[4].)

Even though it is not included in the paragraph 8 list of exceptions, and despite the Statement's insistence that the APB 23 indefinite reversal criteria cannot be extended to analogous transactions, deferred taxes would not be provided for cumulative translation adjustments in situations where, under APB 23, deferred taxes need not be provided for unremitted earnings of a subsidiary. This provision in paragraph 23 of FAS 52 has not been amended by FAS 96.

---

way to measure the temporary differences for those net assets. The approach will depend on the method selected when initially adopting the Statement. Chapter 8 discusses these and other topics relating to business combinations in detail.

¶ 2.04 U.S. DOLLAR FUNCTIONAL CURRENCY

When a foreign operation has the U.S. dollar as the functional currency, certain assets and liabilities (e.g., fixed assets) are remeasured into U.S. dollars at historical exchange rates. A change in the exchange rate creates a temporary difference for purposes of calculating foreign deferred taxes. That is, if, as is assumed by FAS 96, an asset is realized at its current dollar carrying amount, its actual realization in the foreign currency will be at a different amount (because of the change in the exchange rate) than is reflected in the operation's foreign-currency financial statements. This temporary difference is measured as the difference between (1) the foreign-currency equivalent, at the *current* exchange rate, of the U.S. dollar carrying amount of each nonmonetary asset or liability and (2) its foreign tax basis.

For purposes of calculating the foreign deferred tax liability in the consolidated financial statements, this temporary difference will reflect two components:

1. The differences between foreign tax bases and the carrying amounts in the pre-remeasurement foreign-currency financial statements, that is, after adjustment to U.S. accounting principles before remeasurement into U.S. dollars.

2. The temporary differences arising in remeasurement, that is, the difference between the historical-rate and current-rate translations of U.S. dollar carrying amounts of nonmonetary items.

The deferred tax balance in the foreign-currency financial statements would reflect the first component of the temporary difference (and, mechanically, it would also likely include the effect of the indexation temporary difference discussed later in this chapter). The second component arises in remeasurement of the foreign-currency statements into U.S. dollars. If the temporary difference is mechanically computed by direct comparison of the U.S. dollar carrying amount of an asset and its foreign tax basis (as illustrated in FAS 96, paragraph 43), the computed deferred tax includes (or is net of) any deferred tax recorded for that asset in the foreign-currency financial statements.

Unless the remeasurement is performed by the foreign operation's personnel, head-office and foreign accounting functions must carefully coordinate to ensure that the reversals of the temporary differences arising in remeasurement are properly scheduled and are dealt with according to the foreign tax law. Also, when the foreign operation is a branch of a U.S. company or is otherwise included in the U.S. consolidated tax return (or when deferred U.S. taxes are provided on unremitted earnings not included in the U.S. return), the deferred foreign tax effects must be considered in the computation of the deferred U.S. tax liability.

[1] Revalued or Devalued

When the foreign currency has *revalued* against the dollar, the reversals of temporary differences arising in remeasurement ordinarily will result in future tax deductions. The deferred tax liability will decrease and/or a deferred tax asset will be recorded. Of course, recognizing the benefit of scheduled future tax deductions is subject to the requirements of FAS 96 (see the requirements at ¶ 4.05).

For many multinationals, foreign operations with U.S. dollar functional currency will be located in countries where the economy is hyperinflationary and where the foreign currency has *devalued* against the dollar. In that circumstance, the reversal of temporary differences arising in remeasurement usually will result in future taxable income.

[2] Indexation

It is possible that the tax law provides for indexation; this is most common in countries where the economy is hyperinflationary. To the extent that fixed assets are subject to indexation for foreign tax purposes, under paragraph 10 of FAS 96, temporary differences are created that provide some measure of offset to the temporary differences arising from remeasurement.

As the temporary difference for indexation is calculated by applying the index at the balance sheet date to the total tax basis, the entire benefit of the upward revaluation of tax basis could be recognized immediately. Under APB 11, only the excess tax depreciation for the year resulting from indexation was recognized in income.

Indexation is identified as a separate temporary difference in FAS 96, but mechanically it probably would be included in the first component of the U.S. dollar functional currency temporary difference described previously. That is, it would be recorded in the foreign-currency financial statements after adjustment to U.S. accounting principles before remeasurement into U.S. dollars.

Where the foreign currency has devalued against the dollar, the net effect of the devaluation and the indexation generally will be to increase the deferred tax liability and decrease net income.

Exhibit 2-3 illustrates the effects of these temporary differences.

[3] Movements in Exchange Rates

When monetary assets and liabilities are denominated in currencies other than the functional currency, the effect of movements in exchange rates is recognized separately in net income as an exchange gain or loss. The temporary difference created with respect to nonmonetary assets and liabilities when the U.S. dollar is the functional currency would cause exchange rate movements, which could be volatile, to be reflected in the foreign deferred tax provision as well. The actual effect on the deferred tax provision and on net income can be computed only by including the cumulative amounts of this temporary difference in the beginning and end-of-year deferred tax liability computations. A company that has in the past entered into forward exchange contracts to hedge the net monetary position in a foreign operation may now wish to consider including this tax effect of exchange rate changes in its hedging policies.

The deferred tax liability for the temporary differences related to remeasurement and indexation would be part of the net monetary position whose remeasurement each period would give rise to a transaction gain or loss. FAS 96 provides that the transaction gain or loss resulting from remeasurement of the deferred tax liability may be included in deferred tax expense (benefit) "if that presentation is considered to be more useful." In any event, the transaction gain or loss must be included in the aggregate gain or loss disclosed for the period.

EXHIBIT 2-3 ──────────────────────────────
U.S. Dollar Functional Currency and Indexing for Inflation

In 1982 Alpha Co. established a subsidiary, Beta Co., in a foreign country where the economy is hyperinflationary. Accordingly, the U.S. dollar is Beta Co.'s functional currency. The only balance sheet item remeasured using historical translation rates is fixed assets. Alpha Co. adopted FAS 96 as of January 1, 1987 and is applying it prospectively.

For purposes of applying FAS 96, Beta Co. has identified two temporary differences—the U.S. dollar functional currency, and indexing of fixed assets for inflation, which is permitted by foreign tax law. At each year-end, the tax bases of fixed assets are revalued upward. Depreciation on the revalued bases is deductible for tax purposes. Under APB 11, Beta Co. had treated the additional tax depreciation resulting from the inflation adjustment as a permanent difference in the year the deduction was taken on the tax return. As the depreciation method and lives used for financial reporting and tax purposes are the same, no deferred taxes had been provided in prior years.

Following is the computation of Alpha Co.'s foreign deferred tax liability arising from Beta Co.'s temporary differences at the beginning and end of 1987. The exchange rate was FC20=$1 and FC40=$1 at January 1 and December 31, 1987, respectively. The average exchange rate during 1987 was FC30=$1.

Step 1: Measure the Temporary Differences

	1987	
	January 1	**December 31**
Book bases of fixed assets at U.S. dollar historical cost	$ 17,100	$ 19,800
Current exchange rate	20	40
U.S. dollar historical cost at current exchange rate	FC 342,000	FC 792,000
Book bases of fixed assets prior to adjustment for indexing for inflation	FC 41,950	FC 95,950
Temporary difference arising from change in exchange rates	FC 300,050	FC 696,050
Book bases of fixed assets in foreign currency	FC 41,950	FC 95,950
Tax bases of fixed assets after adjustment for indexing for inflation	FC 306,340	FC 679,600
Temporary difference arising from indexing for inflation	(FC 264,390)	(FC 583,650)
Net temporary differences	FC 35,660	FC 112,400

(continued)

EXHIBIT 2-3 *(cont'd)*

Step 2: Calculate the Deferred Tax Balance

Net temporary differences	FC 35,660	FC 112,400
Apply the foreign tax rate	30%	30%
Deferred tax liability	FC 10,698	FC 33,720

As no deferred taxes were provided in prior years, the effect of adopting FAS 96 in 1987 is FC10,698, the deferred tax liability at January 1, 1987 calculated in accordance with FAS 96. The 1987 deferred tax provision is FC23,022 (the deferred tax liability at December 31, 1987 less the balance at January 1, 1987).

Step 3: Remeasure Into U.S. Dollars

Deferred tax liability—foreign currency	FC 10,698	FC 33,720
Current exchange rate	20	40
Deferred tax liability—U.S. dollars	$ 535	$ 843

Step 4: Compute the Transaction Gain or Loss

Deferred tax expense
    The net change in the deferred foreign tax liability (FC23,022) multiplied by the average exchange rate (FC1=$0.0333) $ 767

Transaction gain
    Beginning balance of the deferred foreign tax liability (FC10,698) divided by the change in the exchange rate during the year (from FC1=$0.05 to FC1=$0.025, or FC40)   (267)

    The net change in the deferred foreign tax liability (FC23,022) multiplied by the difference between the average and ending exchange rates ($0.0333 less $0.025, or $0.0083)   (192)

    (459)

Net change in the deferred tax balance
    ($843 less $535) $ 308

When the U.S. dollar is the functional currency and there has been a change in the exchange rate, remeasurement of a foreign deferred tax balance will result in a transaction gain or loss that is included in net income of the current period. FAS 52, *Foreign Currency Translation,* requires disclosure of the aggregate transaction gain or loss included in net income but does not specify how to classify the gain or loss in the financial statements. Therefore, the transaction gain or loss resulting from remeasurement of a foreign deferred tax balance may be included in the reported amount of deferred tax benefit or expense "if that presentation is considered to be more useful." In the preceeding example, Alpha Co. would report either (1) deferred tax expense of $308 or (2) deferred tax expense of $767 and an exchange gain of $459. If reported as described under option (1), the transaction gain or loss must still be included in the aggregate transaction gain or loss for the periods for which disclosure is required by FAS 52. An example of this disclosure would be:

> The Company incurred $1,370 in foreign currency transaction losses during the year. This amount is net of a $459 transaction gain that resulted from the translation of the tax effects of the Company's foreign operations.

The format of this example suggests that the temporary differences for indexing and for the change in exchange rates would be computed separately. It is more likely that the deferred tax effect related to the temporary difference for indexing would be recorded in the foreign currency financials and that the temporary difference from the exchange rate change would be recorded in remeasurement by comparing (1) the U.S. dollar historical cost translated into foreign currency at the current exchange rate with (2) the tax bases in foreign currency after indexation. All other temporary differences of the particular foreign operations would have to be included in the deferred tax computation. The difference between (1) the deferred tax computation after including the remeasurement temporary difference and (2) the deferred tax computed at the foreign operations level, will result in the incremental foreign deferred tax that would then be recorded in the consolidated financial statements. The sum translated into U.S. dollars would be the foreign deferred taxes in the U.S. dollar statements.

¶ 2.05 DEFERRED INVESTMENT CREDITS AND GRANTS

Since its first enactment in 1962, the investment credit has been the subject of accounting controversy. The debate has centered on whether investment credit should be (1) "flowed through" to income, to the extent permitted by statutory limitations in the tax computation, in the period generated or (2) deferred and amortized over the life of the related property. Although the investment credit has been repealed by TRA 1986, the FASB had decided beforehand that it would not address the deferred versus flow-through issue in this Statement.

FAS 96 decrees that deferred investment credit is a temporary difference—a reduction in the cost, and in the future book depreciation of the related asset. This view is consistent with the conceptual rationale for deferral and amortization, but deferred investment credit was not treated as a timing difference under APB 11 because it did not enter into the determination of taxable income. (When the 1982 tax law required that tax basis be reduced for certain investment credits, FASB Technical Bulletin 83-1 required that the basis reduction be treated like a timing difference by flow-through companies, and FAS 96 specifically identifies such a basis reduction as a temporary difference for all companies.) As previously discussed in the example in ¶ 1.02, the liability method treats future book depreciation as future taxable income; and the effect of the FAS 96 treatment of deferred investment credit is to reduce the amount of that future taxable income.

One way to explain the FAS 96 requirement is that there are two benefits of the investment credit: the receipt (through lower tax payments) of the credit itself and the nontaxability of the credit. FAS 96 requires immediate accrual, to the extent permitted by the deferred tax computation, of the future tax reductions from nontaxability of the credit. The nontaxability of the credit is somewhat offset by the reduction in tax basis when a 10 percent credit, rather than an 8 percent credit, was elected under the Tax Equity and Fiscal Responsibility Act of 1982. Under TRA 1986, the tax basis is reduced to the extent the credit is claimed on transition property, and thus there is, with respect to such property, no benefit from nontaxability of the credit.

To appreciate the effect of the FAS 96 treatment, consider a purchase of $100 of qualified property and an investment credit of $10, which, before 1983, did not reduce the tax basis of the property. Under FAS 96, the deferred tax liability computation on the date of acquisition would include a temporary difference of $10 for a company electing deferral and amortization of the investment credit. The scheduling exercise would include taxable income equal to the book depreciation, net of investment credit amortization, for each future year and tax deductions equal to expected tax depreciation. The tax benefit of the future $10 excess tax over book depreciation (tax basis and future tax deductions of $100 versus effective book basis and future taxable income of $90) of the related asset would be recorded at the date of purchase unless precluded by the Statement's restrictions on recording tax debits (see ¶ 4.05). Effectively, then, a company electing deferral of the investment credit would immediately be required to "flow through" this deferred tax benefit to income. (This effect would be partially or wholly offset for post-1982 additions by any requirement to reduce tax basis for the investment credit.)

As the investment credit is amortized to income (without actual tax effect) in future years, the amount included in the scheduling exercise and thus in the deferred tax computation will be reduced correspondingly. The effect will generally be that the tax benefit recognized at the date of purchase would be charged to deferred tax expense in future years in relation to the amount of credit included in income.

[1] Foreign Investment Credits and Grants

Similar treatment would be appropriate for similar tax credits, which have been deferred, arising in foreign tax calculations. Some foreign countries make investment grants that are not dependent on tax reductions for realization and that may not be taxable. It appears that generally deferred grants should be treated as temporary differences in the deferred foreign tax liability computation, potentially with the flow-through effect described previously for U.S. investment credits.

[2] Effect on Leases

This FAS 96 treatment of deferred investment credit will affect the after-tax income patterns for direct-financing leases. For direct-financing leases, the great weight of practice has been to defer the investment credit and amortize it as additional return on the lessor's investment. Thus, assuming retroactive application, there could be (1) a tax benefit reflected in income in the period the investment credit is generated and used and (2) offsetting tax charges in later periods. In prospective adoption, a tax benefit related to the unamortized balance of the investment credit would be recorded (assuming the restrictions on tax debits are met) at the date of adoption as part of the effect of adopting the Statement.

For leveraged leases, deferral of any available investment credit is a condition for, using the FAS 13, *Accounting for Leases*, leveraged-lease model. The effect of treating the deferred investment credit from a leveraged lease as a temporary difference is discussed at ¶ 3.17.

CHAPTER **3**

Scheduling

If identifying temporary differences is a strenuous task, scheduling their reversal may prove to be a real muscle builder. The scheduling exercise is tantamount to preparing a separate tax return for each future year in which temporary differences reverse.

¶ 3.01   AGGREGATE CALCULATION

A detailed scheduling exercise may not always be necessary. For example, if the difference between the deferred tax balance computed by applying the tax rate to temporary differences in total (the aggregate method) is not materially different from the balance calculated on reversals scheduled by future year, the aggregate method can be used. However, it may be difficult to assess the materiality of the difference between the two methods without actually performing both for a number of years.

Paragraph 18 of FAS 96 suggests an approach that in some cases could reduce the extent of scheduling (see Exhibit 3-1), although

---

EXHIBIT 3-1 ———————————————————————————
The Aggregate Approach

FAS 96 suggests the following approach for determining if scheduling is necessary:

1. Identify the type and nature of each temporary difference.

2. For each type of temporary difference, determine whether the tax law precludes or effectively precludes tax-planning strategies (see Chapter 5).

3. If the tax law precludes or effectively precludes tax-planning strategies, scheduling the reversal of some or all temporary differences of this type might be necessary to determine that deductible amounts in future years offset taxable amounts.

4. All other types of temporary differences would be available for offsetting in the deferred tax computation.

It appears that the reversals applicable to the temporary differences in step 4 would be available to offset the results of scheduling in step 3 to obtain the minimum tax liability.

---

it is unlikely that scheduling would be completely eliminated. In fact, certain situations preclude using the aggregate method (described in Exhibit 3-2). In addition, as discussed at ¶ 9.08, alternative minimum tax (AMT) may eliminate the aggregate-approach option entirely for U.S. deferred tax computations.

¶ 3.02 SCHEDULING REVERSALS

In some cases, the Statement specifies the reversal pattern of temporary differences. In other cases, the information gathered while identifying and measuring temporary differences will enable companies to predict the reversal pattern. Exhibit 3-3 illustrates how to schedule reversals.

EXHIBIT 3-2
Required Scheduling

Some scheduling may be required in any of the following scenarios:

1. The company has a classified balance sheet, in which case the scheduling must be performed for at least the first year after the balance sheet date to determine the amount to be classified as current.

2. Future net tax deductions occur in years beyond the last year in which future taxable income is scheduled to occur and carryback availability is limited. Conversely, future net taxable income is scheduled to occur in years beyond the years in which, in the scheduling exercise, net operating loss (NOL) and/or credit carryforwards would expire unused. (In either situation, if tax-planning strategies cannot be applied, scheduling of all temporary differences will be necessary.)

3. Future net tax deductions are scheduled in years for which a carryback to a prior year is permitted or required and carryback would generate a higher deferred tax asset or lower deferred tax liability than if the deduction were carried forward.

4. The tax jurisdiction has graduated rates (unless the rates are phased out over a certain level and that level will be exceeded in each "scheduled" year) or different rates or limitations on various types of income (e.g., capital gains).

5. Enacted tax laws or rates are phased in over a transition period (e.g., in the United States, the reduction to a 34 percent tax rate and the reduction in investment tax credit used after 1986).

For scenarios 2–5 of this exhibit, it may be possible to perform overall estimates for time spans of several years or calculations on an exception basis if:

- Significantly large net deductible amounts not qualifying for recognition of a tax benefit based on the recognition requirements of FAS 96 can be identified.
- Net taxable amounts are at least sufficient to utilize an NOL or tax credit carryforward before the carryforward period expires.
- Net taxable or deductible amounts arising in the years of a phased-in change in tax law or rates can be estimated.

¶ 3.03 SPECIAL SCHEDULING PROBLEMS

[1] Depreciation

For many companies, depreciation will be the largest temporary difference. When a temporary difference arises from using different depreciation methods and/or lives, companies do not schedule only the reversal of the temporary difference at the balance sheet date; they schedule the *difference* between book and tax depreciation for each remaining year of each asset's life. Effectively, this requires scheduling both book and tax depreciation for each future year. In following this procedure, companies may be scheduling future originating differences and their reversals. An illustration of this reversal pattern is contained in Exhibit 3-3.

For newer depreciable assets, it is likely that additional deductions in the first few years that will reverse in later years will be scheduled. This provision has two effects. The first is that many companies will have "losses" (net deductions scheduled in a given future year) that can be carried back to a year when the tax rate was 46 percent (see Exhibit 4-2). The second, more complex effect concerns AMT and is discussed in ¶ 9.07.

There will be certain assets for which tax lives are longer than book lives. For example, under the Tax Reform Act of 1986 (TRA 1986), certain leasehold improvements (whether made by tenants or landlords) are generally amortized over the tax life of the building. High technology equipment may have a shorter book than tax life. In such cases, consistent with the assumptions used in preparing the financial statements (i.e., that the asset will be abandoned or taken out of service and disposed of at the end of its book depreciable life), tax depreciation would be scheduled only over the book life. In the last year of the book life, any residual or salvage value for book purposes would be scheduled as taxable income, and the remaining balance of tax basis would be scheduled as a deduction.

Office buildings (and certain other real estate) in the United Kingdom are not depreciated for tax purposes. Rather, the tax basis of the property is indexed, commencing in 1982, for inflation increases, and a capital gain or loss is measured from the indexed

EXHIBIT 3-3
Scheduling the Reversals of Temporary Differences

Delta Inc. has identified four temporary differences at December 31, 1987:

1. Organization costs were expensed as incurred for book purposes but capitalized for tax purposes. At December 31, 1987, those costs have a remaining tax life of three years and are being amortized on a straight-line basis.

2. FAS 96 requires that originating, as well as reversing, depreciation differences be considered in the scheduling exercise. To compute the amount to be scheduled in each future year, a comparison of book and tax depreciation in those future years must be made. The future pattern of depreciation expense for assets existing at December 31, 1987, is as follows:

	Book depreciation	Tax depreciation	Difference
1988	$600	$900	($300)
1989	600	300	300
1990	600		600
1991	600		600

3. Undeveloped land was acquired by Delta Inc. in a nontaxable exchange. The land is being held as a long-term invest-ment. Therefore, reversal of the temporary difference (the excess of acquisition cost for book purposes over carryover basis for tax purposes) is scheduled to occur sometime in the indefinite future.

4. It is expected that ligitation costs, accrued for book purposes in the current year, will be paid and thus deductible for tax purposes in 1990.

Based on this information, Delta Inc.'s schedule of temporary difference reversals would be as follows:

	Total temporary difference	Future years					
		1988	1989	1990	1991	1992	Indefinite
Organization costs	($60)	($20)	($20)	($20)			
Depreciable assets	1,200	(300)	300	600	$600		
Land	350						$350
Litigation accrual	(2,000)			(2,000)			
Taxable income (deductions) resulting from the reversals of temporary differences	($510)	($320)	$280	($1,420)	$600	$0	$350

tax basis upon disposition. Use of capital losses is limited, as in the United States, to offset against capital gains; there is no carryback and an unlimited carryforward. The question arises as to whether, as for other depreciable assets, all future book and tax amounts must be scheduled. If so, then taxable income equal to book depreciation would have to be scheduled for each future year, with immediate accrual of the resulting deferred tax liability; effectively a tax would be provided on the entire carrying amount (less any book residual value). It would be unlikely that any tax benefit could be ascribed to the capital loss scheduled on disposition (at an assumed proceeds equal to the then carrying amount). The alternative, which Price Waterhouse prefers, would be to consider only the temporary difference at the balance sheet date (i.e., the excess of tax basis over depreciated book value) and to schedule its reversal as a capital loss at expected disposition. The effect of this alternative would be to treat annual book depreciation as a "permanent difference" in that year's tax computation. The FASB staff have not yet reached a tentative position as to the appropriate treatment.

[2] Leasing

A scheduling procedure similar to that used for depreciable assets is also appropriate for leases that are treated as "true leases" (i.e., operating leases) for tax purposes but that are classified by a lessor as sales-type or direct-financing or by a lessee as capital leases. In these cases, the scheduling should technically only consider realization of assets and settlement of liabilities and should not include future interest income (lessor) or interest expense (lessee). Thus, for a capital lease, future book amounts to be scheduled for each year would be the amortization of the leased asset; future tax amounts for each year would be the portion of the deductible lease payment that is applied to reduce the principal amount of the capitalized leasehold obligation. For direct-financing and sales-type leases, the annual tax depreciation would be scheduled as would the portion of the annual taxable lease payments that is applied for book purposes to reduce the recorded investment in the lease (but not the amount to be included in interest income). Generally, the same result would be obtained by simply scheduling total book and tax amounts to be reported for each future year; this would include, in both the book and tax amounts, equal and offsetting amounts of future interest income or expense in each year. Complications could arise, however, when lease payments are not level over the lease term.

When, in an operating lease that is a true lease for tax purposes, lease payments are scheduled to increase over the lease term, paragraph 15 of FAS 13 and FASB Technical Bulletin 85-3 will typically require that the amount of expense (income) recognized by the lessee (lessor) run ahead of the lease payments and of tax deductions (income) although some acceleration for tax purposes may be required. In its financial statements, the lessee (lessor) will record an accrued liability (receivable) for the difference. The accrual, like depreciation temporary differences, will accumulate over a period of years and reverse over a period of years, and the amounts of accumulation and reversal by year are known from the beginning of the lease term. In the years during which the accrual is accumulating, should, as for depreciable assets, all future book and tax amounts be scheduled? Because the remaining accumulations (originating differences) represent book expense (income), it appears inappropriate to include them in the scheduling exercise. Rather, the intervening years of accumulation should be ignored, and the reversal of the accumulated accrual should be assigned to reversal years based on an arbitrary assumption (e.g., LIFO, FIFO, pro rata) that, once adopted, must be applied consistently.

Exhibit 3-4 contains examples of how FAS 96 would be applied to various leasing situations.

[3] Construction in Progress

A temporary difference related to construction in progress may exist at the balance sheet date, or the book and tax bases may be the same. When the completed asset will be owned and depreciated in the future, a question arises as to whether both book and tax depreciation (for construction expenditures accum-

(continued on page 3-18)

EXHIBIT **3-4** _____
Scheduling Leases

This exhibit illustrates the scheduling of a lease that is a true lease (i.e., an operating lease) for tax purposes in three different circumstances:

1. By a lessee that capitalizes the lease;

2. By a lessor that treats the lease as a direct-financing lease; and

3. By a lessor that is a manufacturer and treats the lease as a sales-type lease.

All cases use the same lease for purposes of the illustration. It is assumed that the leased property is equipment and that the commencement of the lease term is December 31, 1987. Other assumptions about the lease are as follows:

First rent payment (in arrears)	6/30/88
Payment intervals	Semiannual
Lease term	10 years
Number of payments	20
Periodic rental payments	$1,400
Minimum lease payments (aggregate periodic rents)	$28,000
Fair value of equipment at lease inception (equivalent to cost to direct-financing lessor and to the normal selling price of the sales-type lessor)	$15,000

Case 1: Lessee That Capitalizes the Lease

The lessee does not know the lessor's implicit rate and accordingly uses its incremental borrowing rate of 16 percent to classify (under the paragraph 7d test of FAS 13) and to record the lease at the commencement of the lease term. The lessee's computation of the present value of minimum lease payments is shown at Schedule 1A. The computation results in a present value of $13,745 that (inasmuch as it does not exceed the fair value of the leased property) is recorded as the leased asset and the capitalized lease obligation at December 31, 1987.

At year-end 1987, there is no net temporary difference between book and tax amounts. In the financial statements, there is an asset of $13,745, representing future taxable income when the asset is recovered through future amortization; the lessee depreciates similar owned property straight-line, and amortization of the leased asset will also be straight-line. There is a liability of the same amount, $13,745, which will result in future tax deductions as the "principal" portion of the deductible lease payments is deducted for tax purposes. The calculation of the annual reduction of the liability is shown in Schedule 1B. Thus, the book asset and liability net to zero at December 31, 1987, although there will subsequently be a difference between their balances until the end of the lease term that will give rise to a net temporary difference between book and tax balance sheets. See Schedule 1C.

Even though there is no temporary difference at December 31, 1987, the future tax taxable income and deductions that will result from realization of the asset and settlement of the liability will be scheduled from the commencement of the lease term. (This presumes that the FASB staff will not take the position, discussed under ¶ 3.03[7], that the existence of a temporary difference is necessary before all future book and tax amounts are scheduled.) Schedule 1C, column I, shows the net amount that would be scheduled for each future year.

Case 2: Direct-Financing Lease

In this case, the lessor estimates that the residual value of the leased equipment at the end of the lease will be $2,000. (Although the $2,000 residual does not meet the IRS 20 percent guideline for a "true" lease, it is assumed that the true lease treatment can nonetheless be sustained.) The lessor's accounting is based on the equation:

$$\begin{array}{c} \text{Present value of} \\ \text{minimum lease} \\ \text{payments} \end{array} + \begin{array}{c} \text{Present} \\ \text{value of} \\ \text{residual} \end{array} = \begin{array}{c} \text{Fair value} \\ \text{of leased} \\ \text{property} \end{array}$$

Solving this equation for the unknown (the interest rate used for discounting to present value at the commencement of the lease term), the lessor's implicit rate of 14.56 percent (compounded semiannually) is derived.

At December 31, 1987, the lessor records its investment in the lease as follows:

Minimum lease payments	$28,000
Unguaranteed residual	2,000
Gross investment	30,000
Unearned income	15,000
Net investment in the lease (i.e., asset cost)	$15,000

The lessor will apply a portion of each taxable lease payment received to recovery of its investment, as shown in columns E and J on Schedule 2A. The annual recovery of the investment in column K is reflected in the scheduling exercise as future taxable income; see column F on Schedule 2B.

The lessor's annual tax depreciation, shown in column E on Schedule 2B, is computed using straight-line modified accelerated cost recovery system (MACRS), under which the asset is depreciated over the recovery period instead of its useful life. Salvage value is not taken into account. The tax recovery period is seven years. One half year of depreciation is taken in the year of acquisition and in the year of disposal. The annual depreciation is reflected in the scheduling exercise as future tax deductions.

Schedule 2B also shows the temporary difference at each year-end in column D and the net taxable (deductible) amount to be scheduled for each future year in column G.

(continued)

EXHIBIT 3-4 *(cont'd)*

Case 3: Sales-Type Lease

In this case, it is assumed that the lessor manufactured the leased property at a cost of $11,000. Otherwise, the same assumptions (as to residual value and tax depreciation method and life) are made as for the direct-financing lessor in Case 2.

The lessor in this case would recognize a gross profit of $4,000 at December 31, 1987, representing the excess of its $15,000 selling price of the leased property (considered to be fair value) over its $11,000 cost. Revenues and cost of sales would be recognized in 1987 in the amount of $14,500 and $10,500, representing the $15,000 and $11,000 each reduced by the $500 present value of the residual. The lessor's recorded investment at December 31, 1987 is the same as for the lessor in Case 2, and its recognition of financing revenue and its recovery of investment are the same as that on Schedule 2A.

This lessor's annual depreciation and tax basis at year-end are indicated in columns E and C of Schedule 3.

Schedule 3 also shows the temporary difference at each year-end in column D and the net taxable (deductible) amount to be scheduled for each future year in column G.

SCHEDULE 1A
Lessee Capital Lease
Present Value of Minimum Lease Payments

(A)	(B)	(C)	(D)	(E)	(F)
	Rent payment	Minimum Lease Payments		Present value factor	Present value of minimum lease payments
Year	dates	Periodic	Annual	using 16%	(C×E)
1988	6/88	$ 1,400		0.9259259259	$ 1,296
	12/88	1,400	$ 2,800	0.8573388203	1,200
1989	6/89	1,400		0.7938322411	1,111
	12/89	1,400	2,800	0.7350298528	1,029
1990	6/90	1,400		0.6805831971	953
	12/90	1,400	2,800	0.6301696269	882
1991	6/91	1,400		0.5834903953	817
	12/91	1,400	2,800	0.5402688845	756
1992	6/92	1,400		0.5002489671	700
	12/92	1.400	2,800	0.4631934881	648
1993	6/93	1,400		0.4288828593	600
	12/93	1,400	2,800	0.3971137586	556
1994	6/94	1,400		0.3676979247	515
	12/94	1,400	2,800	0.3404610414	477
1995	6/95	1,400		0.3152417051	441
	12/95	1,400	2,800	0.2918904676	409
1996	6/96	1,400		0.2702689514	378
	12/96	1.400	2,800	0.2502490291	350
1997	6/97	1,400		0.2317120641	324
	12/97	1,400	2,800	0.2145482074	300
		$28,000	$28,000		$13,745

SCHEDULE 1B
Lessee Capital Lease
Amortization of Obligation

(A) Year	(B) Rent payment dates	(C) Minimum Lease Payments Periodic	(D) Minimum Lease Payments Annual	(E) Interest expense at 16%	(F) Principal Repayments Periodic	(G) Principal Repayments Annual	(H) Balance of obligation
Commencement							$13,745
1988	6/88	$ 1,400		$ 1,100	$ 300		13,445
	12/88	1,400	$ 2,800	1,076	324	$ 624	13,121
1989	6/89	1,400		1,050	350		12,771
	12/89	1,400	2,800	1,022	378	728	12,393
1990	6/90	1,400		991	409		11,984
	12/90	1,400	2,800	959	441	850	11,543
1991	6/91	1,400		923	477		11,066
	12/91	1,400	2,800	885	515	992	10,551
1992	6/92	1,400		844	556		9,995
	12/92	1,400	2,800	800	600	1,157	9,394
1993	6/93	1,400		752	648		8,745
	12/93	1,400	2,800	700	700	1,349	8,045
1994	6/94	1,400		644	756		7,289
	12/94	1,400	2,800	583	817	1,573	6,472
1995	6/95	1,400		518	882		5,590
	12/95	1,400	2,800	447	953	1,835	4,637
1996	6/96	1,400		371	1,029		3,608
	12/96	1,400	2,800	289	1,111	2,140	2,497
1997	6/97	1,400		200	1,200		1,297
	12/97	1,400	2,800	103	1,297	2,497	0
		$28,000	$28,000	$14,255	$13,745	$13,745	

(continued)

EXHIBIT 3-4 (cont'd)

SCHEDULE 1C
Lessee Capital Lease
Scheduling of Temporary Difference

(A) Year	(B) Unamortized asset balance	(C) Unamortized obligation balance	(D) Net book basis (B less C)	(E) Tax basis	(F) Temporary difference at year-end (D less E)	(G) Asset amortization straight-line over 10 years	(H) Obligation amortization (from Schedule 1B)	(I) Net taxable (deductible) for year (G less H)
Commencement	$13,745	$13,745	$ 0	$0	$ 0			
1988	12,370	13,121	(751)	0	(751)	$ 1,375	$ 624	$ 751
1989	10,995	12,393	(1,398)	0	(1,398)	1,375	728	647
1990	9,620	11,543	(1,923)	0	(1,923)	1,375	850	525
1991	8,245	10,551	(2,306)	0	(2,306)	1,375	992	383
1992	6,870	9,394	(2,524)	0	(2,524)	1,375	1,157	218
1993	5,495	8,045	(2,550)	0	(2,550)	1,375	1,349	26
1994	4,120	6,472	(2,352)	0	(2,352)	1,375	1,573	(198)
1995	2,745	4,637	(1,892)	0	(1,892)	1,375	1,835	(460)
1996	1,370	2,497	(1,127)	0	(1,127)	1,375	2,140	(765)
1997	0	0	0	0	0	1,370	2,497	(1,127)
						$13,745	$13,745	$ 0

¶ 3.03[3]

SCHEDULE 2A

Lessor's Amortization of Investment in the Lease

(A) Year	(B) Rent payment dates	(C) Gross investment at period end (C less F)	(D) Balance of unearned income at period end (D less H)	(E) Net investment at period end (C less D)	(F) Minimum Lease Payments* Periodic	(G) Minimum Lease Payments* Annual	(H) Recognition of Financing Revenue Periodic (E×7.284%)	(I) Recognition of Financing Revenue Annual	(J) Amortization of Net Investment Periodic (F less H)	(K) Amortization of Net Investment Annual
Commencement										
1988	6/88	$30,000	$15,000	$15,000	$1,400		$1,093		$307	
	12/88	28,600	13,907	14,693	1,400	$2,800	1,070	$2,163	330	$637
1989	6/89	27,200	12,837	14,363	1,400		1,046		354	
	12/89	25,800	11,791	14,009	1,400	2,800	1,020	2,067	380	734
1990	6/90	24,400	10,771	13,629	1,400		993		407	
	12/90	23,000	9,778	13,222	1,400	2,800	963	1,956	437	844
1991	6/91	21,600	8,815	12,785	1,400		931		468	
	12/91	20,200	7,884	12,317	1,400	2,800	897	1,828	503	971
1992	6/92	18,800	6,986	11,814	1,400		861		540	
	12/92	17,400	6,126	11,274	1,400	2,800	821	1,682	579	1,119
1993	6/93	16,000	5,305	10,695	1,400		779		621	
	12/93	14,600	4,526	10,074	1,400	2,800	734	1,513	666	1,287
1994	6/94	13,200	3,792	9,408	1,400		685		715	
	12/94	11,800	3,107	8,693	1,400	2,800	633	1,318	766	1,481
1995	6/95	10,400	2,473	7,927	1,400		577		823	
	12/95	9,000	1,896	7,104	1,400	2,800	517	1,095	882	1,705
1996	6/96	7,600	1,378	6,222	1,400		453		947	
	12/96	6,200	925	5,275	1,400	2,800	384	837	1,016	1,963
1997	6/97	4,800	541	4,259	1,400		310		1,090	
	12/97*	3,400	231	3,169	3,400	4,800	231	541	3,169	4,259
		0	0							
					$30,000	$30,000	$15,000	$15,000	$15,000	$15,000

*Includes residual value

(continued)

EXHIBIT 3-4 (cont'd)

SCHEDULE 2B
Direct-Financing Lease
Scheduling of Temporary Difference

(A) Year	(B) Net investment at year-end (from Schedule 2A)	(C) Tax basis at year-end (C less E)	(D) Temporary difference at year-end (B less C)	(E) Tax depreciation straight-line over 7 years	(F) Book realization of asset (from Schedule 2A)	(G) Net taxable (deductible) for year (E plus F)
Commencement	$15,000	$15,000				
1987	15,000	13,929	$1,071	($1,071)	$ 0	($1,071)
1988	14,363	11,786	2,577	(2,143)	637	(1,506)
1989	13,629	9,643	3,986	(2,143)	734	(1,409)
1990	12,785	7,500	5,285	(2,143)	844	(1,299)
1991	11,814	5,357	6,457	(2,143)	971	(1,172)
1992	10,695	3,214	7,481	(2,143)	1,119	(1,024)
1993	9,408	1,071	8,337	(2,143)	1,287	(856)
1994	7,927	0	7,927	(1,071)	1,481	410
1995	6,222	0	6,222	0	1,705	1,705
1996	4,259	0	4,259	0	1,963	1,963
1997	0	0	0	0	4,259	4,259
				($15,000)	$15,000	$ 0

SCHEDULE 3
Sale-Type Lease
Scheduling of Temporary Difference

(A) Year	(B) Net investment at year-end (from Schedule 2A)	(C) Tax basis at year-end (C less E)	(D) Temporary difference at year-end (B less C)	(E) Tax depreciation straight-line over 7 years	(F) Book realization of asset (from Schedule 2A)	(G) Net taxable (deductible) for year (E plus F)
Commencement*	$15,000	$11,000	$4,000			
1987	15,000	10,213	4,787	($787)	$ 0	($787)
1988	14,363	8,642	5,721	(1,571)	637	(934)
1989	13,629	7,071	6,558	(1,571)	734	(837)
1990	12,785	5,500	7,285	(1,571)	844	(727)
1991	11,814	3,929	7,885	(1,571)	971	(600)
1992	10,695	2,358	8,337	(1,571)	1,119	(452)
1993	9,408	787	8,621	(1,571)	1,287	(284)
1994	7,927	0	7,927	(787)	1,481	694
1995	6,222	0	6,222	0	1,705	1,705
1996	4,259	0	4,259	0	1,963	1,963
1997	0	0	0	0	4,259	4,259
				($11,000)	$15,000	$4,000

*Reflects $4,000 of income recognized for book purposes at commencement of the lease.

ulated at the balance sheet date) should be scheduled for future years, commencing with the year when the asset under construction is expected to be placed in service.

At the March 31, 1988 meeting of the Implementation Group, the FASB staff indicated that, in its view, the reference to "existing depreciable assets" in paragraph 42 of FAS 96 was intended to specifically preclude the scheduling of both future book and tax depreciation on construction in progress. When no book/tax basis difference for construction in progress amounts exists, no scheduling is appropriate. In the event that a net temporary difference does exist, reversal of only the net amount would be scheduled. For example, if the book basis exceeded the tax basis, the net temporary difference would be scheduled to reverse, commencing when the asset is expected to be placed in service, using the book life and pattern of depreciation. Conversely, if the tax basis exceeded the book basis, the difference would reverse over the tax life using the pattern of tax depreciation.

The accounting firm of Price Waterhouse disagrees with the staff's tentative views, however, stating that the fact that the recorded asset will be placed in service and depreciated in future years is a future event inherent in the financial statements at the balance sheet date. Therefore, both book and tax depreciation of the recorded amount should be scheduled for all future years, commencing with the year when the asset under construction is expected to be placed in service. According to Price Waterhouse, scheduling the reversal of these temporary differences in any other manner (or not scheduling at all in the case where there is no basis difference) could significantly affect the tax provision in the year the asset is placed in service, merely as a result of management carrying out its intent.

The two approaches are illustrated at Exhibit 3-5. The FASB staff's position is still tentative.

[4] Goodwill

In certain foreign jurisdictions, goodwill is separately valued for tax purposes in a purchase business combination, and the tax

EXHIBIT 3-5
Construction in Progress

Alpha Co. adopted FAS 96 in 1987 and applied it prospectively. At January 1, 1987, the date FAS 96 was initially applied, Alpha Co. had one temporary difference relating to a depreciable plant owned and operated by the company. (For simplicity of illustration, all other book/tax basis differences have been ignored.) The plant was fully depreciated for tax purposes and had a book basis of $540. At the beginning of 1987 it had a remaining useful life for financial reporting purposes of six years. At January 1, Alpha Co. scheduled taxable income of $90 (equal to expected book depreciation) for each of the years 1987–1992.

During 1987, Alpha Co. began construction on a new plant. The company expects that the plant will be completed and placed in service in 1991. At December 31, 1987, Alpha Co.'s temporary differences were calculated as shown:

	Book basis	Tax basis	Temporary difference
Plant	$ 450	$ 0	$450
Construction in progress	1,000	1,000	0
	$1,450	$1,000	$450

In calculating the deferred income tax liability at December 31, 1987, a question arises as to whether, with respect to construction in progress, both book and tax depreciation (for the $1,000 expenditures accumulated at the balance sheet date) should be scheduled for future years, commencing in 1991, the year when the plant under construction is expected to be placed in service. (Once the plant is placed in service, the company intends to depreciate it over 25 years straight-line for book purposes and over 10 years using MACRS for tax purposes—the 10 year tax life is unrealistic and has been used for purposes of illustration only.) Alternatively, no scheduling for expenditures made to date would be performed, as no temporary difference exists at the balance sheet date. The scheduling under both alternatives follows.

(continued)

EXHIBIT 3-5 (cont'd)

Alternative 1: Schedule Both Book and Tax Depreciation

	Temporary difference at 12/31/87	1988	Future years				
			1989 through 1990	1991 through 1992	1993 through 2000	2001	2002 through 2015
Plant	$450	$90	$180	$180	($367)	$7	$560
Construction in progress	0			(200)			
	$450	$90	$180	($20)	($367)	$7	$560

Alternative 2: Schedule Only the Reversal of Temporary Differences

	Temporary difference at 12/31/87	1988	Future years				
			1989 through 1990	1991 through 1992	1993 through 2000	2001	2002 through 2015
Plant	$450	$90	$180	$180	$0	$0	$0
Construction in progress	0						
	$450	$90	$180	$180	$0	$0	$0

Later chapters will illustrate how important the amount of taxable income or deductions scheduled to occur in specific years can be in computing the deferred tax liability.

Price Waterhouse believes that the approach to scheduling construction in progress expenditures as outlined in Alternative 1 more accurately reflects the assumptions inherent in the financial statements with respect to recovery of the asset recorded for construction in progress. Under the FASB staff's position taken at the March 31, 1988 meeting of the Implementation Group, however, Alternative 2 should be followed in this situation. The FASB staff's position is presently tentative.

basis is subsequently amortizable. Even though the Statement prohibits recognition of a deferred tax liability related to goodwill (paragraphs 8 and 23), the accounting firm of Price Waterhouse believes that this prohibition is intended to apply to goodwill that either has no tax basis or for which the deductibility for tax purposes would be dependent upon discontinuance of an operation. To the extent that goodwill is itself amortizable for tax purposes, Price Waterhouse believes that it should be treated in the same manner as depreciable assets: all future book and tax amortization should be scheduled. At the March 31, 1988 meeting of the Implementation Group, however, the FASB staff expressed the view that deferred taxes could not be provided with respect to goodwill and that tax benefits actually realized from its amortization for tax purposes should be credited directly to goodwill. The staff did agree, after discussion, to consider the propriety of treating goodwill that is amortizable for tax purposes in the same manner as depreciable assets in the deferred tax computation.

[5] Certain Intangibles

The FASB staff have suggested that, for intangible assets that have tax basis but that are not amortizable for tax purposes, it may be appropriate to schedule *all* book amortization from date of acquisition. In this case, the temporary difference will originate over a period of years as a result of book amortization but will reverse as tax deductions in a single year, usually in the indefinite future when sale or liquidation of an operation or product line occurs. If no benefit can be ascribed to actual tax deductions, applying such an approach would have the effect of accruing, at date of acquisition, a deferred tax on taxable income equal to book basis, scheduled to occur based on book amortization in each future year. The justification for this approach would be that realization of the intangible by future operations is an assumption inherent in the financial statements and there is, accordingly, a deferred tax consequence equal to the tax on taxable income that will be reported as a result of the assumed realization each year of the book amortization.

[6] Other

The use of scheduling procedures that include future originations is generally limited to the situations described previously, but it could also be appropriate in other circumstances where a temporary difference both accumulates over a period of years and reverses over a period of years. Generally, these procedures do not apply to liabilities that are recorded at their net present values, such as deferred compensation obligations, because interest that is expected to accrete in future years is not considered in the scheduling process.

[7] Trigger Point

When the scheduling exercise takes into account future originations and their reversals, the question arises whether there must be a temporary difference with respect to a particular asset before this scheduling of all future book and tax amounts enters into the deferred tax computation. If so, a fixed asset purchase for cash, with the same book and tax basis at date of acquisition, would not be considered in the scheduling exercise until either book or tax depreciation had been taken. Or, if the accumulated book and tax depreciation happened to be equal at any balance sheet date then future book/tax differences would not be scheduled.

The most important effect of such a position would probably be in a purchase business combination if the same amount were assigned to a depreciable asset for both book and tax purposes. There would be *no* scheduling, and thus no effect on the purchase price allocation, at date of acquisition, but there would be full scheduling of all future book and tax amounts at the end of the next reporting period. There could be purchase business combinations in which either the exact same amount could be ascribed to an asset for both book and tax or, alternatively, there could be some minor difference—but a temporary difference nonetheless—between the amounts assigned. This obviously could provide considerable potential for "managed" effects on reported results.

While this issue has not been on the agenda of the Implementation

Group, it has been discussed at both the January 29, 1988 and March 31, 1988 meetings. At the March meeting, it appeared at first that the FASB staff had reached a tentative position that would require the existence of a temporary difference before an asset would be considered in scheduling. After discussion, they agreed that they would give further consideration to this issue.

¶ 3.04 OTHER TEMPORARY DIFFERENCES

Many items, such as warranty reserves, reverse in a fairly predictable pattern and the data may already have been captured for cash flow planning. But computing the reversal pattern of other temporary differences may not be so clear-cut and will require estimates and judgment.

Exhibit 3-6 contains a list of typical temporary differences and some guidelines for determining their reversal patterns. As with any set of guidelines, there will be exceptions. The company should carefully evaluate its own circumstances to determine the appropriate pattern of reversals.

¶ 3.05 LIFO INVENTORIES

A temporary difference related to LIFO inventories can come about in one of four ways:

1. A purchase business combination (either nontaxable or different amounts assigned for book and tax);
2. LIFO for books and FIFO for tax (typically would apply only to foreign operations);
3. Different pools or other attributes for book and for tax; or
4. A different basis stemming from TRA 1986's new uniform capitalization rules.

FAS 96 indicates that any temporary difference arising from LIFO inventories be considered to reverse on a flow-of-goods basis. For

(continued on page 3-29)

EXHIBIT **3-6** _____
Reversal Patterns of Certain Temporary Differences

The reversal patterns included in this exhibit are based on the tax law as currently written (i.e., enacted through December 31, 1987). In addition, the reversal patterns cited pertain to the regular tax law only and are not appropriate when attempting to determine the reversal pattern of a temporary difference created by AMT.

Temporary Difference	Reversal Pattern
Depreciation	Financial statement and tax depreciation are scheduled for the remaining useful life of each asset. The difference, including originating differences, between these two amounts for each future year is then scheduled.
Leasing	See discussion at ¶ 3.03[2].
Intangible assets (e.g., television franchises or trademarks) that are not amortizable for tax purposes	Reversal would generally be indefinite because it would be dependent upon sale or liquidation of an operation or product line. See discussion at ¶ 3.03[5].
Specific reserves for bad debts	Reversal should be scheduled in the year that the receivable is expected to be charged off. Historical pattern may be of some use but management judgment must also come into play. The scheduling of write-offs after the third year should be rare.
Specific reserves for loan losses	As with bad debts, the reversal should be scheduled in the future year in which each loan is expected to be charged off. The use of historical patterns may not be appropriate if the environment in which the financial institution operates has changed significantly. Management judgment is required.

Temporary Difference	Reversal Pattern
Unallocated reserves for bad debts/loan losses	While the specific reserves can be scheduled with reference to an individual loan or trade receivable, this is not the case with unallocated reserves. Future tax deductions should be scheduled based on management's best estimate of when receivables or loans outstanding at the balance sheet date will result in actual charge-offs for tax purposes. For financial institutions to assume the sale or exchange of loans (to generate deductions), the loans would have to be carried at market value because the assumed sale could not, under FAS 96, be expected to generate a book loss. The carrying amount would of course consider the loan loss reserves to the extent that they have been provided to cover loss on sales or swaps.
Inventory reserves, excluding LIFO reserves	Reversal should be scheduled as the related inventory is scheduled to turn on a flow-of-goods basis. Obsolete inventory may be anticipated to be sold over, say, a three-year period while damaged inventory may be expected to be sold for scrap in the next period. The reversals should be scheduled accordingly.
LIFO inventories	The reversal pattern is on a flow-of-goods basis. See discussion at ¶ 3.05.
Units of production depreciation	Reversal should be scheduled on the basis of the anticipated pattern of units that will be produced over the remaining productive life of the asset.

(continued)

EXHIBIT 3-6 *(cont'd)*

Temporary Difference	Reversal Pattern
Lower of cost or market reserves for marketable equity securities	The reversal period is dependent on management's intentions with respect to the securities. Clearly, a current classification of the security would call for a reversal in the first subsequent year. The reversal of reserves related to investments classified as noncurrent must be based on the period in which management intends to sell the assets and should be consistent with the operating plans of the company; the benefit allocated to equity would be determined under the Statement's rules for intraperiod allocation (see Chapter 7). Note that the reversal of such reserves may constitute capital losses that may limit offset opportunities.
Pensions	See discussion at ¶ 3.06.
Deferred investment tax credits	The reversal is identical to the amortization pattern of the deferred income tax credit (ITC). Special problems arise with respect to direct-financing and leveraged leases, as discussed at ¶ 2.05[2].
Unremitted earnings of foreign subsidiaries	If deferred taxes are provided, scheduling should be based on the expected form of repatriation. Dividends should be scheduled in the expected year of remittance. Provision should be made for any foreign withholding taxes. If sale or liquidation of the subsidiary is contemplated in some future period, reversal of the remaining cumulative temporary differences should be considered to occur in that period. Related tax attributes, such as foreign tax credits, should also be scheduled.
Deferred intercompany profits	See discussion at ¶ 3.07.

Temporary Difference	Reversal Pattern
Bad debt reserves of savings and loan associations	Deferred taxes are rarely, if ever, provided on these temporary differences. If provided, and absent a significant event that would likely require a provision for tax to be classified as current, reversal should be consistent with the reason for the provision. If not provided, reversal for purposes of computation of the unrecognized tax liability to be disclosed (see ¶ 12.01) would generally be assumed to be at sale or liquidation.
Policyholders' surplus accounts of stock life insurance companies	
Statutory reserve funds of U.S. steamship companies	
Reserves for litigation	The reversal of accruals such as these should be scheduled in a pattern that is consistent with management's intentions and the basis of the accrual. For example, if management intends to "vigorously contest" any claim, the reversal should take into account the sometimes ponderous pace of the legal process. If, on the other hand, management intends to settle and expects to have the ability to do so, reversal in the near term would be expected.
Discontinued operations	Reversal should be scheduled in the periods in which the loss from future operations and the losses on disposal are expected to be deducted for tax purposes.
Warranty reserves	The reversal pattern should be based on the period in which the claims are expected to be paid. Historical trends would generally be used to estimate the pattern of the reversals. The reversal period should not exceed the warranty period, except for processing delays.

(continued)

EXHIBIT 3-6 *(cont'd)*

Temporary Difference	Reversal Pattern
Tax accounting changes	See discussion at ¶¶ 3.08, 3.09.
Installment receivables	See discussion at ¶ 3.10.
Completed-contract accounting	Reversal should be scheduled in the year that each contract is expected to be completed. See discussion at ¶ 3.11.
Deferred compensation	The years in which payment is expected to be made should establish the reversal pattern. The reversal period will depend on the terms of the contract—whether payments will be made for a stipulated period or whether they will be made for the remaining life of the employee. In the latter case, presumably the actuarial assumption used in providing the accrual will be used in scheduling the reversal. As the amount provided in the financial statements is part of the "principal" that, on retirement, "funds" the deferred compensation payments, its reversal should be scheduled on an interest method (i.e., in increasing amounts). The method of payment (lump sum versus annuity), as well as early or late retirement options, may be at the employee's election. Absent any data on likely employee options that are expected to be selected, management judgment will be required.
Deferred gain on sale-leaseback	See discussion at ¶ 13.12.
Excess cash surrender value of life insurance over cumulative premiums paid	See discussion at ¶ 3.13.
Change in equity in net assets of subsidiary resulting from its own capital transactions	See discussion at ¶ 3.14.

Temporary Difference	Reversal Pattern
Oil and gas properties	The majority of temporary differences related to oil and gas properties will reverse based on a projected future unit of production rate. The projection of a single overall rate may be more appropriate for an entity utilizing full cost accounting; entities utilizing successful efforts accounting may need to project separate rates for individually significant properties and an overall rate for other properties.
Stock options	See discussion at ¶ 3.15.
Stock appreciation rights	Reversal of any compensation expense recognized for book purposes should generally be scheduled based on the dates when employees are expected to exercise the related rights. (It appears that this assumption is necessary even though the accrued compensation expense may in fact be reversed in intervening periods by market price declines.)

example, when inventories are estimated to turn over at least once a year, the temporary difference would be scheduled to reverse in the next year. Deferred taxes must be provided even though the company has no intention of invading low-value base-year LIFO layers. One could logically assert that the inventory will be replaced, thus preventing the recognition of a decrement and taxable income. But such an assertion assumes a future event—consideration of which FAS 96 strictly prohibits.

¶ 3.06 PENSIONS

Accounting for pensions under FAS 87, *Employers' Accounting for Pensions*, and FAS 88, *Employers' Accounting for Settlements* and *Curtailments of Defined Benefit Pension Plans and for Termination Benefits*, can give rise to a number of temporary differences.

For financial reporting purposes, a pension asset results from any, or a combination, of the following:

- Funding in excess of net periodic pension cost
- Net periodic pension income
- Curtailment gains
- Settlement gains

Conversely, a pension liability will be reported as a result of:

- Net periodic pension cost in excess of funding
- Special termination benefits to be paid by the pension plan
- Curtailment losses
- Settlement losses

Further, commencing with fiscal years beginning after December 15, 1988, FAS 87 requires the recognition of an additional minimum liability at least equal to the difference between (1) the unfunded accumulated benefit obligation and (2) any liability already recognized as unfunded accrued pension cost and/or a prepaid pension asset. An amount equal to unrecognized prior service cost shall be recognized as an intangible asset. Any excess minimum liability would be recognized as a reduction of equity. In those situations where the additional minimum liability and the intangible asset are equal (i.e., no reduction of equity is required) and amortization of the asset coincides with reversal of the liability, no scheduling will be required. However, scheduling the separate reversal of both the asset and the liability may be desirable if, as a tax-planning strategy, the company would pre-fund the liability to accelerate future deductions. (Tax-planning strategies are discussed in Chapter 5.) Use of such a strategy, however, changes the character of the related intangible asset to that of a prepaid pension asset. Alternative approaches to scheduling the reversal of the prepaid asset and other pension-related temporary differences are discussed in the following text.

A deduction, up to a specified maximum, is allowed for tax purposes if the amount is paid on or before the extended due date of the tax return. Actual contributions exceeding the maximum allowable deduction may be carried forward and deducted in a subsequent year. In that situation, an asset would be reflected on the tax basis balance sheet. (Excess contributions in the future will be rare as TRA 1986 imposes a 10 percent nondeductible excise tax on those contributions.)

Any difference between a pension liability or asset recorded for financial reporting purposes and the amount reflected on the tax basis balance sheet is a temporary difference. How those temporary differences will reverse, however, is subject to interpretation.

At its January 29, 1988 meeting, the Implementation Group discussed the reversal pattern of one specific pension-related temporary difference—a pension asset arising from an overfunded plan. The FASB staff expressed their tentative belief that, if the company plans to terminate the pension plan, reversal should be scheduled for the year of termination. However, if there are no plans for termination, reversal of the temporary difference should be scheduled at an indefinite future date. In their view, the asset represents a receivable for overfunded pension cost; as FAS 96 prohibits consideration of future events, it cannot be assumed that the overfunded position will be reduced by incurring net periodic pension cost in the future. Therefore, the excess plan assets will revert to the company, and the receivable "collected," at the point in time that all pension obligations existing at the balance sheet date are settled.

Many Implementation Group members, however, have raised objections to scheduling the reversal at an indefinite future date as unrealistic. The FASB staff has agreed to reconsider its tentative view in the broader framework of the reversal pattern for all pension-related temporary differences.

The primary question with respect to scheduling the reversal of pension temporary differences is the extent to which future events (e.g., future service costs) are inherent in realization of pension-related assets or settlement of pension-related liabilities. If consideration of future events is deemed appropriate, then each component of net periodic cost in future years (i.e., future service and interest costs, amortization of a net transition asset, and so forth) would be scheduled based on the existing plan participants and the current actuarial assumptions. In addition, funding requirements for each future year would also be actuarially determined and scheduled.

A second approach would be to assume that a pension asset/liability recorded under FAS 87 reverses in a pattern based solely on events that have already occurred. Under this scenario, the company would assume no future service or interest costs and no return on plan assets. Conceptually, the balance sheet asset or liability represents some portion of the net "off–balance sheet" funded status of the plan. That portion will ultimately become taxable or deductible without regard to future service. Therefore, the reversal pattern would be based on book pension expense consisting solely of amortization of prior service cost, net actuarial gains or losses, and any transition amount compared to contributions that would be deductible if there were no future service costs or interest. In most instances, a consulting actuary would be required to project the reversal pattern of the book/tax pension asset/liability. Based upon comments of the FASB staff at the January 29, 1988 meeting of the Implementation Group, they will presumably favor this basic approach, which ignores future service and interest costs, if it can reasonably be applied to all the pension-related questions.

A third approach would be to schedule the reversal based on an ordering assumption. For example, if a pension asset were assumed to reverse on a FIFO basis, then the related temporary difference would reverse in the earliest year(s) subsequent to the balance sheet date; reversal each year would be measured by the estimated amount of the deductible contribution based on current plan participants and current assumptions. Of course, once an ordering assumption had been selected, it would have to be applied consistently for both pension assets and liabilities and for all subsequent years.

The reversal of pension-related temporary differences is complex, and it is unlikely that this question will be resolved in the immediate future. Price Waterhouse believes that any of the approaches suggested in the preceding text would be acceptable. However, until such time as more definitive guidance is available, the selected approach should be applied consistently.

¶ 3.07 DEFERRED INTERCOMPANY PROFITS

Under APB 11, the tax paid by the seller on intercompany profit was deferred in consolidation. Under FAS 96, the focus is on the difference between the book and tax basis, and it is the tax basis of the buyer (which would exceed the book basis in consolidation) that is relevant. The scheduling and deferred tax computation performed by the buyer would have to be recomputed in consolidation to include reversal of the excess of the buyer's tax basis over consolidated book basis. The pattern of reversals would depend upon the asset: Inventory differences would reverse, on a flow-of-goods basis, in the period of expected sale, and a fixed asset would have all future book and tax depreciation included in the scheduling. Where effective tax rates of buyer and seller are different, it should be noted that an intercompany transfer could affect net income by the difference between the current tax paid by the seller and the effect in consolidation on the buyer's deferred tax liability. Disclosure may be warranted in certain circumstances. See also ¶ 5.05.

When the foreign currency is the functional currency of a foreign subsidiary, the intercompany profit on sales of inventory by the U.S. parent is, under FAS 52, based on exchange rates in effect on the date of transfer, and the amount of deferred intercompany profit is fixed in terms of U.S. dollars at that date. The carrying amount in the buyer-subsidiary's statements—its cost and its basis for foreign tax purposes—is recorded in the foreign currency at the exchange rate at the date of transfer. The U.S. dollar carrying amount of the inventory in the consolidated balance sheet fluctuates with exchange rate changes as the subsidiary's cost is translated into U.S. dollars at the current rate at the balance sheet date; and the fixed U.S. dollar amount of the parent's deferred profit is deducted to arrive at the carrying amount in the consolidated statements. The FASB staff was asked how, in these circumstances, to measure the temporary difference resulting from the intercompany profit deferral, which exists in the buyer's tax jurisdiction. At the March 31, 1988 ... meeting of the Implementation Group, the FASB staff took the position that the temporary difference is measured as the excess of the tax basis of the buyer over the consolidated carrying amount translated from U.S. dollars into its foreign currency equivalent by using the current exchange rate. Generally, this excess can be derived by translating the deferred profit of the U.S. parent at the current exchange rate.

¶ 3.08 TRA 1986 ACCOUNTING CHANGES

A peculiar set of temporary differences was created by TRA 1986, which mandated changes in various tax accounting methods. As a result of some of these changes, where book and tax accounting methods will continue to differ after the tax accounting change, some assets or liabilities will have two temporary differences to schedule. There will be the effect of the tax accounting change (the cumulative difference at the date of change between the old and the new tax methods) and the difference between the book basis and the tax basis under the new method.

In general, the law prescribes that the cumulative effect of the tax accounting change be spread at the rate of 25 percent per year for four years. However, for certain accounting changes, the recognition in taxable income may be accelerated. For example, for a cash-to-accrual accounting change, an amount of receivables that is, for two successive years, one-third below that measured as of the effective date of the method change would cause any balance of the income spread to be accelerated into the second of the two successive years. The same acceleration would be required for the spread of taxable income resulting from the uniform capitalization rules if inventories for two successive years are one-third below the amount at the date of the method change.

In both cases, a cessation of the trade or business would result in immediate recognition of any remaining balance of the income spread.

At the January 29, 1988 meeting of the Implementation Group, the FASB staff took the position that the pattern of taxable income resulting from the spread should be that which would result under the tax law if assets and liabilities were realized at their carrying amounts and there were no other future events. In the view of the FASB staff, FAS 96 would, with respect to recorded receivables and inventories classified as current, accrue the tax effect of realization of carrying amounts in the succeeding year with no assumption of future sales or future replacements of inventories.

Under this view, scheduling at December 31, 1986 of one of the described accounting changes would be 25 percent of the spread in 1987 and 75 percent in 1988; scheduling at December 31, 1987 (after 25 percent has been included in 1987 taxable income) would be 25 percent in 1988 and 50 percent in 1989. The FASB staff observed that FAS 96 does not contemplate discontinuance of the trade or business (if it did, any balance of the spread—100 percent at December 31, 1986 and 75 percent at December 31, 1987—would be included in the succeeding year in scheduling). Scheduling the reversal of a TRA 1986 accounting change temporary difference is illustrated at Exhibit 3-7.

FAS 96 requires that the effects of a change in tax laws or tax rates be reflected in the period of enactment as opposed to the effective date of the change. This can further complicate the accounting for TRA 1986 tax accounting changes. For example, the TRA 1986 uniform capitalization rules for inventory apply for tax years beginning on January 1, 1987 or later, and the cumulative effect between the old and new tax methods—the amount to be spread—is calculated based on opening inventories in the first year the rules apply. To give effect to this change in tax law on October 22, 1986 (the enactment date), according to the FASB staff, a calendar-year company would have to estimate that portion of its inventory on hand at October 22 that would remain unsold on January 1, 1987. Then the cumulative effect of the new tax rules on that portion of the inventory would be

EXHIBIT 3-7 _____

Scheduling the Reversal of TRA 1986 Accounting Changes

Delta Inc. adopted FAS 96 in 1987 and is applying the new Statement prospectively. Delta Inc.'s largest asset is LIFO inventories. TRA 1986 mandated that new uniform capitalization rules be adopted for tax purposes effective January 1, 1987. Delta Inc. has not adopted the new uniform capitalization rules for financial reporting purposes. The tax accounting change resulted in a cumulative effect (or spread) of $100. TRA 1986 prescribes that the spread enter into taxable income at the rate of 25 percent per year for four years. Recognition will be accelerated, however, if inventories for two successive years are one-third below the inventory balance at January 1, 1987.

When applying FAS 96 at January 1, 1987, there are actually two temporary differences for which Delta Inc. must provide deferred taxes. The first difference is equal to the cumulative difference at the date of change between the old and the new tax methods. (Spreading the cumulative effect to future periods creates, in effect, a deferred credit on Delta Inc.'s tax basis balance sheet representing the future taxable income to be recognized.) The second temporary difference is equal to the difference between the book basis and the tax basis of LIFO inventories under the new method.

	Book basis	Tax basis	Temporary difference
LIFO inventories	$900	$1,000	($100)
Deferred credit resulting from tax accounting change	0	(100)	100
	$900	$ 900	$ 0

Delta Inc.'s inventories turn at least once a year. Therefore, FAS 96 requires that reversal of the temporary difference arising from the difference in basis of LIFO inventories be scheduled to occur in the following year. The temporary difference arising from the cumulative difference of the tax accounting change at January 1, 1987 must be scheduled to reverse in accordance with the tax law. As noted above, recognition of the spread will be accelerated if inventories decline for two successive years. As FAS 96 prohibits the anticipation of future inventory replacement (a future event not inherent in the balance sheet), the spread in the scheduling exercise would be that which would result if there were no inventories at December 31, 1988 or 1989. Thus, the spread will be scheduled on an accelerated basis—25 percent in year 1 and 75 percent in year 2.

	Temporary difference at 1/1/87	Future years				
		1987	1988	1989	1990	1991
LIFO inventories	($100)	($100)				
Deferred credit resulting from tax accounting change	100	25	$75			
	$ 0	($75)	$75	$0	$0	$0

estimated, and that effect would be spread as indicated previously in the scheduling as of October 22. While this appears to be conceptually correct, Price Waterhouse believes that short-cuts or estimates will usually be adequate.

¶ 3.09 OTHER TAX ACCOUNTING CHANGES

Tax accounting changes are sometimes made at the election of the taxpayer, although usually only with the permission of the IRS. In these cases, the cumulative difference between the old and new methods is included in taxable income generally pro rata over six years, but sometimes in other patterns as specified by the IRS. However, there are typically provisions in the election agreement with the IRS that specify acceleration of the spread based on factors similar to those that would accelerate the spread for TRA 1986 changes, and the same approach would be used for scheduling the spread. When permission of the IRS is necessary, the change would be reflected in tax computations made for financial statement purposes from the date IRS approval is granted.

¶ 3.10 INSTALLMENT RECEIVABLES

Discussions of accounting for deferred taxes have typically cited installment accounting for profit recognition on sales as the most prominent example after accelerated tax depreciation. In scheduling reversals of temporary differences relating to installment receivables, deferred gross profit would be scheduled to enter into taxable income ratably with scheduled collections. However, use of installment accounting has been largely eliminated for U.S. federal tax purposes by TRA 1986 and the Revenue Act of 1987.

TRA 1986 repealed the installment method of accounting on revolving credit sales. In addition, TRA 1986 accelerated, based on the amount of outstanding debt, the taxation of certain installment obligations arising from dispositions of real and personal property. Exceptions were provided, however, for dispositions of property used or produced in farming and, provided the taxpayer elected to pay interest, for dealer dispositions of timeshares and residential lots. The Revenue Act of 1987 generally repealed, for dealer dispositions after December 31, 1987, the installment sales method of accounting except for dispositions of property used or produced in farming and, subject to provisions for payment of interest on deferred tax, for dispositions of residential lots and timeshares and nondealer dispositions of real estate.

Under TRA 1986, the gain remaining to be recognized from revolving credit sales was taken into income over a period not to exceed four years. The TRA 1986 "proportionate disallowance" of profit deferrals on the amount of outstanding debt is effective for taxable years ending after December 31, 1986 for dispositions after February 28, 1986; and under transition rules, its effect in taxable years ending in 1987 and 1988 should be recognized ratably over a three- and two-taxable-year period, respectively. While the resulting taxable gain for sales of real property is the ratable spread, the increased tax (from including the resulting taxable gain in the computation of the current year's taxable income and tax liability) is the ratable spread for sales of personal property. Thus, the former would be included in the scheduling exercise while the latter would be reflected as an actual tax liability with the portion payable after one year classified as noncurrent.

Under the provisions of the Revenue Act of 1987, the proportionate disallowance rules are continued (for applicable sales made after February 28, 1986 and before January 1, 1988) in taxable years beginning before January 1, 1988. Any gain remaining to be recognized on these sales as of the first day of the first taxable year beginning after 1987 is taken into income over a period not to exceed four years.

Nondealer dispositions of real property made after August 16, 1986 and before January 1, 1988 continue to be subject to the proportionate disallowance rules. Alternatively, a nondealer taxpayer may elect to apply the Revenue Act of 1987 provision, which requires an interest payment on the deferred tax, to these installment receivables.

Thus, except for retroactive application, scheduling reversals for installment receivables may consist largely of scheduling spreads from tax accounting changes, and due consideration should be given to the points discussed at ¶ 3.08. Of course, the scheduling as of any particular date should reflect the tax law enacted as of that date, and the effect of the Revenue Act of 1987 would be reflected only after its enactment on December 22, 1987. For purposes of scheduling after enactment of TRA 1986 but before December 22, 1987, the proportionate disallowance applies to the first collections due; for affected receivables, it would be the last maturities that are scheduled. Of course, for installment receivables remaining from dispositions occurring before February 28, 1986, all future collections would have to be scheduled.

¶ 3.11 CONTRACT ACCOUNTING

TRA 1986 prescribes either the percentage-of-completion method or a hybrid completed-contract percentage-of-completion method, with percentage-of-completion measured using cost-to-cost, except for small contractors. Under the hybrid method, percentage-of-completion is applied to 40 percent—raised to 70 percent by the Revenue Act of 1987—of the profit on each contract; the balance can continue to be accounted for on a completed-contract method. (For AMT purposes, completed-contract accounting will not be available for contracts entered into after February 28, 1986.)

There can be two separate temporary differences resulting from contract accounting.

1. For the 60 percent or 30 percent for which completed contract is used for tax purposes under the hybrid method and for contracts entered into before February 28, 1986 that are 100 percent completed contract, profits recognized on a percentage-of-completion method in the financial statements will reverse in the period when the contract completion will occur for tax purposes. Estimates of years in which such completion dates will occur will be necessary.

2. It is quite possible that the percentage-of-completion measure used for financial accounting will differ from the prescribed application of cost-to-cost for tax purposes. It may be that this temporary difference would be one that originates over several periods and reverses over several periods, raising the question whether—as for depreciation—all future book and tax amounts should be scheduled. However, this would involve future book income and therefore does not seem to be an appropriate application. It would be an acceptable approach to estimate all future book and tax amounts and to consider the accumulated differences at the balance sheet date to be originating differences. Scheduling their reversal would require an arbitrary assumption—such as FIFO, LIFO, or average—that, once adopted, would have to be applied consistently.

Scheduling the reversal of temporary differences resulting from contract accounting is illustrated in Exhibit 3-8.

¶ 3.12   SALE-LEASEBACK

It is not uncommon for capital gains tax to be incurred on sales of real estate. Under APB 11, when gain was deferred because of a leaseback, any related capital gains tax was also deferred. Under FAS 96, any benefit of a lower capital gains rate would be reflected in the current tax provision, and the deferred gain would be treated in the scheduling as future ordinary deductions (i.e., the excess of future ordinary deductions for lease payments

EXHIBIT 3-8
Contract Accounting

Theta Co. was awarded a long-term contract in 1988 to produce 10,000 units of a customized version of its principal product over the next five years. The contract is for $9,000, which will be billed to the customer as the units are shipped. The total contract cost is expected to be $6,000.

Theta follows the percentage-of-completion method measured using units shipped for financial reporting purposes. Theta is not considered to be a "small contractor" as defined by TRA 1986. Consequently, Theta is required to use the 70 percent hybrid completed-contract percentage-of-completion method using cost-to-cost for tax purposes. Prior to TRA 1986, Theta had followed the completed-contract method for tax purposes.

The following information depicts the estimated pattern of financial and taxable income over the life of the contract and the resulting temporary differences.

Financial Income	Actual 1988	1989	Projected 1990	1991	1992
Percentage-of-completion using units shipped					
Units shipped	0	2,000	3,000	3,000	2,000
Revenue, at $0.90 per unit	$ 0	$1,800	$2,700	$2,700	$1,800
Cost, at $0.60 per unit	0	1,200	1,800	1,800	1,200
Gross profit for year (A)	0	600	900	900	600
Gross profit recognized in prior years	0	0	600	1,500	2,400
Cumulative gross profit (B)	$ 0	$ 600	$1,500	$2,400	$3,000

(continued)

3-41

EXHIBIT 3-8 *(cont'd)*

Taxable Income

Percentage-of-completion using cost-to-cost

Current period costs	$1,000	$1,800	$1,200	$1,200	$ 800
Costs previously incurred	0	1,000	2,800	4,000	5,200
Costs incurred to date	1,000	2,800	4,000	5,200	6,000
Total projected costs	6,000	6,000	6,000	6,000	6,000
Percentage complete	17%	47%	67%	87%	100%
Cumulative income to be recognized ($9,000 contract amount × percentage complete)	$1,500	$4,200	$6,000	$7,800	$9,000
Less amounts previously recognized	0	1,500	4,200	6,000	7,800
Current period income	1,500	2,700	1,800	1,800	1,200
Current period costs	1,000	1,800	1,200	1,200	800
Gross profit (C)	$ 500	$ 900	$ 600	$ 600	$ 400

Completed Contract

Taxable income	$ 0	$ 0	$ 0	$ 0	$9,000
Contract costs	0	0	0	0	6,000
Gross profit (D)	$ 0	$ 0	$ 0	$ 0	$3,000

Total Taxable Income

Percentage-of-completion (C) at 70%	$ 350	$ 630	$ 420	$ 420	$ 280
Completed-contract (D) at 30%	0	0	0	0	900
Total for year	350	630	420	420	1,180
Total taxed in prior years	0	350	980	1,400	1,820
Cumulative taxable income (E)	$ 350	$ 980	$1,400	$1,820	$3,000

Aggregate Temporary Difference

Cumulative taxable income (E)	$ 350	$ 980	$1,400	$1,820	$3,000
Cumulative financial income (B)	0	600	1,500	2,400	3,000
Aggregate temporary difference	$ 350	$ 380	($100)	($580)	$ 0

Originating (Reversing) Amounts by Component

Taxable income using percentage-of-completion	$ 350	$ 630	$ 420	$ 420	$ 280
Financial income (A) at 70%	0	420	630	630	420
	350	210	(210)	(210)	(140)
Taxable income using completed-contract	0	0	0	0	900
Financial income (A) at 30%	0	180	270	270	180
	0	(180)	(270)	(270)	720
Aggregate (net) originations (reversals)	$ 350	$ 30	($480)	($480)	$ 580

This example is surprising, compared to what would have been expected before TRA 1986 and the Revenue Act of 1987, in that taxable income runs ahead of financial income. This results from the fact that the cost-to-cost measurement used for the tax percentage-of-completion component runs ahead of the units-shipped measurement used for financial income; the financial income measurement, of course, runs ahead of the tax completed-contract component. Because the two components of taxable income create temporary differences running in opposite directions, it raises the question whether the reversal of temporary differences should be scheduled by reference to aggregate (or net) originations and reversals (applying an arbitrary assumption of reversal pattern). Price Waterhouse believes that scheduling reversals should respect the separate components.

(continued)

3-43

EXHIBIT 3-8 *(cont'd)*

In this example, Theta Co. assumed a FIFO reversal pattern for the tax percentage-of-completion component. At December 31, 1988, there is a $350 temporary difference (taxable income in excess of financial income), all of which relates to the tax percentage-of-completion component. Theta Co. would schedule reversals (future tax deductions) of $210 for 1990 and $140 for 1991.

If actual 1989 costs, production, and shipments equalled year-end 1988 projections and if projections for future years had not changed then, at December 31, 1989, Theta Co. would have a temporary difference of $380 (taxable income in excess of financial income) consisting of $560 excess taxable income from the percentage-of-completion component net of $180 excess financial income from the completed-contract component. It would schedule reversals as follows:

	1990	1991	1992
Percentage-of-completion component	$210	$210	$140
Completed-contract component	0	0	(180)
Aggregate (net) reversals—future tax deductions (taxable income)	$210	$210	($40)

Note: In calculating the preceding temporary difference, we have not compared book and tax bases of assets and liabilities related to the contract. Rather, we have taken the simple shortcut of comparing cumulative taxable income and financial income. Since costs incurred, billings rendered, and collections received would be balance sheet entries for both book and tax, the aggregate or net difference between book and tax bases of contract-related assets and liabilities would be the difference between the book and tax income measurements.

over future book expense, whether rent in an operating lease or depreciation in a capital lease).

Exhibit 3-9 illustrates the application of FAS 96 to a sale-leaseback situation.

¶ 3.13 EXCESS CASH SURRENDER VALUE

When the company owns life insurance policies, typically it is management's intent to maintain the policy in force until the death of the insured, in which case proceeds of the policy would be nontaxable (except for potential effect in the AMT calculation). However, if the policy is surrendered for its cash value, any excess of cash surrender value over cumulative premiums paid would be taxable. Because the asset recorded for an insurance policy is its cash surrender value, FAS 96 requires treatment as a temporary difference of any excess that would be taxable on surrender of the policy. The question is, in what future year should this taxable income, which the company never expects to report, be scheduled?

It is usually difficult to correlate timing of expected realization of the asset with the basis for its measurement. The FASB staff has taken the view that, given the basis for measurement of the asset, the presumption is that it will reverse in the next year. However, if actual surrender is not intended, management should choose another year (occurring before the actuarially expected death of the insured) if it would minimize the deferred tax liability.

It has been suggested that it would be appropriate to carry the investment in a life insurance policy not at its cash surrender value but at its net loan value (the maximum amount that the company can contractually borrow against the policy) if the company intends to retain the policy in force until the death of the insured and to borrow against the policy to meet any cash requirements. This valuation of the asset would be consistent with management's intent to hold the policy until the death of the insured, when proceeds would be nontaxable. Under this view, the amount recognized as the investment in the policy would not be a

EXHIBIT **3-9** _____
Sale-Leaseback

Omega Corp. owned an office building that housed its headquarters until December 31, 1985. On that date, Omega sold the building to a third party for $24 million and leased the building back for a period of 25 years. The building had been purchased new for $10 million in December 1969. In 1985, the tax rates applicable to ordinary income and to capital gains were 46 percent and 28 percent respectively.

Omega adopted FAS 96 in 1988 and restated to January 1, 1985. Omega has other temporary differences related to depreciation on equipment and other buildings in amount and reversal patterns sufficient to offset the future deductions related to the sale-leaseback temporary difference.

The computation of the gain and the related tax paid was as follows:

	Financial statements	Tax return
Sales price	$24,000,000	$24,000,000
Basis		
Original cost	10,000,000	10,000,000
Less: Accumulated depreciation	4,000,000	4,600,000
	6,000,000	5,400,000
Gain	$18,000,000	$18,600,000
Tax on $600,000 ordinary income at 46%		$ 276,000
Tax on $18,000,000 capital gain at 28%		5,040,000
		$ 5,316,000

Gain on the sale was taxed at the ordinary rate to the extent of tax depreciation previously claimed in excess of the straight-line amount, for which Omega Corp. had provided deferred taxes. The entire gain was deferred for financial reporting purposes. Under its net change application of APB 11, Omega Corp. deferred the actual tax paid, $5,316,000, and there was no effect of the transaction on 1985 net income as originally reported.

Under FAS 96, however, the deferred gain will result in future ordinary deductions (the lease payments), and in scheduling reversals as of any date after adoption of FAS 96, amortization of the deferred gain would be scheduled accordingly. If the leaseback is operating, the deferred gain will reverse ratably with recognition of rental expense, typically straight-line, over the term of the leaseback, 25 years in this case. If the leaseback is capital, the gain will serve to reduce the amount of book depreciation that would otherwise be expensed. It the depreciation method used is straight-line, the deferred gain will also reverse in that pattern.

In applying FAS 96 at year-end 1985, Omega Corp. recorded a deferred tax benefit of $8,280,000 ($18 million at 46 percent). The sale-leaseback then had the following effects on the 1985 restated income statement:

Pretax accounting income		$ 0
Tax provision		
Current		5,316,000
Deferred tax benefit recorded after sale-leaseback	($8,280,000)	
Deferred tax liability recorded on building temporary difference of $600,000 before sale-leaseback	(276,000)	(8,556,000)
		(3,240,000)
Net income		$3,240,000

The benefit to income from the sale-leaseback in the restated 1985 income statement represents the 18 percent differential between ordinary and capital gain rates on the $18,000,000 capital gain.

Note: The mechanics of computation of the deferred tax provision are covered in the later chapters. However, this is a useful illustration of the difference between the deferred taxes provided under APB 11 and under the FAS 96 liability method.

---

temporary difference. The propriety of this approach was supported by a majority of the FASB Emerging Issues Task Force at its March 10, 1988 meeting, but a consensus was not reached. The FASB staff will give this issue further consideration.

¶ 3.14 SUBSIDIARY'S CAPITAL TRANSACTIONS

When the parent company does not participate in the transactions of a subsidiary in its own shares on a pro rata basis to its ownership interest, there is typically a change in the parent's equity in net assets reflected in the consolidated financial statements. Example transactions would be sale of additional shares to the public, repurchase of shares, exercise by employees of options, and conversions of convertible debt. The change may be recorded as a gain or loss in the consolidated income statement, or it may be reflected directly in consolidated shareholders' equity.

The "change in interest" is not a currently taxable event. It is quite similar to the change in the parent's equity in a subsidiary resulting from its unremitted earnings in that management may have the ability and intent to control its reversal. Indeed, its reversal may be even more indefinite because it typically would not result from dividends but would require sale of subsidiary shares by the parent, and, even so, only a pro rata part of the change in interest would reverse.

In FAS 96, note 9 to paragraph 14 and paragraphs 72 and 96 appear to indicate that the change in interest is a temporary difference for which deferred taxes must *always* be provided because the APB 23 indefinite reversal criteria cannot be extended to analogous transactions.

However, at the January 29, 1988 meeting of the Implementation Group, the FASB staff observed that, where a domestic subsidiary is at least 80 percent owned, it would be possible for a change in interest gain to totally escape U.S. tax. This could be accomplished by selling the assets of the subsidiary and then effecting its tax-free liquidation. Alternatively, a sale of all the stock of such a subsidiary might be deemed to be a sale of assets by, and a subsequent tax-free liquidation of, the subsidiary. If such circumstances exist, the FASB staff position is that deferred taxes should not be provided. Obviously, potential tax consequences to the buyer as well as to the seller in these transactions would have to be examined carefully to determine whether the criteria for an acceptable tax-planning strategy are met (see ¶ 5.01).

At the March 31, 1988 meeting of the Implementation Group, the FASB staff took the position that this treatment might be extended to a less than 80 percent owned domestic subsidiary. Where the subsidiary's stock is publicly traded, repurchase of sufficient shares to obtain 80 percent ownership could be assumed in situations where the market price of the subsidiary's stock at the balance sheet date is not more than the carrying amount per share of the minority interest reflected in the consolidated balance sheet. It would have to be feasible to repurchase the requisite shares without driving the price above the carrying amount per share of the minority interest. When the minority is closely held, the minority holders would have to be expected to be willing to sell, and at a price not in excess of the carrying amount per share. These strategies, as well as other possible strategies such as statutory mergers, would have to be evaluated as to whether, giving due consideration to state laws governing appraisal rights and so on, they meet the criteria for tax-planning strategies (see Chapter 5). Any valid strategy would have to be capable of accomplishment at a cost not exceeding the carrying amount per share of the minority interest.

When nontaxability of the change in interest gain, for purposes of the computation of the deferred tax liability, is dependent upon market price at the balance sheet date, market price changes from one year-end to the next could result in the gain's exclusion from scheduled future taxable income when it had been included in the preceding year-end's computation, or vice versa.

For situations in which taxability must be assumed, it appears that reversal should be scheduled, perhaps in an indefinite but far-off future year and, for domestic subsidiaries, as capital gain or loss. Taxation of gain on sale of foreign subsidiaries is quite complex, and it is possible that some portion of the gain would be taxed as dividend income potentially with related deemed paid foreign tax credits.

¶ 3.15 STOCK OPTIONS

In general, actual tax deductions arising from stock options are available upon (1) exercise by the employee of a nonqualified option, in which case the deduction is measured by the excess of market price over exercise price, or (2) disqualifying disposition by the employee of stock received under a qualified plan, in which case the proceeds to the employee over exercise price would be deductible by the corporation. The classification of the tax effects of stock options required by APB Opinion 25, *Accounting for Stock Issued to Employees*, was not amended by FAS 96. Accordingly, if the amount of the tax deduction realized exceeds the amount of book compensation recognized, the "excess" tax benefit realized should be credited to additional paid-in capital.

There could be a question under FAS 96 concepts whether, until exercise occurs, there is a temporary difference for the deductions that the company would receive if all nonqualified options were exercised at the market price at the balance sheet date. Disqualifying dispositions by employees would involve too many imponderables for consideration as a temporary difference.

The FASB staff, at the meeting of the Implementation Group on January 29, 1988, stated that FAS 96 does not change any of the accounting for stock options required by APB 25. Accordingly, no deferred tax benefit should be ascribed to future deductions that the corporation might receive upon exercise of stock options. The FASB will address the implications of FAS 96 on the accounting for stock issued to employees during its reconsideration of APB 25.

¶ 3.16 DEFERRED REVENUE OR INCOME

For many types of revenue entering into taxable income currently but deferred to some future period for financial reporting (e.g., rent received in advance), it may be difficult to discern just how the temporary difference reverses, that is, what the future tax consequence will be of earning the income. Under FAS 96, the deferred revenue indicates a future sacrifice will be required to earn the revenue, and that sacrifice is measured by the amount of the deferred revenue. Thus, it is probably easiest to think of the deferred revenue as a liability which will be settled by a deductible cash payment in the period recognized.

¶ 3.17 LEVERAGED LEASES

The accounting for leveraged leases is prescribed in FAS 13. The FAS 13 model is based on projected after-tax cash flows, and it thus predicts the future actual tax effects arising from the lease. Generally, these tax effects are based on the actual incremental tax effects expected to be realized in future years when the taxable income (loss) resulting from the leveraged-lease transaction will be reported on the tax return. Thus, contrary to the FAS 96 deferred tax computation in which reversals are presumed to be the first items entering into future years' taxable income, application of FAS 13 to leveraged leases is apt to consider their tax effects to be the last items entering into future years' taxable income. Nevertheless, FAS 96 requires that the deferred taxes arising from leveraged leases should be integrated into the overall deferred tax computation. The result is that future reversals of temporary differences from leveraged leases can be offset by net deductions from other temporary differences in the FAS 96 deferred tax computation, reducing the total deferred tax liability. However, there are different interpretations of how this integration should be accomplished.

Under one approach, the reversal of the leveraged lease temporary differences would not be included in the FAS 96 scheduling exercise and deferred tax computation. Rather, if there are unused deductions or credits resulting from the FAS 96 computation, then the deferred taxes provided for leveraged leases under FAS 13 would be considered to determine whether they provide deferred tax credits available for offset in the applicable years.

Under the approach that the accounting firm of Price Waterhouse believes should be applied, leveraged lease reversals would be included with reversals of all other temporary differences in the FAS 96 scheduling exercise and deferred tax computation. This approach to integration could, however, reduce certain tax benefits, that is, leveraged-lease reversals scheduled for 1987–1990 could offset net deductions from other temporary differences that would otherwise result in hypothetical carryback in the deferred tax computation to higher rate years. This effect of carryback to higher rate years is discussed in ¶ 4.05.

Under either approach, however, not all deferred taxes for leveraged leases are available for offset. When there is a change in the estimated future tax effects, FAS 13 requires a recomputation of the leveraged-lease income pattern from the beginning of the lease as if the change in tax effects had been anticipated at inception, and a catch-up adjustment is required. When estimated tax rates change over the term of the lease, one effect is that the deferred taxes recorded for the leveraged lease have no particular relationship to the book/tax basis difference. Further, as discussed at ¶ 2.05[2], FAS 96 treats the deferred investment credit arising under the FAS 13 model as a temporary difference, whereas under FAS 13 it was not considered in deferred tax computations.

Under FAS 96, the temporary difference at the balance sheet date will be computed as the difference between the net book value of the investment in the lease (after deducting deferred investment credit but not deferred taxes) and its tax basis (asset cost after tax depreciation plus accrued lease receivables and less remaining principal of, and accrued interest on, nonrecourse debt—frequently a negative number). Under the approach preferred by Price Waterhouse, the reversal of that temporary difference will be included in the FAS 96 schedule of reversals. The amount of reversal to be included in the scheduling exercise for each year would be determined as the amount expected to occur in each future year of (1) taxable income less (2) pretax income and less (3) amortization of deferred investment credit. Following the Price Waterhouse approach, it is necessary to allocate the deferred taxes for the leveraged lease provided under FAS 13 between (1) those that are "covered" by the FAS 96 computation and (2) those that must be preserved in the balance sheet, not available for offset in the FAS 96 computation, and amortized to income only as that occurs under the FAS 13 leveraged-lease model. (The preceding approach, which would not include leveraged-lease reversals in the FAS 96 scheduling exercise and deferred tax computation, would also have to derive, in some fashion, the leveraged-lease deferred taxes provided under FAS 13 that are available to offset unused deductions or credits arising in the FAS 96 computation.) Under the Price Waterhouse approach, the company's total deferred tax liability would be the sum of the results of the FAS 96 computation (including the reversals of the leveraged-lease temporary differences) and that portion of the FAS 13 deferred taxes for leveraged leases that is unavailable for offset.

The question arises exactly how the allocation is to be made. Price Waterhouse believes that the amount covered by the FAS 96 computation should be determined by multiplying the scheduled reversal for each year (as described previously) by the estimated tax rate used for that year in the FAS 13 projection of cash flows (Schedule 2 in Appendix E to FAS 13). The excess of the total FAS 13 deferred taxes over this amount would appropriately measure the amount that should be unavailable for offset in the FAS 96 computation as it would represent the sum of (1) the disproportionate deferred taxes relative to the cumulative (and thus also the aggregate future reversing) timing differences resulting from the tax rate change and (2) the effect of excluding deferred investment credit from consideration in the FAS 13 deferred tax calculation. Unusual circumstances in a particular situation or the enactment of tax rate increases might cause Price Waterhouse to reevaluate the propriety of this approach.

Two other possible approaches to allocation of the FAS 13 deferred taxes, when the FAS 96 computation includes the leveraged-lease reversals, would be to measure the amount covered by the FAS 96 computation as:

- The differential in the FAS 96 deferred tax liability computed with and without the reversals of the leveraged leases or
- The deferred taxes that would be provided on the reversals of the leveraged-lease temporary difference, applying the rules of FAS 96 and assuming that only those reversals were included as taxable income (deductions) in future years' tax returns. (Under this approach, the question would arise whether carryback availability or carryforwards existing at the balance sheet date and unrelated to the leveraged lease would be considered in the computation.)

Presumably the FASB staff will provide guidance.

Exhibit 3-10 illustrates the approach preferred by Price Waterhouse in applying FAS 96 to leveraged leases.

(continued on page 3-59)

EXHIBIT **3-10** _____
Application of FAS 96 to Leveraged Leases

As discussed at ¶ 3.17, different approaches have been suggested to "integration" of the FAS 96 deferred tax liability computation and the deferred taxes computed for leveraged leases under FAS 13. This exhibit illustrates the approach preferred by Price Waterhouse. The FASB staff could, in due course, provide guidance that differs from this approach.

The accounting for leveraged leases is illustrated in Appendix E of FAS 13. Schedules 1–4 of Appendix E schedule the projected after-tax cash flows from an example lease and recognize the projected after-tax income at a constant rate of return on net investment during the positive investment period. (Projected after-tax income does not include any secondary earnings—the benefit of the availability of funds from tax deferral during the negative investment period.)

Certain of the information used in Schedules 1–4 of Appendix E is summarized on Schedule 1, Columns A through N. While the net investment in the lease is not given on this schedule (it will be found in FAS 13, Appendix E, Schedule 3), it could be computed as the initial investment of $400,000 less the annual cash flow shown in Column H reduced by the portion allocated to income shown in Column I. Column I presents the recognition of projected after-tax income at a constant rate on net investment. Columns J through L then "explode" the Column I amounts into pretax income, investment credit, and the tax benefit (expense) related to pretax income. The current tax benefit (expense) is shown in Column D, and the deferred tax (expense) benefit is derived as the amount necessary to make the total (or net) tax benefit (expense) equal the amount shown in Column L. Note that, on Schedule 1, an actual tax rate of 50.4 percent is expected for the term of the lease (Column C); the ratio of income tax expense (Column L) to pretax income (Column J) is also 50.4 percent. Columns O and P show the timing differences between taxable income (Column B) and pretax income (Column J).

On Schedule 2, the Appendix E, Schedules 1–4 example is changed to assume tax rate changes enacted in year 7. (For this purpose, the new 40 percent and 34 percent tax rates are assumed to include state tax effects, net of U.S. tax benefit, just as does the 50.4 percent used in Appendix E. Implicit in this assumption is that the computation of taxable income or loss is essentially the same for state as for U.S. tax purposes.) Note that the amounts shown for taxable income (loss) in Column B are the same as in Schedule 1.

As required by paragraph 46 of FAS 13, Schedule 2 (through Column K) recalculates the income from the leveraged lease from its inception giving effect to the enacted rate changes. The amounts shown as pretax income, investment credit, and tax credits for years 1–6 would not have been actually recorded; rather, the amounts shown on Schedule 1 for those years would have been recorded in those years, and a cumulative adjustment would be made in year 7, when the new rates were enacted, to adjust to the recalculated balances. The cumulative adjustment would affect all components of income—pretax income, investment credit, and tax effect of pretax income.

Note that, on Schedule 2, there is a total tax benefit over the life of the lease and that it is 277 percent of the amount of pretax income. Under the FAS 13 model, ignoring investment credit, tax on pretax income will be recognized, cumulatively in year 7 and for each remaining year of the lease, at this 277 percent inverse rate.

Note also that, before the rate change, as indicated on Schedule 1, the deferred tax balance of $315,884 at the end of year 7 equalled 50.4 percent of the $626,756 cumulative timing differences; thus, deferred taxes had been provided at the expected tax rate for future reversals. After the rate change, as indicated on Schedule 2, the deferred tax balance at the end of year 7 was adjusted to $250,016, equal to 40 percent of the future reversing timing differences (the amount of cumulative timing differences is not affected by the rate change). Since the expected rate for future years is only 34 percent, the 6 percent differential will represent a portion of the "excess" deferred taxes provided under FAS 13 that is not available for offset in the FAS 96 computation. (The balance of the "excess" relates to the amount of unamortized investment credit, after adjustment for the rate changes, which is treated as a temporary difference under FAS 96.)

Schedule 3 calculates temporary differences, as defined by FAS 96, for the Schedule 2 situation. The amounts shown in column J would be included as reversals (taxable income) in the FAS 96 scheduling exercise.

Column L of Schedule 2 brings forward temporary differences from Schedule 3. Column M of Schedule 2 then applies to these temporary differences the 34 percent rate used in the FAS 13 calculation to determine the portion of the leveraged lease deferred taxes that would be covered by the FAS 96 deferred tax computation.

Column N of Schedule 2 is the difference between the FAS 13 and the FAS 96 calculations of deferred taxes for the leveraged lease. This amount is not affected by the FAS 96 computation. The lessor's total deferred tax liability at each year-end would be the aggregate of the FAS 96 computation and the amount shown in Column N.

Note:
- The illustration on Schedules 2 and 3 shows only reversing differences for the years after the tax rate change. If the amount of temporary difference from the leveraged lease were going to continue to increase after the balance sheet date before starting to reduce, the FAS 96 scheduling would include all future changes in the temporary difference, including originating differences in early years.
- This Exhibit illustrates prospective application of FAS 96 from the year of enactment of the tax rate changes. If FAS 96 were applied retroactively, the temporary differences used in the FAS 96 computation for years 1–6 would be based on Schedule 1. The temporary differences to be included in FAS 96 scheduling at the end of each year 1–6 would be the timing differences, shown in Column O of Schedule 1, adjusted for amortization of deferred investment credit (Column K).

(continued)

EXHIBIT 3-10 *(cont'd)*

SCHEDULE 1

FAS 13 Leveraged-Lease Example (No Rate Change)

(A)	(B)	(C)	(D)	(E)	(F)	(G)	(H)	(I)	(J) Allocation to Income	(K)	(L)	(M) Deferred Tax	(N)	(O) Timing Differences	(P)
Year	Taxable income (loss)	Tax rate	Current tax reductions (payments)	Loan principal payments	ITC realized	Add back tax depre-ciation	Annual cash flow (sum of columns B, D, E, F & G)	Total	Pretax income	ITC	Income tax benefit (expense)	(Expense) benefit	Year-end balance	(Originating) reversing	Cumulative
Investment							($400,000)								
1	($106,857)	50.4%	$ 53,856	($20,435)	$100,000	$ 142,857	169,421	$ 34,588	$ 9,929	$ 29,663	$ 5,004	($ 58,860)	($ 58,860)	($116,786)	($116,786)
2	(207,059)	50.4%	104,358	(22,274)		244,898	119,923	22,929	6,582	19,664	(3,317)	(107,675)	(166,535)	(213,641)	(330,427)
3	(147,231)	50.4%	74,204	(24,279)		187,075	89,769	14,542	4,174	12,472	(2,104)	(76,308)	(242,843)	(151,405)	(481,832)
4	(111,032)	50.4%	55,960	(26,464)		153,061	71,525	8,037	2,307	6,893	(1,163)	(57,123)	(299,966)	(113,339)	(595,171)
5	(74,637)	50.4%	37,617	(28,846)		119,048	53,182	2,547	731	2,184	(368)	(37,985)	(337,951)	(75,368)	(670,539)
6	(6,054)	50.4%	3,051	(31,442)		53,061	18,616	0	0	0	0	(3,051)	(341,002)	(6,054)	(676,593)
7	49,837	50.4%	(25,118)	(34,272)			(9,553)	0	0	0	0	25,118	(315,884)	49,837	(626,756)
	(603,033)		303,928	(188,012)	100,000	900,000	112,883	82,643	23,723	70,876	(11,956)	(315,884)		(626,756)	
8	52,921	50.4%	(26,672)	(37,357)			(11,108)	0	0	0	0	26,672	(289,212)	52,921	(573,835)
9	56,283	50.4%	(28,367)	(40,719)			(12,803)	0	0	0	0	28,367	(260,845)	56,283	(517,552)
10	59,948	50.4%	(30,214)	(44,383)			(14,649)	0	0	0	0	30,214	(230,631)	59,948	(457,604)
11	63,942	50.4%	(32,227)	(48,378)			(16,663)	719	206	617	(104)	32,123	(198,508)	63,736	(393,868)
12	68,296	50.4%	(34,421)	(52,732)			(18,857)	2,222	637	1,906	(321)	34,100	(164,408)	67,659	(326,209)
13	73,043	50.4%	(36,813)	(57,478)			(21,248)	4,045	1,161	3,469	(585)	36,228	(128,180)	71,882	(254,327)
14	78,215	50.4%	(39,420)	(62,651)			(23,856)	6,232	1,789	5,345	(902)	38,518	(89,662)	76,426	(177,901)
15	83,855	50.4%	(42,263)	(68,290)			(26,698)	8,834	2,536	7,576	(1,278)	40,985	(48,677)	81,319	(96,582)
16	100,000	50.4%	(50,400)	0		100,000	149,600	11,906	3,418	10,211	(1,723)	48,677	(0)	96,582	0
	$ 33,470		($ 16,869)	($600,000)	$100,000	$1,000,000	$116,601	$116,601	$33,470	$100,000	($16,869)	$ 0		$ 0	

Source: October 1, 1986 letter to the FASB staff from Mr. Jeffrey A. Riley, Vice-President, Administration & Control, GATX Leasing Corporation.

SCHEDULE 2

FAS 13 Leveraged-Lease Example (Assuming Tax Rate Change in Year 7)

(A) Year	(B) Taxable income (loss)	(C) Tax rate	(D) Current tax reductions (payments)	(E) Annual cash flow*	Allocation to Income			(I) Income tax benefit (expense)	Deferred Tax		(L) Temporary difference	Deferred Taxes on Leveraged Lease	
					(F) Total	(G) Pretax income	(H) ITC		(J) (Expense) benefit	(K) Year-end balance		(M) Related to temporary difference	(N) Excess
Investment				($400,000)									
1	($106,857)	50.4%	$ 53,856	169,421	$ 50,591	$ 7,487	$ 22,368	$20,736	$ 33,120	($33,120)			
2	(207,059)	50.4%	104,358	119,923	35,563	5,263	15,724	14,576	(89,782)	(122,902)			
3	(147,231)	50.4%	74,204	89,769	24,893	3,684	11,006	10,203	(64,001)	(186,903)			
4	(111,032)	50.4%	55,960	71,525	16,686	2,469	7,378	6,839	(49,121)	(236,024)			
5	(74,637)	50.4%	37,617	53,182	9,751	1,443	4,311	3,997	(33,620)	(269,644)			
6	(6,054)	50.4%	3,051	18,616	4,258	630	1,883	1,745	(1,306)	(270,950)		$199,960	
7	49,837	40.0%	(19,934)	(4,369)	2,440	361	1,079	1,000	20,934	(250,016)	$588,119		$50,056
	(603,033)		309,112	118,067	144,182	21,337	63,749	59,096	(250,016)				
8	52,921	34.0%	(17,993)	(2,429)	3,303	489	1,460	1,354	19,347	(230,669)	537,147	182,630	48,039
9	56,283	34.0%	(19,136)	(3,572)	4,028	596	1,781	1,651	20,787	(209,882)	483,241	164,302	45,580
10	59,948	34.0%	(20,382)	(4,817)	4,989	738	2,206	2,045	22,427	(187,455)	426,237	144,921	42,534
11	63,942	34.0%	(21,740)	(6,176)	6,229	922	2,754	2,553	24,293	(163,162)	365,971	124,430	38,732
12	68,296	34.0%	(23,221)	(7,657)	7,798	1,154	3,448	3,196	26,417	(136,745)	302,277	102,774	33,971
13	73,043	34.0%	(24,835)	(9,270)	9,752	1,443	4,312	3,997	28,832	(107,913)	234,989	79,896	28,017
14	78,215	34.0%	(26,593)	(11,029)	12,159	1,799	5,376	4,984	31,577	(76,336)	163,949	55,743	20,593
15	83,855	34.0%	(28,511)	(12,946)	15,092	2,233	6,673	6,186	34,697	(41,639)	89,000	30,260	11,379
16	100,000	34.0%	(34,000)	166,000	18,639	2,759	8,241	7,639	41,639	(0)	0	0	0
	$ 33,470		$ 92,701	$226,171	$226,171	$33,470	$100,000	$92,701	($ 0)				

*Annual cash flow is the amount shown in Column H of Schedule 1 adjusted in years 7–16 for the difference between the amounts in Column D on this schedule and those in Column D on Schedule 1.

Source (for columns through column K): October 1, 1986 letter to the FASB staff from Mr. Jeffrey A. Riley, Vice-President, Administration & Control, GATX leasing Corporation.

(continued)

EXHIBIT 3-10 (cont'd)

SCHEDULE 3

Calculation of Leveraged-Lease Temporary Differences Under FAS 96 (Using Lease Example in Schedule 2)

(A)	(B)	(C)	(D)	(E)	(F)	(G)	(H)	(I)	(J)
		Book Basis				Tax Basis*			
Year	Net receivable plus residual	Unearned income	Deferred ITC	Net	Asset	Unpaid debt principal	Net	Temporary difference	Change in temporary difference
Investment	$433,470	($33,470)	($100,000)	$300,000	$1,000,000	($600,000)	$400,000		
1	(15,565)	7,487	22,368	314,290	(142,857)	20,435	277,578		
2	(15,565)	5,263	15,724	319,712	(244,898)	22,274	54,954		
3	(15,565)	3,684	11,006	318,837	(187,075)	24,279	(107,842)		
4	(15,565)	2,469	7,378	313,119	(153,061)	26,464	(234,439)		
5	(15,565)	1,443	4,311	303,308	(119,048)	28,846	(324,641)		
6	(15,565)	630	1,883	290,256	(53,061)	31,442	(346,260)		
7	(15,565)	361	1,079	276,131		34,272	(311,988)	$588,119	
	324,515	(12,133)	(36,251)		100,000	(411,988)			
8	(15,564)	489	1,460	262,516		37,357	(274,631)	537,147	($ 50,972)
9	(15,564)	596	1,781	249,329		40,719	(233,912)	483,241	(53,906)
10	(15,565)	738	2,206	236,708		44,383	(189,529)	426,237	(57,004)
11	(15,564)	922	2,754	224,820		48,378	(141,151)	365,971	(60,266)
12	(15,564)	1,154	3,448	213,858		52,732	(88,419)	302,277	(63,694)
13	(15,565)	1,443	4,312	204,048		57,478	(30,941)	234,989	(67,288)
14	(15,564)	1,799	5,376	195,659		62,651	31,710	163,949	(71,040)
15	(15,565)	2,233	6,673	189,000		68,290	100,000	89,000	(74,949)
16	(200,000)	2,759	8,241	0	(100,000)	0	0	0	(89,000)
	$ 0	$ 0	$ 0		$ 0	$ 0			($588,119)

*For an accrual-basis taxpayer, computation of the tax basis would also have to include any accrued lease receivable and any accrued interest payable on the debt. Such amounts are not included on this schedule because, in the FAS 13 Appendix E example, lease payments and interest payments are made on the last day of the year.

With respect to leveraged leases acquired in a purchase business combination, the rules prescribed by FASI 21, *Accounting for Leases in a Business Combination*, including net-of-tax valuation of the leases at date of acquisition, will be continued. Thus, the future tax effects that enter into that valuation will not be integrated. However, post-acquisition deferred taxes generated by purchased leveraged leases under the FASI 21 model would be integrated with the FAS 96 computation in the same manner as deferred taxes for other leveraged leases.

¶ 3.18 AGGRESSIVE TAX POSITIONS

In past practice under APB 11, it generally was unnecessary to be concerned in deferred tax computations about potential adjustments to tax returns by the taxing authority when the adjustments would affect only timing differences. Deferred taxes were provided on all timing differences, and the total tax provision charged to income typically was not affected by what was reported on the current year's tax return or by when timing differences were expected to reverse. Thus, a revenue agent's adjustment to accelerate taxable income (e.g., by capitalizing items expensed on the originally filed tax return) generally would result only in reclassification of deferred tax credits to current taxes payable. The provision for increased tax resulting from such adjustments was automatically covered by deferred taxes; if disallowances were anticipated, accrual only for potential interest was necessary.

Because the FAS 96 deferred tax computation can be importantly affected by the years for which specific reversals are scheduled, it may be necessary to review aggressive tax positions to determine whether the position currently being taken on tax returns is expected to be sustained. The company should look at the most recent revenue agent's reports and consider whether scheduling properly reflects the adjustments. If interest has been accrued for potential assessments, the company should investigate whether the expected disallowances for past returns involve issues that will also affect the pattern of future reversals. The scheduling of reversals in the deferred tax computation should reflect the tax positions expected to be ultimately sustained. Assessment of whether adjustment of reversal patterns is needed should be coordinated with determination of carryback availability discussed at ¶ 4.06.

In documenting the computations accountants must keep in mind the potential exposure to increased taxes and remember that the IRS has authority, although it is seldom used, to summon and examine the records of the company or its independent accountants.

Carrybacks and Carryforwards

Using the material provided in the previous chapters, the company should now have a schedule that spreads its temporary differences to the years in which those differences will reverse, similar to the schedule shown in Exhibit 3-3. Adding up the amounts for each year will provide either net taxable income or net tax deductions for each future year. Sometimes the amounts net to zero for a given year or no reversals are scheduled for that year. The totals include only the reversal of temporary differences. No future income or loss may be considered, and with limited exceptions, such as depreciation and leasing, there will be no originating temporary differences.

¶ 4.01   EXISTING NET OPERATING LOSS CARRYFORWARDS

At this point the actual tax net operating loss (NOL) carryforward, if any, enters the computation. It should be used to the company's best advantage to reduce future taxable income.

¶ 4.02   FUTURE NET DEDUCTIONS

For book purposes, net deductions scheduled in future years are considered NOLs. They can first be carried back to actual prior years' tax returns and to the provision for taxes payable in the current year to obtain a hypothetical refund. NOLs can also offset net taxable income scheduled for other future years, thus reducing the overall deferred tax balance. The mechanics to be used are the carryback and carryforward rules contained in the provisions of the applicable tax regulations.

In the United States, the Internal Revenue Code generally provides for a three-year carryback and a 15-year carryforward. However, in the United Kingdom, for example, the carryback is only one year, although there is an indefinite carryforward period. There may be different rules for carrybacks and carryforwards in each city, state, and applicable foreign taxing jurisdiction. Exhibit 4-1 contains a state-by-state summary of corporate net operating loss carryback/carryforward rules.

¶ 4.03   UNUSED DEDUCTIONS

The company's schedule could result in its being unable to use all its future tax deductions to offset future taxable income or get hypothetical refunds of prior years' taxes paid and current taxes payable.

If the company has future taxable income of $100 that will occur over the next 15 years (e.g., excess of book over tax depreciation) and future tax deductions of $100 that occur after year 20 (e.g., deferred compensation), then even with the carryback of three years, an offset is out of reach. Absent a tax-planning strategy (see Chapter 5), the company would have to record a deferred tax liability for the $100 of future taxable income without ascribing *any* benefit to the $100 of future tax deductions—and that's a big problem.

Some might argue that the problem is limited to a few companies that have deferred compensation or dismantlement accruals. This may be true today, but the scenario could easily change. The FASB is currently considering a requirement to accrue a liability for postretirement benefits. If such a requirement is included in a future FASB pronouncement, more companies will be faced with the problem.

¶ 4.04 FORGO A CARRYBACK

One of the more obscure provisions in the Internal Revenue Code is the election to forgo the carryback of a loss. A company might make the election if, for example, it has used foreign tax credits to reduce or even eliminate the actual taxes payable in the preceding three years. To that extent, the loss carryback will not result in a refund but will only free up the foreign tax credits. However, given the short carryforward period of five years for foreign tax credits in the United States and other restrictive limitations on their use, these foreign tax credits might expire unused. What the company can do instead is file an election in the year of the loss to carry it forward.

There may be other circumstances in which credits that would be freed up by carryback of a loss could in turn be used by further carryback to claim refund of taxes paid in years preceding the three-year NOL carryback period. In such cases, carryback benefit at or approaching the full statutory rate may be available.

The company can elect to forgo a carryback in the scheduling process only if it minimizes the deferred tax liability. Presumably, the election would be made if the deferred tax computation represented the company's actual tax position. Note that the

EXHIBIT 4-1

Corporate Net Operating Losses: State-by-State Summary
As of January, 1988

| State | Number of Years Allowed | | Election to |
	Carrybacks	Carryforwards	Forgo Carryback?
Alabama[2]	0	15	N/A
Alaska	3	15	Yes
Arizona	0	5	N/A
Arkansas			
Years prior to 1987	0	3	N/A
Years after 1986	0	5	N/A
California[3]			
Years prior to 1985	0	0	N/A
1985–1986	0	3	N/A
1987–1991	0	15	N/A
Colorado	0	15	N/A
Connecticut	0	5	N/A
Delaware	3	15	Yes
District of Columbia[4]	3	15	Yes
Florida	0	15	N/A
Georgia			
Years prior to 1987	3	7	Yes
Years after 1986	3	15	Yes
Hawaii	3	15	Yes
Idaho[5]	3	10	Yes
Illinois	3	15	Yes
Indiana	3	15	Yes[1]
Iowa	3	15	Yes[1]
Kansas	3	7	Yes[1]
Kentucky	3	15	Yes
Louisiana	3	5	Yes
Maine	3	15	Yes[1]
Maryland	3	15	Yes[1]
Massachusetts[6]	0	5	N/A
Michigan	0	10	N/A
Minnesota	0	15	N/A
Mississippi	0	5	N/A
Missouri	3	15	Yes
Montana	3	7	No
Nebraska	0	5	N/A

State	Number of Years Allowed		Election to Forgo Carryback?
	Carrybacks	Carryforwards	
Nevada	N/A	N/A	N/A
New Hampshire	0	0	N/A
New Jersey	0	7	N/A
New Mexico	3	15	Yes[1]
New York	3	15	Yes[1]
North Carolina	0	15	N/A
North Dakota	3	15	Yes[1]
Ohio	0	15	N/A
Oklahoma	3	15	Yes[1]
Oregon	0	15	N/A
Pennsylvania	0	3	N/A
Rhode Island	3	15	Yes[1]
South Carolina	0	15	N/A
South Dakota	N/A	N/A	N/A
Tennessee	0	7	N/A
Texas	N/A	N/A	N/A
Utah	3	5	No
Vermont[7]	3	15	Yes[1]
Virginia	3	15	Yes[1]
Washington	N/A	N/A	N/A
West Virginia	3	15	Yes[1]
Wisconsin	0	15	N/A
Wyoming	N/A	N/A	N/A

[1] Permitted only if election to forgo carryback is also made for federal tax purposes.

[2] Net operating loss carryforward is limited to $600,000 per year.

[3] California allows 50 percent of a NOL to be carried forward against income for years beginning on or after January 1, 1987. A NOL incurred in a fiscal year ending in 1985 is prorated based on the month in which the year ends. NOLs generated in 1985 may be carried forward three years starting with the year beginning in 1987. NOLs generated in years 1987 through 1991 may be carried forward 15 years. Special rules apply to NOL carryforwards generated by a small business.

[4] These rules apply to tax years beginning after December 31, 1987. No losses may be carried back to years ending before January 1, 1988. For years beginning before December 31, 1987, no carrybacks or carryforwards are permitted.

[5] NOL carryback is limited to $100,000.

[6] NOL carryback is allowed only during the corporation's first five taxable years.

[7] NOL carryback refund is limited to $10,000 for any one taxable year.

company can make the election year by year—that is, make the election to carry *forward* a loss scheduled in 1997 but carry *back* a loss scheduled in 1996.

As with any FAS 96 tax-planning strategy, (see ¶ 5.07), circumstances may change in succeeding years that would cause the company to reverse a carryforward decision. The scheduled pattern of reversing differences can change from year to year, and taxes actually paid or recovered will vary from amounts "scheduled" in previous years' deferred tax computations. When the carryforward election no longer results in the minimum liability, it would not be an appropriate tax-planning strategy.

¶ 4.05 DEFERRED TAX ASSET

A deferred tax asset is justified only if future net deductions could be carried back to reduce taxes paid in the current or a prior year or, when the balance sheet is classified, to claim a refund of a deferred tax liability classified as current. (Actually, in the classification of deferred taxes in the balance sheet (see ¶ 7.01), all noncurrent amounts are aggregated so noncurrent deferred tax "assets" may be netted against, or reduced by, noncurrent deferred tax liabilities. Similarly, in an unclassified balance sheet, all deferred taxes related to a single jurisdiction would be presented as a single asset or liability.)

Some unusual effects can be generated in these circumstances (Exhibit 4-2 illustrates one). TRA 1986 mandated a phase-in of tax rate decreases. As a result, a scheduled loss in 1987, 1988, or 1989 that is carried back to 1986 or prior years could generate a deferred tax benefit at a 46 percent rate. A loss in 1990 carried back to 1987 could yield a deferred tax benefit at a 40 percent rate. If, in the future, this "loss" is absorbed by taxable income from sources other than scheduled reversals, the company will receive only a 34 percent benefit when the deduction is claimed in 1988, 1989, or 1990 (40 percent in 1987). Stated another way, taxable income in one of those years will attract tax expense at the higher carryback rate to the extent that it causes loss of the carryback previously scheduled. The net result is that the company

EXHIBIT 4-2
Lower Effective Rate Due to Carryback

ABC Company adopted the liability method of accounting for deferred taxes in 1987. During 1987, ABC Company had recorded, for financial reporting purposes, a $2,000 accrual relating to plant shutdown costs. It is not expected that these costs will be paid, and thus be deductible for tax purposes, until 1989. ABC Company has no other temporary differences.

In applying the liability method at December 31, 1987, the $2,000 net deduction scheduled to occur in 1989 is carried back to offset actual taxable income as reported on ABC Company's 1986 tax return. As a result, a deferred tax asset of $920 is established at the balance sheet date (the $2,000 net deduction of 46 percent tax-effected at the rate 1986 taxes were paid).

In 1989, the plant shutdown costs were paid and deducted on ABC Company's tax return, yielding a tax benefit at the statutory tax rate of 34 percent. The effect on the effective tax rate in 1987, 1988, and 1989 of establishing a deferred tax asset at a higher tax rate than the actual benefit derived is shown:

	1987	1988	1989
Pretax financial reporting income	$5,000	$7,000	$7,000
Plant shutdown accrual	2,000		(2,000)
Taxable income as reported on the tax return	7,000	7,000	5,000
Tax rate	40%	34%	34%
Current income tax expense	2,800	2,380	1,700
Deferred income tax provision (benefit)	(920)	0	920
Total income tax provision	$1,880	$2,380	$2,620
Effective tax rate	38%	34%	37%

The income tax journal entries to be recorded by ABC Company at each year-end, assuming that the plant shutdown accrual is the only temporary difference, are shown below. Note that the noncurrent deferred tax asset established at December 31, 1987 is reclassified to current at December 31, 1988 (see ¶ 7.01).

December 31, 1987:
Debit: Current tax expense	$2,800	
Credit: Current taxes payable		$2,800
Debit: Noncurrent deferred tax asset	$ 920	
Credit: Deferred tax benefit		$ 920

(continued)

EXHIBIT 4-2 *(cont'd)*

December 31, 1988:

Debit: Current tax expense	$2,380	
Credit: Current taxes payable		$2,380
Debit: Current deferred tax asset	$ 920	
Credit: Noncurrent deferred tax asset		$ 920

December 31, 1989:

Debit: Current tax expense	$1,700	
Credit: Current taxes payable		$1,700
Debit: Deferred tax expense	$ 920	
Credit: Current deferred tax asset		$ 920

A reconciliation between the "expected" tax expense (benefit) for 1987, 1988, and 1989 (computed by applying the U.S. federal tax rate to earnings before income taxes) is as follows:

	1987	1988	1989
Tax expense at the statutory rate of 40% in 1987 and at 34% in 1988 and 1989	$2,000	$2,380	$2,380
Effect of recognizing the benefit of plant shutdown expenses at a higher rate (46%) than the current statutory rate (40%) ($2,000 at 6%)	(120)		
Effect of realizing the benefit of plant shutdown expenses at a lower rate (34%) than previously recognized (46%) ($2,000 at 12%)			240
	$1,880	$2,380	$2,620

---

will show an illusory benefit in one year that it will "pay back" in a future year.

It might look appealing to make an election to forgo carrying back the loss to avoid this situation—but the company cannot. A valid tax-planning strategy is one that the company *would* use if it *had* to in order to obtain or preserve a tax benefit. Accordingly, it would be difficult to represent plausibly that the company would *not* carry back a loss to get a *46* percent benefit but *would* carry it forward to get a *34* percent benefit. (Tax-planning strategies are discussed in detail in Chapter 5.)

As noted in ¶ 3.03[1], this situation can be widespread among capital-intensive companies because their largest temporary difference is likely to be depreciation, and excess tax over book depreciation may be scheduled to occur in years that can be carried back to 46 percent and 40 percent years. But the problem can also result from the scheduling of warranty or other accrual reversals.

This effect is expected to be controversial. Recording an asset that will not subsequently be realized is counterintuitive. The FASB's rationale for this treatment is that the 46 percent (or 40 percent) benefit is implicit in the book/tax basis differences in the balance sheet; when other sources of taxable income arise in future years that lessen the actual benefit, the result is an event companies will recognize in those future years.

The FASB staff has taken the position that management must actively search for tax-planning strategies that will maximize net deductions scheduled for 1987–1990 to the extent that carryback will generate a higher tax benefit than would use of deductions in other later years. Companies that are concerned about the effect of recording a 46 percent/40 percent carryback benefit and writing off a portion in subsequent years may wish to delay adoption of FAS 96 until 1989 and perhaps then will wish to restate at least 1988 so that a similar charge is lodged in the prior year's comparative results (see ¶¶ 12.01, 12.02).

¶ 4.06 CARRYBACK TO CUSHION

As discussed in ¶ 3.18, the scheduling of reversals should reflect tax return positions expected to be ultimately sustained. Similarly, amounts of taxable income available for carryback should be that expected after any revenue agent adjustments. This may be especially important for tax years preceding the TRA 1986 rate reduction. When adopting the liability method, deferred taxes provided at 46 percent should not be adjusted downward to 34 percent if it is probable that the related taxable income will eventually have to be included in pre-1988 tax returns.

Approaching the assessment of cushion from the opposite direction, the deferred tax liability computation in some cases may be importantly affected by the amount of carryback availability, which may sometimes be the only basis for recording certain tax benefits. At year-end 1987, the amount of carryback availability is important even for companies that have no problem recognizing all potential tax benefits. That is, carryback from 1988, 1989, and 1990 is to 46 percent and 40 percent years, and the measurement of the amount of tax benefit could be affected. Thus, it is important to use in the carryback computation the ultimate tax liability expected to be paid in each prior year.

While the potential return adjustments that could affect scheduling would generally involve acceleration of taxable income, carryback availability should also consider expected adjustments representing permanent disallowances (e.g., taxable income reported as capital gains that might be reclassified to ordinary income on examination). Sometimes the cushion is an amorphous amount intended to cover a range of issues. In applying FAS 96, it may be important to assign such cushion to specific tax years to determine whether it is available for carryback. In other words, management should focus on the issues for which the cushion is provided.

Management should be aware of the conflict involved between the need to adequately document the deferred tax computation and the potential exposure to increased taxes attributable to the seldom-used authority of the IRS to summon and examine the records of the company or its independent accountants.

Tax-Planning Strategies

After applying all the carryback and carryforward rules, there may still be years in which there is net taxable income while the company also has net deductions in other years. *Or* there may be loss carryforwards that will not be fully used against taxable income scheduled during the carryforward years and years with net taxable income beyond the carryforward period.

The concept of tax planning became an integral part of FAS 96 to help alleviate the problem of unused deductions and credits. The FASB reasoned that, faced with a specific pattern of taxable income and loss, any company would attempt to minimize its net tax liability through tax planning. Therefore, the objective of a tax-planning strategy for the deferred tax computation is to accelerate or delay the reversal of temporary differences.

On the surface, it seems that the objective of tax-planning strategies conflicts with a basic principle of FAS 96—that is, no consideration can be given to future events. Essentially, a tax-planning strategy can only be concerned with the timing of realization of a recorded asset or settlement of a recorded liability (or timing of taxable income or deductions when there is no balance sheet item related to the temporary difference). Therefore, a distinction is made between two types of future events, so that tax-planning strategies mesh with the conceptual underpinnings of the Statement. Both types of future events result in taxable or deductible amounts in future years. However, the future taxable or deductible amounts resulting from one type of future event is attributable to temporary differences existing at the balance sheet date. The deferred tax consequences of those differences are inherent in the balance sheet and are recognized in the current year. The future taxable or deductible amounts resulting from the second type of future event are attributable to the generation of income (losses) in those future years. The tax consequences from that type of future event should be recognized in the year the event occurs.

Tax-planning strategies as defined by FAS 96 apply only to the first type of future event described previously. Their use cannot result in the anticipation of net additional future income or net additional future deductions.

¶ 5.01 GROUND RULES

A tax-planning strategy must be a feasible, prudent action over which management has discretion and control. Put another way, FAS 96 sees a tax-planning strategy as what a company would do if it had

EXHIBIT 5-1 _____
Acceptable Tax-Planning Strategies

The following strategies may be used if they reduce a deferred tax liability or increase a deferred tax asset.

- Selling operating assets and simultaneously leasing them back for a long period of time.
- Accelerating the repatriation of foreign earnings for which deferred taxes were previously provided.
- Electing to forgo the carryback of a net operating loss (NOL) deduction.
- Funding a liability before the expected payment date. The prefunding must be deductible on the tax return. In addition, any interest discount and subsequent accretion would be ignored.
- Filing a consolidated tax return.
- Electing to deduct foreign taxes paid or accrued rather than treat them as creditable foreign taxes.
- Prefunding a pension obligation. See discussion at ¶ 3.06.

---

to in order to avoid losing a tax benefit. Further, it must not involve significant cost to the company.

Since FAS 96 does not define "feasible," "prudent," "discretion," "control," or "significant," their meaning is subject to some interpretation. FAS 96 states that management must have both the ability and the intent to carry out a tax-planning strategy, but the FASB staff has stated that the intent requirement does not imply discretionary selection of strategies (see ¶ 5.06). Exhibit 5-1 offers some tax-planning strategies that would be acceptable in the appropriate circumstances.

¶ 5.02   SALE-LEASEBACK STRATEGY

A potential tax-planning strategy not mentioned in Exhibit 5-1 is an outright sale of operating assets. Any outright sale of assets could entail economic considerations that go well beyond those typically involved in actual tax-planning strategies. For example, they could include whether the company wants to remain in certain business lines, products, or marketing areas. In most cases, it would be difficult to make a realistic assessment whether the outright sale of operating assets would meet the prudent and feasible tests of FAS 96. A concurrent long-term operating leaseback of the assets, however, would appear to solve any problem in this area.

As noted previously, a tax-planning strategy can only accelerate or delay the reversal of temporary differences. Therefore, the assumed proceeds for such a sale-leaseback would be equal to the net book value of the asset at the date of the sale, not the net book value or the fair value at the current balance sheet date. The assumption of the sale would reverse any temporary differences accumulated to the date of sale. There would be no further temporary differences to schedule for the asset after the date of sale because rent expense and deductible rent should be equal under the operating leaseback.

Exhibit 5-2 illustrates the use of a sale-leaseback tax-planning strategy in a FAS 96 deferred tax calculation.

¶ 5.03 SALE-LEASEBACK AT A "LOSS"

The question arises whether it is acceptable for a tax-planning strategy to assume sale-leaseback of an asset whose current fair value is below its present carrying amount and/or whose fair value at the sale date in the proposed strategy is expected to be less than its carrying amount at that time. The asset is not impaired; recovery of its carrying amount is expected through use in operations rather than by sale.

When there is a loss on a sale-leaseback, however, it must generally be recognized immediately under FAS 13. This seems to conflict with the FAS 96 assumption of realization of assets at their carrying amounts. The accounting firm of Price Waterhouse believes that, when the leaseback is long-term, the loss on the sale is not an economic loss, and realization of the carrying amount through operations will not be affected. The loss on the sale will be recovered through lower rent payments under the leaseback. Thus, they conclude that there is no basic conflict between the sale-leaseback of a depreciated asset and the FAS 96 assumption of recovery of carrying amounts of assets.

EXHIBIT 5-2
Sale-Leaseback Tax-Planning Strategy

Gamma Corp. adopted FAS 96 in 1988 and is applying it prospectively. Several years ago, Gamma Corp. acquired an operating facility (land and buildings) in a nontaxable purchase business combination. The book and tax bases of those assets at January 1, 1988 are as follows.

	Book basis	Tax basis	Temporary difference
Land	$ 8,000	$3,000	$ 5,000
Buildings	12,000	5,000	7,000
	$20,000	$8,000	$12,000

The buildings have a remaining useful life of 20 years for financial reporting purposes and 10 years for tax purposes. The straight-line method of depreciation is being used in both cases. Thus, book depreciation will be $600 annually through 2007, and tax depreciation will be $500 annually through 1997. Gamma Corp. has no other temporary differences.

In recent years, Gamma Corp. has experienced losses for both book and tax purposes and, at January 1, 1988, there is a tax NOL carryforward of $5,000, most of which expires in 2002. For purposes of applying FAS 96, Gamma Corp. has scheduled the reversal of the identified temporary differences; the results of that exercise are as follows.

(continued)

5-5

EXHIBIT 5-2 *(cont'd)*

	Temporary difference at 1/1/88	Future years					
		1988	1989–1997 (nine years)	1998–2002 (five years)	2003	2004–2007 (four years)	Indefinite future
Land	$ 5,000						$5,000
Buildings	7,000	$100	$900	$3,000	$600	$2,400	5,000
	$12,000	100	900	3,000	600	2,400	5,000
Tax NOL used	($ 4,000)	(100)	(900)	(3,000)	—	—	—
Taxable income resulting from reversal of temporary differences		0	0	0	600	2,400	5,000
Enacted tax rate		34%	34%	34%	34%	34%	34%
Deferred tax liability	$ 2,720	$ 0	$ 0	$ 0	$204	$ 816	$1,700

In the preceding schedule, the temporary difference relating to land is shown as reversing in the very indefinite future, presumably when the company is liquidated. Reversal of the temporary difference relating to the buildings results in taxable income in each future year as book depreciation exceeds tax depreciation in each year of the assets' remaining 20-year book life. As the U.S. tax law only allows for a 15-year carryforward of NOLs, taxable income scheduled to occur in years 2003 and thereafter cannot be offset by NOL carryforwards existing at the balance sheet date. Absent the use of a tax-planning strategy, Gamma Corp. would be required to report a deferred tax liability of $2,720 and a book NOL carryforward of $1,000 ($5,000 tax NOL less $4,000 NOL used in the scheduling exercise).

In order to recognize the entire benefit of the NOL carryforward, taxable income scheduled to occur in 2003 and subsequent years must be accelerated into the carryforward period (2002 or earlier). A sale and long-term operating leaseback of the buildings would accomplish that objective. (The land would be excluded from the sale-leaseback. Gamma Corp. would retain title to the land and lease it to the buyer of the buildings for a term exceeding the buildings' lives.) The buildings' current value is well in excess of their carrying amounts, and there is no indication that the values would decline, at any future date, below the then carrying amounts. In addition, in the opinion of management, a sale-leaseback would be prudent and feasible and would not result in significant cost to the company. The strategy assumes that the sale-leaseback would occur in 2002 because that optimizes the benefit. Thus, any taxable income originally scheduled to occur after that date (the excess of book basis, which is assumed to be the sales price, over the tax basis of the buildings) would be realized in 2002. A schedule incorporating the sale-leaseback tax-planning strategy is as follows.

	Temporary difference at 1/1/88	Future years					
		1988	1989–1997 (nine years)	1998–2002 (five years)	2003	2004–2007 (four years)	Indefinite future
Land	($ 5,000)						$5,000
Buildings	7,000	$100	$900	$3,000	$600	$2,400	
	$12,000	100	900	3,000	600	2,400	5,000
Sale-Leaseback tax-planning strategy				3,000	(600)	(2,400)	
		100	900	6,000	0	0	5,000
Tax NOL used	($ 5,000)	(100)	(900)	(4,000)	—	—	
Taxable income resulting from reversal of temporary differences		0	0	2,000	0	0	5,000
Enacted tax rate		34%	34%	34%	34%	34%	34%
Deferred tax liability	$ 2,380	$ 0	$ 0	$ 680	$ 0	$ 0	$1,700

Incorporating the sale-leaseback tax-planning strategy into the deferred tax calculation reduces the deferred tax liability by $340, and it results in the minimum deferred tax liability in this situation.

Note: The effects of alternative minimum tax (AMT) have been ignored in this example. In general, the AMT rules preclude the use of an NOL carryforward to completely eliminate tax.

FAS 96 requires that both book and tax amounts for all future years be scheduled for depreciable assets. To apply this literally to sale-leaseback of a depreciated asset:

- For tax purposes, there would be taxable income or loss in the period of sale equal to the difference between expected sales price and tax basis at that date. There would be no future tax effects to schedule because, for the portion of the carrying amount represented by the sale price, future rent expense would equal deductible lease payments.
- For book purposes, to realize the carrying amount as it would be recorded, there would be income in the year of sale equal to the loss on sale. In effect, recognition of the loss in this situation is merely an acceleration of future years' book depreciation into the year of sale.

Because the loss is artificial and not economic, Price Waterhouse believes that it should be appropriate simply to depreciate the loss (i.e., to schedule taxable income) over the leaseback term. Limitation to the remaining depreciable book life would be appropriate to avoid arbitrary assumptions of leaseback term that could thus spread forward taxable income in the scheduling exercise. This would reflect the economic basis for the amount at which the asset is carried, that is, its recovery through use in operations.

This question was discussed by the Implementation Group at its March 31, 1988 meeting, and the FASB staff has tentatively taken the position that, if sale-leaseback would result in recognition of an accounting loss, it could not be used as a tax-planning strategy.

¶ 5.04 DEFERRED COMPENSATION

Deferred compensation frequently results in scheduling deductions in periods beyond those in which offset against taxable income from other reversals is possible. To what extent can tax-planning strategies be adopted to accelerate the pattern of deductions of deferred compensation? With respect to individual deferred compensation contracts, it might be possible to assume accelerated payout if the executives are willing to accept taxable income before the contractual dates and if shareholders can be expected to find accelerated payout acceptable. When a formal plan covers a number of employees, management trustees may have the authority to change the plan or the payout.

It must be remembered that a change in deferred compensation payout must be a feasible tax-planning strategy and management must be able to implement it. In many situations, the decision does not rest unilaterally with management; care must be taken to consider whether the strategy could in fact be accomplished with no significant cost.

¶ 5.05 DEFERRED INTERCOMPANY PROFITS

The scheduling of deferred intercompany profits was discussed at ¶ 3.07. There may be situations in which the deduction available to the buyer could not be used in the scheduling exercise. A possible tax-planning strategy would have the buyer sell the inventory or fixed assets back to the original seller. If this is considered a sale (and, on the other end, a purchase) for tax purposes by the respective taxing authorities, it could solve the problem. The cost of the transaction would have to be considered. For example, freight costs of shipping the asset back to the original seller cannot be significant. In other cases, it might be possible to accomplish a sale for tax purposes without the need to ship the asset.

Rather than resorting to a hypothetical tax-planning strategy, a company may consider an actual transaction—instead of selling the assets to the subsidiary, shipping them on consignment. The tax regulations of the consignor and the consignee jurisdictions would have to be reviewed regarding consignment. Also, any costs associated with the consignment would have to be considered (e.g., insurance and property taxes). Such costs may affect tax-basis intercompany pricing. But consignment would avoid the deferred intercompany profit and the resultant deferred tax problem. The only effect in the consolidated financial statements would be on the deferred tax as the intercompany profit is eliminated in any case.

¶ 5.06 THE OBJECTIVE IS NOT ELECTIVE

When computing the deferred tax balance, companies have an overriding objective: to reduce a deferred tax liability or increase a deferred tax asset as much as possible. Tax-planning strategies were designed to help meet that objective—their use is not elective. If there is an available tax-planning strategy that meets the FAS 96 criteria and the use of that strategy reduces the deferred tax balance, it must be incorporated in the calculation.

As use of tax-planning strategies is mandatory, the question arises as to what extent management must actively search for usable strategies. One view could be that management has a positive obligation to derive the minimum possible deferred tax liability (or maximum asset). In a complex tax situation, this potentially could involve testing numerous scenarios with a variety of strategies. Another view is that management need only consider strategies that are obviously available. A third view is somewhere in between: A reasonable effort should be undertaken to find usable strategies.

The FASB staff has taken the position that management has a positive obligation to derive the minimum possible deferred tax liability (or maximum asset). As much diligence must be applied to achieving this objective as would be applied to appropriate measurement of any other balance sheet account (e.g., counting or costing physical inventories). If a tax-planning strategy is discovered after publication of the financial statements in which it could have appropriately been employed, the FASB staff believes that it is a subsequent discovery of facts existing at the balance sheet date, and restatement of the previously issued financials to correct the resulting error would be called for. The staff has, further, made an observation with respect to companies that have taxable income in 1987 and prior years that is available for carryback recovery at the full 46 percent or 40 percent rates. As discussed in ¶ 4.05, the FASB staff has stated that management should aggressively search for tax-planning strategies that would maximize the net deductions scheduled for years through 1990 and result in recording tax benefits at the higher rates.

The question arises how this mandated use of tax-planning strategies does not conflict with the requirement that management have the positive intent to employ a strategy if necessary. The intent criterion suggests that management could avoid use of an available strategy at a particular balance sheet date by stating at that time that the strategy would not be used or that they are undecided.

The FASB staff has stated that management's intent cannot be uneconomic. The SEC staff has also expressed concern about the potential manipulation of earnings that could result from discretionary employment of tax-planning strategies and has stated that intent or lack of intent could not be used as a justification for "management" of reported results.

There is, in the view of the FASB staff, no question as to whether it is probable or even reasonably possible that a strategy will in actual fact ever be employed. The focus is not on what the projected actual future tax position will be but rather the optimum tax position that management could prudently and feasibly achieve if future taxable results were only those resulting from reversal of temporary differences. Not only federal tax must be considered; there may be state, local, and foreign tax computations where tax-planning strategies can minimize the deferred tax liability.

In general, a search for strategies to reduce federal taxes would be indicated in the following circumstances:

- There are unused net deductions, credits or carryforwards;
- There is actual or deferred AMT liability that cannot be recovered by use of minimum tax credits in the deferred tax computation;
- The company's income tax can be affected by rate bracket adjustments, and there is a possibility of increasing the benefit in the deferred tax computation; or
- There is unused carryback availability and the tax benefits ascribed to net deductions will be increased if they can be accelerated into years from which carryback is allowed.

When there are foreign operations, additional considerations could be introduced into the federal computation. Tax-planning strategies must also be applied to taxes in other jurisdictions; strategies that reduce taxes in one jurisdiction may increase taxes in another.

¶ 5.07 CHANGE IN FACTS AND CIRCUMSTANCES

These tax-planning strategies are hypothetical. They are for use in an artificial environment—one that assumes there will be no other taxable income or loss except for the reversal of the temporary differences. As each year passes, facts and circumstances change. Taxable income or loss in future years will be different from the amount scheduled at the preceding year-end(s), and the amount and timing of reversals of temporary differences will change. Often, these changes will obviate the need for a tax-planning strategy used in the prior year. This situation is illustrated in Exhibit 5-3.

In the discussion in Chapter 4 of electing to forgo the carryback of an NOL (see ¶ 4.04), it was pointed out that a company can change its mind with respect to its hypothetical election if a change in facts and circumstances warrants it. Suppose, when calculating the deferred tax liability in 1987, the company elected as a tax-planning strategy to forgo a loss carryback in 1991. If 1988 brings altered facts and circumstances and an election to forgo the carryback would no longer result in the minimum deferred tax balance, the company would no longer plan to make the election.

¶ 5.08 CONSISTENT USE

Tax-planning strategies that assume transactions affecting the timing of deductions and taxable income must be used consistently for federal and state tax purposes and for a parent company and its subsidiaries. In addition, as discussed in ¶ 9.08, the same tax-planning strategies used for regular tax purposes must also be used in the AMT calculation and this could potentially add considerable complexity to the search for effective strategies. Of course, when different tax elections are allowed in different tax jurisdictions, it may be necessary to make different elections—for example, whether to file consolidated or separate returns—in different jurisdictions to arrive at the minimum tax.

(continued on page 5-18)

EXHIBIT 5-3
Tax-Planning Strategies—A Change in Facts and Circumstances

As discussed in Exhibit 5-2, Gamma Corp. adopted FAS 96 in 1988. During 1988, a deferred compensation arrangement was established for certain individuals in upper-management positions. The deferred compensation arrangements provide for a lump-sum payment to each individual in the year 2010. At December 31, 1988, a deferred compensation liability of $1,000 had been accrued for financial reporting purposes.

Gamma Corp.'s 1988 pretax loss was $300. A reconciliation from pretax loss to taxable income follows. (Note that, as in Exhibit 5-2, the effects of AMT have been ignored in this example. In general, the AMT rules preclude the use of an NOL carryforward to completely eliminate tax.)

1988 pretax loss	($ 300)
Add: Deferred compensation expense	1,000
Excess book depreciation	100
Taxable income before use of NOL	800
Use of NOL carryforward	(800)
Taxable income and current tax expense	$ 0

The remaining tax NOL, most of which expires in 2002, is $4,200 ($5,000 tax NOL at the beginning of the years less $800 used in the current year).

For purposes of calculating the deferred tax liability at December 31, 1988, Gamma Corp. has scheduled the reversal of temporary differences existing at the balance sheet date before consideration of any tax-planning strategies. The results of its scheduling exercise are as follows.

(continued)

EXHIBIT 5-3 (cont'd)

Schedule of Temporary Difference Reversals
No Tax-Planning Strategies Considered

	Temporary difference at 12/31/88	1989	1990 through 1997 (eight years)	1998 through 2002 (five years)	Future years 2003 through 2006 (four years)	2007	2008	2009	2010	Indefinite future
Land	$ 5,000									$5,000
Buildings	6,900	$100	$800	$3,000	$2,400	$600			($1,000)	
Deferred compensation	(1,000)									5,000
	$10,900	100	800	3,000	2,400	600	0	0	(1,000)	5,000
Tax NOL used	($ 3,900)	(100)	(800)	(3,000)						
Carryback from 2010						(600)			600	
Taxable income resulting from reversal of temporary differences		0	0	0	2,400	0	0	0	(400)	5,000
Enacted tax rate		34%	34%	34%	34%	34%	34%	34%	34%	34%
Deferred tax liability	$ 2,516	$ 0	$ 0	$ 0	$ 816	$ 0	$ 0	$ 0	$ 0	$1,700

Prior to consideration of tax-planning strategies, Gamma Corp. is unable to use all of the remaining tax NOL. In addition, no benefit can be ascribed to $400 of the deferred compensation deduction scheduled to occur in 2010 as taxable income scheduled to occur in the indefinite future is beyond the allowable carryforward period. Accordingly, Gamma Corp. recomputed its deferred tax liability at December 31, 1988 assuming that the buildings would be sold and leased back in 2002, which is consistent with the tax-planning strategy used at the beginning of the year as shown in Exhibit 5-2.

Schedule of Temporary Difference Reversals
Tax-Planning Strategy Consistend With Prior Year

	Temporary difference at 12/31/88	1989	1990 through 1997 (eight years)	1998 through 2002 (five years)	2003 through 2006 (four years)	2007	2008	2009	2010	Indefinite future
					Future years					
Land	$ 5,000									$5,000
Buildings	6,900	$100	$800	$3,000	$2,400	$600				
Deferred compensation	(1,000)								($1,000)	
	$10,900	100	800	3,000	2,400	600	0	0	(1,000)	5,000
Sale-leaseback tax-planning strategy				3,000	(2,400)	(600)				
		100	800	6,000					(1,000)	5,000
Tax NOL used	($ 4,200)	(100)	(800)	(3,300)						
Taxable income resulting from reversal of temporary differences		0	0	2,700	0	0	0	0	N/A	5,000
Enacted tax rate		34%	34%	34%	34%	34%	34%	34%	34%	34%
Deferred tax liability	$ 2,618	$ 0	$ 0	$ 918	$ 0	$ 0	$ 0	$ 0	$ 0	$1,700

Incorporating the same tax-planning strategy as used in the deferred tax calculation at the beginning of the year allows full use of the remaining tax NOL. However, no benefit can be ascribed to the deferred compensation deduction scheduled to occur in 2010 as taxable income scheduled to occur in 1998–2002 precedes the three-year carryback period permitted under U.S. tax law, and taxable income scheduled to occur in the indefinite future is beyond the allowable carryforward period. The net effect results in a higher deferred tax liability than if no tax-planning strategies were used. Had Gamma Corp. assumed that the land was sold and leased back in 2010, as opposed to a sale-leaseback of the buildings in 2002, a lower deferred tax liability would have resulted, as follows.

(continued)

5-15

EXHIBIT 5-3 (cont'd)

Schedule of Temporary Difference Reversals
Tax-Planning Strategy Changed From Prior Year

	Temporary difference at 12/31/88	1989	1990 through 1997 (eight years)	1998 through 2002 (five years)	2003 through 2006 (four years)	2007	2008	2009	2010	Indefinite future
					Future years					
Land	$ 5,000									$5,000
Buildings	6,900	$100	$800	$3,000	$2,400	$600				
Deferred compensation	(1,000)								($1,000)	
	$10,900	100	800	3,000	2,400	600	0	0	(1,000)	5,000
Sale-leaseback tax-planning strategy									5,000	(5,000)
Tax NOL used	($ 3,900)	(100)	(800)	(3,000)						
Taxable income resulting from reversal of temporary differences		0	0	0	2,400	600	0	0	4,000	0
Enacted tax rate		34%	34%	34%	34%	34%	34%	34%	34%	34%
Deferred tax liability	$ 2,380	$ 0	$ 0	$ 0	$ 816	$204	$ 0	$ 0	$1,360	$ 0

A change in facts and circumstances is justification for changing tax-planning strategies previously used. In fact, if a new tax-planning strategy minimizes the deferred tax liability, and assuming that it satisfies the tax-planning strategy criteria of FAS 96 (for example, the sale-leaseback of land illustrated above might not be "prudent" because it only reduces deferred taxes by $136), then the FASB staff has indicated that the new strategy must be used. This could require several iterations of the deferred tax calculation.

In the preceding example, incorporating a tax-planning strategy to sell and lease back the land in 2010 results in a lower deferred tax liability than incorporating a strategy to sell and lease back the buildings in 2002 or incorporating no tax-planning strategies. However, $300 of the tax NOL would still expire unused, and Gamma Corp. must investigate whether any other strategies might reduce its deferred tax liability even further. Possibilities that would have to be investigated include:

• Whether it would be possible to sell and lease back the buildings in 2002, retaining title to the land, and subsequently in 2010 sell and lease back the land (subject to the lease of the buildings' owner).

• Whether it would be possible to accelerate payments under the deferred compensation agreements.

Both of these potential strategies would entail critical examination of whether they could be structured to achieve the desired tax effect and whether, with respect to the deferred compensation arrangements, acceleration of payments would even be possible.

¶ 5.09 TAX PLANNING IS NOT DEALER'S CHOICE

The discussion up to this point has focused chiefly on what a valid tax-planning strategy can do. There are, however, several things a valid tax-planning strategy cannot do.

1. A new factor cannot enter into the deferred tax computation. For example, the assumed sale of marketable securities at a price in excess of book value does not qualify as a tax-planning strategy; only the difference between the book and tax bases of the securities counts. Similarly, a tax-planning strategy cannot look to liquidation of LIFO inventories carried at amounts considerably below current cost or realization of unrealized appreciation in real estate.

2. As noted, a tax-planning strategy must not involve significant cost. In assessing what is significant, the tax savings from entering into a hypothetical transaction cannot be considered a reduction of the cost. The cost "must be of a minor, incidental nature," but the Statement does not provide quantitative guidelines. It is presently the position of Price Waterhouse that a cost is significant when it exceeds 5 percent of the amount of taxable income or deductions that is accelerated or delayed by the strategy. Price Waterhouse would not differentiate between costs that are deductible for tax purposes and those that are not because that would entail measuring tax benefit of the cost; the strategy itself is undertaken because all tax benefits cannot be used in the scheduling exercise and deferred tax computation.

3. Expenditures other than those accrued cannot be assumed. For example, if an asset with a book/tax basis difference could not be sold without a significant cash expenditure—for example, to demolish an old building on a piece of land—selling the land cannot be considered a valid tax-planning strategy as it would not be feasible absent significant cost. Note that this is the case even if the cash expenditure could be recovered with a higher sales price. Of course, in this particular situation, it may be feasible to assume that both the land and the building are sold and the buyer demolishes the building.

When a tax-planning strategy involves remittance of dividends from foreign subsidiaries, the question arises whether any foreign withholding tax should be considered in determining whether there is a significant cost. Price Waterhouse believes that a decision to repatriate foreign undistributed earnings, including its optimal form, is one that considers all tax attributes, foreign as well as U.S. While foreign withholding tax may require a cash outflow (an expenditure) separate from the reduction in U.S. taxes payable, Price Waterhouse believes that the objective of the tax-planning strategy is to reduce aggregate tax expense. Since the benefit of the strategy, the reduction in tax expense, is net of foreign withholding tax, the withholding tax should not itself be considered a cost in assessing whether the criteria for a tax-planning strategy are met.

¶ 5.10 RECALCULATE

After completing the tax-planning exercise, recalculate the effect of loss carrybacks and carryforwards, including any elections to forgo a carryback. (This is necessary because effective tax-planning strategies rearrange the pattern of taxable income or losses subject to the carryover rules.) This is the stage where the net taxable or deductible amounts on a year-by-year basis generate the smallest tax liability and maximum asset. But the company must still consider the effect of tax-planning strategies on tax credits and AMT (see ¶¶ 6.08, 9.07).

CHAPTER **6**

The Tax Computation

This chapter discusses the actual computation of the tax liability. Note again that a company must respect the tax laws of the specific income-taxing jurisdiction for which it is making the calculations.

¶ 6.01 IGNORE NET DEDUCTIONS

Perhaps the hardest restriction to accept when computing the tentative deferred tax liability is that, after the carryback and carryforward potential and all tax-planning strategies have been exhausted, any amounts that are net deductions in a given year *must be ignored*. FAS 96 does not permit companies to benefit from a scheduled future tax deduction unless (1) it would result in a carryback refund or (2) there is also scheduled future taxable income against which it can be offset. Even if the company is confident it will have taxable income from other sources by the time the year in question rolls around, the Statement does not permit the assumption of any future events, including taxable income that will be earned. Exhibit 6-1 demonstrates the effect of this proscription.

If future net deductible amounts cannot be used in the deferred tax calculation in the current year, they may be used in the calculation or on an actual tax return in a future year as illustrated in Exhibit 6-2. In the meantime, they are considered net operating loss (NOL) carryforwards for financial statement purposes.

¶ 6.02 RECOGNITION OF NET OPERATING LOSS CARRYFORWARDS

FAS 96 has changed the classification of NOL benefit recognition. Under APB 11, benefits from recognizing NOL carryforwards (after the loss period) were (with exceptions for purchased and pre-quasi reorganization NOLs) classified as extraordinary items. Under FAS 96, however, such benefits are generally now classified in the same manner as the source of income that gives rise to their recognition; consequently, classification could require intraperiod tax allocation, as illustrated in Exhibit 7-2. There are three situations where the source of loss determines treatment of the benefit: (1) purchase business combinations (see ¶ 8.02[1]), (2) certain quasi reorganizations (see ¶ 10.06), and (3) stock compensation deductions that, under APB 25, must be credited to additional paid-in capital (see ¶ 3.15).

EXHIBIT 6-1 _____
Loss of Tax Benefit Due to Net Deductions

ABC Company had scheduled the reversal of temporary differences existing at December 31, 1987. After using all available tax-planning strategies, the following pattern of future years' net taxable income and deductions emerged:

	Future years					
	1988	1989	1990	1991	1992	1993
Taxable income (deductions) resulting from the reversal of temporary differences	$400	$600	$0	$0	$0	($300)

ABC Company is now ready to compute its deferred tax balance. No NOL carryforwards exist at the balance sheet date. During 1987, a $300 temporary difference arose that will reverse as a net deductible amount in 1993. When performing the deferred tax computation, no benefit can be ascribed to the $300 net deduction as (1) there is no future taxable income to which it can be carried forward to offset and (2) the net deduction cannot be carried back to 1988 or 1989 because only a three-year carryback period is permitted by U.S. tax law. Therefore, the deferred tax liability that would be reflected on the balance sheet at December 31, 1987 would be $340 (taxable income in 1988 and 1989 tax-effected at the enacted rate of 34 percent).

The deferred tax liability at the beginning of 1987 was $420. 1987 pretax income was $280, and taxable income was $780. ABC Company made the following journal entries at December 31, 1987 to record the income tax provision:

Debit: Current tax expense	$312	
Credit: Current taxes payable		$312
(1987 taxable income of $780 at 40 percent)		
Debit: Deferred tax liability	$ 80	
Credit: Deferred tax benefit		$ 80
(Difference between the $340 deferred tax balance at the end of 1987 and the $420 balance at the beginning of 1987)		

(continued)

EXHIBIT 6-1 *(cont'd)*

ABC Company reported the following in its 1987 financial statements:

Pretax income		$280
Current tax expense	$312	
Deferred tax benefit	(80)	
Total tax provision		232
Net income		$ 48
Effective tax rate		83%

The following is the reconciliation of the effective tax rate to the statutory rate of 40 percent.

Expected tax at 40%	$112
Change in scheduled tax deductions for which no tax benefit can be ascribed ($300 at 40%)	120
	$232

¶ 6.03 TAX LAWS

As illustrated in Exhibits 6-3 and 6-4, the operative tax laws and rates are those that have been enacted in each jurisdiction as of the balance sheet date. In the United States specifically, as noted, companies must consider the effect of alternative minimum tax (AMT) for calculations for balance sheet dates after the October 22, 1986 enactment.

As the scheduling process effectively entails preparing a tax return for each future year, companies must apply all the tax rules and regulations. In the United States, city and state taxes are deductible when computing the federal tax liability. If the scheduling process generates deferred city or state tax effects, they should be included by year in scheduling the federal temporary differences.

¶ 6.04 APB 23 AND APB 24 TAXES ON UNDISTRIBUTED EARNINGS

APB Opinion 24, *Accounting for Income Taxes—Investments in Common Stock Accounted for by the Equity Method (Other than Subsidiaries and Corporate Joint Ventures)*, mandated that deferred taxes be provided with respect to undistributed earnings of investees included within its scope. APB 24 has now been superseded by FAS 96, while APB 23 (FAS 60, *Accounting and Reporting by Insurance Companies*, with respect to policyholders' surplus of stock life insurance companies) has been left in place, amended as necessary to delete references to measurement that are at variance with FAS 96.

Even before APB 11 was superseded by FAS 96, many people believed that APB 23 and APB 24 called for a liability rather than a deferred approach to measurement of the applicable deferred taxes. However, in that application of the liability method, the future tax effects were commonly measured as the expected incremental effect on actual taxes payable (or, alternatively, tax expense) in the years of expected inclusion in taxable income. Under FAS 96, these items are included with other book/tax differences, and the future tax effect is measured in the same way. Again, FAS 96's measurement of the deferred tax liability assumes no future taxable income (loss) other than reversal of these differences.

When repatriation of undistributed earnings of foreign subsidiaries does not meet the indefinite reversal criteria and when there are foreign nonsubsidiary equity investees, the effects of reversal include, for U.S. tax computations, the potential gross-up and related credit for foreign taxes deemed paid, as well as, when the repatriation is expected by dividends, any foreign withholding taxes and the related U.S. deduction or credit. Differences between accumulated earnings and profits determined for U.S. tax purposes and U.S. generally accepted accounting principles undistributed earnings may also have to be considered. Calculations can be extremely complex, and effects on the deferred tax liability can vary considerably depending upon the repatriation scenario. Given the FAS 96 mandate for tax-planning strategies to reduce

EXHIBIT 6-2
Use of Long-Term Net Deductions

As shown in Exhibit 6-1, at December 31, 1987, ABC Company had been unable to ascribe a benefit to long-term deductions arising in the scheduling of temporary differences. In March 1988, ABC Company purchased a large piece of equipment, which it is depreciating on an accelerated basis for tax purposes. This transaction results in a pattern of temporary difference reversals at December 31, 1988 that differs from the prior year's. During 1988, ABC Company reported a tax loss of $226, which has been carried back to 1987 and prior years and there are no available NOL carryforwards and no carryback availability.

The computation of ABC Company's deferred tax balance at December 31, 1988, is as follows. As demonstrated in the calculation, the $300 net deduction scheduled to occur in 1993, to which no benefit could be ascribed in the prior year's deferred tax calculation, is now used to offset scheduled taxable income generated by excess book depreciation scheduled to occur in later years.

	Future years					
	1989	1990	1991	1992	1993	1994–1998
Taxable income (deductions) resulting from the reversal of temporary differences (excluding depreciation on equipment purchased in the current year)	$600	$ 0	$ 0	$ 0	($300)	$ 0
Taxable income (deductions) resulting from the reversal of temporary differences on equipment purchased in the current year	(145)	(75)	(25)	10	25	275
Net taxable income (deductions) resulting from the reversal of temporary differences	455	(75)	(25)	10	(275)	275
Carryback/carryforward net deductions:						
1990 carryback	(75)	75				
1991 carryback	(25)		25			
1993 carryback				(10)	10	
1993 carryforward					265	(265)
	355	0	0	0	0	10
Enacted tax rate	34%	34%	34%	34%	34%	34%
Deferred tax liability	$121	$ 0	$ 0	$ 0	$ 0	$ 3

THE TAX COMPUTATION

At December 31, 1988, ABC Company would establish a deferred tax liability of $124 on its balance sheet. The deferred tax provision for 1988 would reflect a benefit of $216—the difference between $124 (the deferred tax liability at the end of the year) and $340 (the deferred tax balance at the beginning of the year, as shown in Exhibit 6-1). The journal entries to be made are as follows:

Debit: Current tax refundable $ 97
Credit: Current tax benefit $ 97

> (The current tax benefit is the actual refund that results from the carryback of the 1988 tax loss. ABC Company paid taxes at a 40 percent rate in 1987 and at a 46 percent rate in 1986 and prior years. The carryback benefit is at an aggregate 43 percent rate.)

Debit: Deferred tax liability $216
Credit: Deferred tax benefit $ 216

> (Difference between the $124 deferred tax balance at the end of 1988 and the $340 balance at the beginning of 1988.)

ABC Company reported the following in its 1988 financial statements:

Pretax loss		($561)
Current tax benefit	($ 97)	
Deferred tax benefit	(216)	
Total tax provision		(313)
Net loss		($248)
Effective benefit rate		56%

The following is the reconciliation of the effective tax rate to the statutory rate of 34 percent.

Expected benefit at 34%	($191)
Carryback of current-year NOL to recover taxes paid at higher rates	(20)
Benefit of scheduled utilization of tax deductions for which tax benefit was not previously ascribed ($300 at 34%)	(102)
	($313)

The preceding example illustrates how changes in a company's facts and circumstances from one year to the next can affect the deferred tax balance. That effect can be managed to some extent. For example, accelerating or postponing the actual purchase of fixed assets will alter the scheduled pattern of temporary difference reversals.

deferred taxes to a minimum amount, conceivably the tax consequences of a variety of alternatives would have to be computed. The specifics of the problems involved in this computation are outside the scope of this book.

The treatment under FAS 96 of undistributed earnings of a nonsubsidiary investee carried at equity was discussed at the March 31, 1988 meeting of the Implementation Group. The FASB staff position, in which the SEC Observer concurs, is that future taxable income should be scheduled based on the expected method of realization (i.e., dividends, liquidation, or sale). If a tax-planning strategy were available to the investor that would reduce the deferred tax liability, that strategy should be incorporated in the scheduling exercise. However, the FASB staff observed that, as the investor does not control the investee, generally the only strategy available would be sale of the investment. Generally it would be inappropriate to assume that realization would occur through receipt of dividends because dividends are typically paid from current year's earnings. If there is evidence that future dividends will be paid from undistributed earnings at the balance sheet date, then the dividend assumption could be appropriate. Such evidence could take the form of a history of dividend payments by the investee in excess of its current earnings or, when the investor's basis exceeds its equity in net assets of the investee, dividend receipts in excess of equity earnings. Because it has been common under APB 11 to provide for APB 24 taxes based on the dividend assumption, FAS 96 will likely require a change in practice in this respect.

¶ 6.05 APPORTIONMENT FACTORS

Many state tax jurisdictions assess a tax based on the portion of taxable income earned in the jurisdiction. The amount of taxable income is usually computed using three factors: sales within the jurisdiction compared with total sales, assets within the jurisdiction compared with total assets, and payroll within the jurisdiction compared with total payroll.

How should these allocation factors be treated under FAS 96? Price Waterhouse believes the most reasonable approach is to use the apportionment factors expected to be applicable in future years (using current factors as a guide) in each state that follows an apportionment formula. Applying those factors to enacted rates in future years may yield the most realistic answer.

Deferred state income taxes should be provided based on scheduled reversals of temporary differences even for jurisdictions where the company's actual tax liability is expected to be based on factors other than income.

¶ 6.06 CHANGING RATES AND RATE-BRACKET ADJUSTMENTS

The tax rates that should be used for any year-end calculation are those that have been enacted before that year-end. This is not as simple as it sounds when new tax rates are phased in over a number of years. The Tax Reform Act of 1986 (TRA 1986) rates are a good case in point. For a calendar-year company, the tax rate is 46 percent in 1986, 40 percent in 1987, and 34 percent in 1988 and after. When computing the deferred tax liability as of December 31, 1987, net deductions scheduled for 1988 to 1990 may result in carryback refunds up to 46 percent, but 34 percent would otherwise generally be applied to scheduled net taxable income in future years. Companies must also consider the potential effect of the rate-bracket adjustment (or surtax exemption) on scheduled net taxable income.

This is a major change from the provisions of APB 11, which mandated using the rates in effect in the current year for the current year's tax computation. Exhibit 6-3 illustrates this effect of applying graduated tax rates to future reversing taxable income. Exhibit 6-4 illustrates the effect of graduated tax rates when there has been a change in rates.

EXHIBIT 6-3
Graduated Tax Rates

ABC Company adopted FAS 96 in 1987 and elected to restate prior years. In computing the required deferred tax liability as of December 31, 1985, ABC Company must apply the tax rates enacted as of that date to the scheduled reversal of temporary differences, including any rate-bracket adjustments.

			Future years			
	1986	1987	1988	1989	1990	Total
Net taxable income resulting from the reversal of temporary differences	$1,500,00	$290,000	$230,000	$120,000	$800,000	$2,940,000
Tax on $100,000	25,750	25,750	25,750	25,750	25,750	
46% tax on income over $100,000	644,000	87,400	59,800	9,200	322,000	
5% tax on income over $1 million but less than $1.405 million	20,250	—	—	—	—	
Future tax liability resulting from the reversal of temporary differences	$ 690,000	$113,150	$ 85,550	$ 34,950	$347,750	$1,271,400
Effective tax rate	46%	39%	37%	29%	43%	43%

ABC Company's deferred tax liability at December 31, 1985, as restated, would be $1,271,400, which is equivalent to applying a 43 percent rate to total temporary differences at the balance sheet date. Had ABC Company merely applied the enacted statutory rate of 46 percent to total temporary differences, the deferred tax liability would have been overstated by $81,000.

EXHIBIT 6-4
Changing Tax Rates

In restating the 1986 financial statements, the deferred tax liability must reflect the lower tax rates enacted by TRA 1986 for future years, including the blended marginal rate in effect during 1987. The deferred tax liability resulting from applying those rates at December 31, 1986, is as follows.

		Future years				
	1987	1988	1989	1990	1991	Total
Net taxable amounts resulting from reversal of temporary differences	$1,300,000	$320,000	$180,000	$650,000	$1,200,000	$3,650,000
Tax on income of $75,000		13,750	13,750	13,750	13,750	
Tax on income of $100,000	23,988					
34% tax on income over $75,000		83,300	35,700	195,500	382,500	
39.95% tax on income over $100,000	479,400					
5% tax on income between $100,000 and $335,000		11,000	4,000	11,750	11,750	
2.52% tax on income between $100,000 and $335,000	5,922					
2.48% tax on income between $1 million and $1.405 million	7,440					

(continued)

6-11

EXHIBIT 6-4 *(cont'd)*

| | Future years | | | | | |
	1987	1988	1989	1990	1991	Total
Future tax liability resulting from the reversal of temporary differences	$ 516,750	$108,050	$ 53,450	$221,000	$ 408,000	$1,307,250
Effective tax rate	40%	34%	30%	34%	34%	36%

The resulting deferred tax liability at December 31, 1986, as restated, is equivalent to applying a 36 percent rate to total temporary differences. The higher rate results from the blended marginal rates in effect for 1987 less the effect in other years of rate-bracket adjustments.

¶ 6.07 TAX CREDITS

Now comes the last step in determining the deferred tax balance—applying any available tax credits. Here, too, companies must follow the applicable tax laws. For example, if investment tax credits are carried forward from 1986, the 1987 amount must be reduced by 17.5 percent and later-year amounts reduced by 35 percent to take into account the TRA 1986 provisions. Recognizing the statutory limitations on investment or foreign tax credits is another example of applying the tax law. Note that the scheduled usage of investment credits in 1987 versus 1988 and later years can vary from subsequent actual usage on the tax returns.

¶ 6.08 TAX-PLANNING STRATEGIES AND OVERALL CHECK

Is this the end? Perhaps not. An appropriate tax-planning strategy can increase the use of available tax credits. If so, the company should go back to the calculation steps discussed in Chapters 4 and 5, then recompute.

When the company can do nothing more to reduce its deferred tax liability, it is ready to make the adjustment. Check the computations, by comparing the total tax provision (current and deferred) to pretax income multiplied by the statutory tax rate. The company should be able to account for the rate differentials (that is, the items causing a difference between the tax provision and the amount derived by applying the federal statutory rate to pretax income). These rate differentials include at least eight variables.

1. The effect on deferred tax balances of rate changes enacted in the current year to apply to future years.
2. The rate differential on certain differences (e.g., other than depreciation on assets in place at the beginning of the year) originating in the current year and scheduled to reverse in a year for which a different rate has been enacted.
3. Different rates applicable to a year to which a carryback is assumed.

4. Use of tax deductions in the current year at a lower rate than recorded in the prior-year deferred tax computation when carryback to higher rate years was assumed.

5. When the tax rate will change in the succeeding year, the effect of recalculating the deferred tax liability related to LIFO inventories from the current year's rate used at the preceding year-end to the succeeding year's rate used at the current year-end (or the tax effect of any other temporary difference that was scheduled to reverse in the current year but in fact did not).

6. Changes from the beginning of the year to year-end in the amount of tax benefits from deductions (including tax loss carryforwards) and credits that cannot be recognized in the deferred tax computation.

7. Use of permanent differences or tax credits in the calculation of taxes payable.

8. Higher or lower statutory rates in other jurisdictions that are included in the consolidated financial statements.

These amounts must be disclosed in the notes to the financial statements.

CHAPTER **7**

Making the Adjustment

¶ 7.01 BALANCE SHEET CLASSIFICATION

In an unclassified balance sheet, all deferred taxes related to a single jurisdiction would be presented as a single asset or liability. When the balance sheet is classified and there is more than one jurisdiction, four possible balance sheet classifications relate to deferred taxes: current asset, noncurrent asset, current liability, and noncurrent liability. The results of the scheduling process determine the proper amount for each balance sheet caption.

[1] Current Reversals

Generally, in each jurisdiction, the amount of tax (asset or liability) for temporary differences scheduled to occur in the year after the balance sheet date represents the current portion; taxes scheduled for all other years should be aggregated and classified as a net noncurrent asset or liability. When the operating cycle is longer than one year, however, the classifications may differ (see ¶ 7.01[2]).

FAS 96 specifies how to determine the amount scheduled to reverse in the first year following the balance sheet date. Assume, for example, that net taxable income of $650,000 is scheduled to occur in year one and net tax deductions of $600,000 are scheduled to occur in year four. If the required deferred tax liability is reduced by the carryback of the year four deductions to year one, what amount should be shown as current?

If no other events occur, income taxes will be paid in year one and recovered in year four. Therefore, the balance sheet should reflect a current deferred tax liability (the taxes to be paid in year one) and a noncurrent asset (the future recovery). In other words, the net amount of deferred taxes on the balance sheet (even if zero) may need to be disaggregated to reflect the current and noncurrent amounts. Exhibit 7-1 illustrates the appropriate balance sheet classification of the deferred tax balance.

[2] Operating Cycle

Some companies classify their balance sheets on the basis of an operating cycle exceeding one year. Accordingly, determining the current deferred tax asset or liability based on reversals in the first subsequent year may not be meaningful. The concept of the reversal period has been expanded to appropriately reflect the longer operating cycle.

The current portion of the deferred tax liability or asset comprises the tax effects of temporary differences that (1) will reverse in the next year, (2) are related to an asset or liability classified as current because of an operating cycle that is longer than one year,

EXHIBIT 7-1
Balance Sheet Classification

ABC Company has scheduled the reversal of temporary differences existing at December 31, 1987 (the balance sheet date), for each tax jurisdiction within which it operates. Based on the scheduled amounts, as follows, a deferred state income tax liability of $191 must be established.

	1988	1989	1990	1991	1992	1993	Total
Taxable income (deductions) resulting from the reversal of temporary differences	$650	$500	$650	($600)	$525	$400	$2,125
Carryback of net operating loss (NOL) resulting from the reversal of temporary differences	(600)	—	—	600	—	—	0
Net taxable income (deductions) resulting from the reversal of temporary differences	50	500	650	0	525	400	2,125
Enacted state tax rate	9%	9%	9%	9%	9%	9%	9%
State deferred tax liability	$ 5	$ 45	$ 58	$ 0	$ 47	$ 36	$ 191

At December 31, 1987, ABC Company would record a current state deferred income tax liability of $58 ($650 tax-effected at 9 percent) and a noncurrent state deferred income tax liability of $133 (the total liability of $191 less the current portion of $58). A benefit is attributed to the net deductions scheduled to occur in 1991 as the amount can be carried back to offset net taxable amounts scheduled to occur during the carryback period permitted by the tax laws of that jurisdiction. However, as the net deductions are not scheduled to occur in the year immediately after the balance sheet date, the benefit is considered to be noncurrent in nature under the provisions of FAS 96. Therefore, the current deferred tax liability is the tax effect of temporary difference reversals in 1988 before use of the NOL carryback from 1991.

or (3) are not related to an identifiable asset or liability for financial reporting but other related assets and liabilities are classified as current because of an operating cycle that is longer than one year.

An example of this last item would be the use by a contractor of the percentage-of-completion method for financial reporting purposes and the percentage-of-completion/capitalized-cost method for tax purposes. The contractor might have a balance sheet caption titled "Costs and profits in excess of billings," a current asset, that represents the total costs incurred on its contracts plus any earned profit less any amounts billed. The tax-basis balance sheet would contain two captions: "Work in process," representing the accumulated costs, and "Deferred revenue," representing any amounts billed.

These two tax-basis balance sheet items have no direct correlation to any item in the financial statements. However, since they relate to an asset classified as current, the deferred tax effects of these temporary differences must also be classified as current.

In the scheduling exercise, the reversals beyond one year of temporary differences for assets and liabilities classified as current based on the operating cycle will, of course, be included with reversals of temporary differences related to noncurrent assets or liabilities. When the tax effect of only a portion of the net taxable income or deductions scheduled for a particular year is to be classified as current, arbitrary assumptions may be necessary in complex situations to determine the tax effects to be classified as current.

Alternatively, the current portion of deferred tax could be computed by a scheduling exercise including only the reversals of temporary differences that will occur in the next year and those whose tax effects are to be classified as current. The residual of the deferred tax balance would be classified as noncurrent.

[3] Classify by Jurisdiction

A company rarely operates in only one taxing jurisdiction, and the classification procedure must be completed for each applicable jurisdiction. Netting of deferred tax balances arising from different tax jurisdictions is not permitted. As a result, all four possible classifications may appear on the balance sheet.

For example, a current asset and a long-term liability might arise for deferred federal tax purposes while a current liability and a noncurrent asset arise from the computation of the deferred tax liability to New York state. The current asset receivable from the U.S. government and the current liability payable to New York state cannot be offset.

[4] Effect on Working Capital

The FAS 96 classification rules may significantly affect the working capital of many companies. As noted, amounts scheduled to reverse in the first year following the balance sheet date will be included in the current classification. That classification will now include a portion of originating depreciation temporary differences and usually any temporary difference related to purchased LIFO inventories (frequently not tax-effected in the purchase price allocation prior to FAS 96). These items could have a material effect on working capital—one generally positive, one generally negative. Debt covenants based on working capital may need revision prior to adoption of FAS 96 to avoid technical default.

¶ 7.02 MAKE THE ADJUSTMENT

After all the hard work determining the deferred tax balance, making the adjustment is easy. Since the company performed the computations according to FAS 96, it must simply compare the ending balance with the beginning balance—the difference is generally the deferred tax provision. Although this is the rule stated in FAS 96, there are some obvious exceptions:

- The change in deferred taxes at the date of a purchase business combination (see ¶ 8.01[2])
- Any transaction gain or loss on the U.S. dollar functional currency temporary difference that is not included in deferred tax expense (see ¶ 2.04[3])

- The portion reflected in the currency translation adjustment account of the change in the deferred tax liability of an operation using a foreign functional currency (see ¶ 11.06)
- Adjustments for the effects of NOLs and investment tax credits if the "gross" presentation of tax expense is followed (see ¶ 12.01)

Certain other adjustments will likely be buried in the overall adjustment of the deferred tax balance sheet accounts, such as provision-to-return and revenue-agent-report adjustments as a result of an IRS audit. No separate adjustment to the deferred tax balance is needed because the temporary differences have been corrected to reflect the new facts. It may, however, require additional disclosures when reconciling the statutory and effective rates.

¶ 7.03 INTEREST AND PENALTIES

Many companies included any provision for interest and penalties payable on settlement of prior years' returns as an element of tax expense. FAS 96 precludes such treatment. Many companies may be reluctant to include these items as a component of interest expense since they could provide a clue to examining agents about the amount of expected adjustments. However, the only basis for failing to follow the FAS 96 mandate is that the effect is immaterial.

¶ 7.04 INITIAL APPLICATION

In the year of initial application of FAS 96, the effect of changing to the new accounting method must be calculated and recorded. The "cumulative effect of a change in accounting principle" is defined in APB Opinion 20, *Accounting Changes*, as the difference between (1) the amount of retained earnings at the beginning of the period of a change and (2) the amount of retained earnings that would have been reported if the new accounting principle had been applied retroactively for all prior periods. The effect of adopting FAS 96, however, may not meet the APB 20 definition.

The primary reason for the distinction is the special transition rule for purchase business combinations, which is discussed in Chapter 8. If a prior year in which a purchase business combination was consummated is not restated (i.e., the "shortcut" method is applied), the effect of adopting FAS 96 clearly is not the cumulative difference between applying FAS 96 and APB 11 in prior years. It is simply the difference between the deferred tax balance computed by applying FAS 96 at the date of initial application and the existing balance of deferred taxes. The computed effect of adoption is reflected as the last item before net income of the year of earliest application, except when adoption utilizes certain loss carryforwards that must be credited directly to additional paid-in capital (under the quasi reorganization and APB 25 stock compensation rules) or to goodwill and other intangible assets (purchased NOLs).

¶ 7.05 INTRAPERIOD ALLOCATION

Prior to FAS 96, the rules for intraperiod tax allocation were not very precise, but generally the allocation was made by considering the effects on pretax income adjusted for permanent differences of income from continuing operations and other categories (hereafter the other categories) recognized during the current period (i.e., discontinued operations, extraordinary items, and direct entries to equity). It was generally considered appropriate to make the allocation by proceeding sequentially down the face of the income statement, first computing the tax effects of income from continuing operations, then computing the differential in taxes resulting from inclusion of each subsequent category.

FAS 96 provides relatively precise rules for making the intraperiod allocation, and the computations could be much more complicated. In contrast to APB 11's single computation of tax expense based on pretax income adjusted for permanent differences, the calculation under FAS 96 of the current tax provision and the deferred tax provision are completely separate computations. The FAS 96 rules for intraperiod allocation of income taxes could conceivably result in several separate computations of the current and the deferred tax provisions including, for each deferred tax computation, a revised scheduling exercise.

It should be noted that, under both FAS 96 and the prior rules, certain categories recognized during the period are excluded from the computation of total tax expense for the period because their tax effects are measured by reference to prior periods. In this latter group are (1) accounting changes adopted either by retroactive restatement of prior periods or by cumulative catch-up adjustment as of the beginning of the period and (2) corrections of errors in prior years' financials. For these, the tax effects that should be recorded should be the effects that would have been recorded if the newly adopted accounting method or the correct accounting had been used in the prior periods. (The example of intraperiod allocation in paragraph 74 of FAS 96 includes the cumulative effect of an accounting change. This would be erroneous except in a rare situation, where it is specified by the transition requirements of a Statement that the cumulative effect would enter into the computation of the current year's tax expense.)

As discussed at ¶ 12.01, it is unclear whether disclosure of current and deferred tax expense should be before or after use of NOL carryforwards and investment credits. Exhibit 7-2, which illustrates intraperiod allocation when there is an NOL carryforward, follows the gross presentation, but the net amounts are also available.

It is clear in FAS 96 that NOL carryforward benefits are generally classified on the basis of the source of income that uses the carryforward rather than the source of the loss that generates the carryforward. There are exceptions for purchase business combinations, certain quasi reorganizations, and certain stock compensation deductions. Presumably, although not specified, the source of income would generally determine classification of tax benefits of other carryforwards, such as tax credit and capital loss carryforwards; the exceptions for purchase business combinations and quasi reorganizations would also apply to credit carry-forwards.

Following are the mechanics prescribed by FAS 96 for performing the intraperiod tax allocation process.

Step 1—Continuing Operations

Under FAS 96, one calculation of the current and the deferred tax provisions is made for income from continuing operations. This computation would include only the effects on current year's taxable income (loss) and the temporary differences resulting from continuing operations. In addition, the tax expense (benefit) allocated to income from continuing operations would include:

- All adjustments to deferred tax balances for changes in tax status and tax laws or rates
- Usage of NOL carryforwards from prior periods to the extent permitted by the tax computations

Note that these latter effects are included in the provision charged to continuing operations regardless of whether the deferred taxes or the carryforwards could be deemed to have arisen from sources other than continuing operations in prior (or presumably even the same) period(s). It is the tax expense resulting from this computation for which the disclosure of significant components (current, deferred, NOL benefits, and so forth) is made, and it is this tax expense that is reconciled to that derived by simply calculating the statutory federal rate times pretax accounting income.

Step 2—Total Tax Expense

If there are, in addition, other categories, there would be another computation—one of total tax expense for the year. This computation would include the effects on taxable income and on temporary differences of all other categories (except for those measured by reference to prior periods), as well as the effects of income from continuing operations.

Step 3—Measure Incremental Effects

If there is more than one other category, then the tax effect of each category on total tax expense must be determined by performing additional computations of tax expense to measure the incremental effects. This entails adjusting the calculation of total current tax expense and total deferred tax expense (including adjusting the scheduled reversals as necessary) by excluding taxable income (loss) and temporary differences generated by the category or group of categories whose incremental effect is being measured. FAS 96 requires the following sequence:

a. Determine the tax benefit allocable to net loss categories.

    i. Measure the incremental tax benefit of the total net loss for all net loss categories.

    ii. Calculate the incremental effect of excluding each net loss category from the calculation of total tax expense.

    iii. Add together the incremental tax effects of all the net loss categories computed individually.

    iv. Apportion the total tax benefit derived in (i) ratably to each net loss category on the basis of the ratio of its individual incremental tax effect derived in (ii) to the total of all incremental tax effects derived in (iii).

b. Determine the difference between tax expense attributable to continuing operations and total tax expense. The difference between this amount and the amount derived in (a)(i) is deemed to apply to total net gain categories and is apportioned ratably to each net gain category on the same basis as the apportionment in respect to net loss categories described previously.

Step 4—Allocate Within a Category

If there is a need to allocate income taxes to different items within a category, the same procedures would be followed as described previously for categories, using the incremental effect on total tax expense of each item.

There may be some question whether, for purposes of intraperiod allocation, the two components of discontinued operations—results of the discontinued operation and gain or loss on disposal—constitute separate categories or items within a category. The example in paragraph 74 of FAS 96 includes discontinued operations as a single category. For convenience of illustration of the steps enumerated in the text, Exhibit 7-2 considers the two components to be separate categories. In the example situation the same procedures would be followed, and the same allocations would be made, if discontinued operations were considered a single category and its two components were items within that category. In that case, however, steps 3(a)(ii), (iii), and (iv) would represent allocations to items within a category rather than allocations between loss categories of the total tax benefit from both loss categories.

EXHIBIT 7-2
Intraperiod Tax Allocation

Alpha Co. applied FAS 96 as of January 1, 1987 on a prospective basis. At January 1, 1988, Alpha Co. had available NOLs for financial reporting purposes of $9,000 representing a $12,000 NOL for tax purposes less $3,000 of temporary differences (net future taxable income), none of which related to operations that were classified as discontinued in 1988.

In 1988, $6,000 of the tax NOL was used. Temporary differences netted to $1,000 at December 31, 1988, representing $5,000 future taxable income related to continuing operations and $4,000 future net deductions related to discontinued operations. Thus the book NOL at that date was $5,000.

The following information related to Alpha Co. for the year ended December 31, 1988:

	Taxable income (tax deductions)		
	Pretax income	Permanent differences	Change in temporary differences
Continuing operations	$14,000	$1,000	($2,000)
Discontinued operations			
Capital loss on sale	(2,000)	500	
Loss from operations	(13,000)	(2,000)	4,000
Gain on extinguishment of debt	4,000		
Totals	$ 3,000	($ 500)	$2,000

Step 1: Continuing Operations

Current Provision	With NOL	Without NOL	Benefit of NOL
Pretax accounting income	$14,000	$14,000	
Permanent differences	1,000	1,000	
Capital loss not usable	0	0	
Change in temporary differences	(2,000)	(2,000)	
Taxable income before NOL	13,000	13,000	
Tax NOL used	(12,000)	0	
Taxable income	1,000	13,000	
Tax rate	34%	34%	
Current provision	$ 340	$ 4,420	$4,080

Deferred Provision	With NOL	Without NOL	Benefit of NOL
Deferred tax balance at 12/31/88			
Temporary differences	$ 5,000	$ 5,000	
NOL used	0	0	
Future taxable income	5,000	5,000	
Tax rate	34%	34%	
	1,700	1,700	
Deferred tax balance at 1/1/88			
Temporary differences	3,000	3,000	
NOL used ($12,000 tax			
NOL)	(3,000)	0	
Future taxable income	0	3,000	
Tax rate	34%	34%	
	0	1,020	
Deferred provision	$ 1,700	$ 680	(1,020)

Effect of Use of NOL Carryforward

Book NOL at 1/1/88	$ 9,000	
Book NOL at 12/31/88	0	
NOL used	9,000	
Tax rate	34%	
NOL benefit	$ 3,060	$3,060

Summary of Tax Provision

Current	$ 4,420
Deferred	680
NOL benefit	(3,060)
Total	$ 2,040

Balance Sheet Accounts

Taxes currently payable	$ 340
Deferred taxes payable	1,700
Total	$ 2,040

(continued)

EXHIBIT 7-2 *(cont'd)*

Step 2: Total Tax Expense

Current Provision	With NOL	Without NOL	Benefit of NOL
Pretax accounting income	$3,000	$3,000	
Permanent differences	(500)	(500)	
Capital loss not usable	1,500	1,500	
Change in temporary Differences	2,000	2,000	
Taxable income before NOL	6,000	6,000	
Tax NOL used ($12,000 tax NOL)	(6,000)	0	
Taxable income	0	6,000	
Tax rate	34%	34%	
Current provision	$ 0	$2,040	$2,040

Deferred Provision			
Deferred tax balance at 12/31/88			
Temporary differences	$1,000	$1,000	
NOL used ($6,000 tax NOL)	(1,000)	0	
Future taxable income	0	1,000	
Tax rate	34%	34%	
	0	340	
Deferred tax balance at 1/1/88			
Temporary differences	3,000	3,000	
NOL used ($12,000 tax NOL)	(3,000)	0	
Future taxable income	0	3,000	
Tax rate	34%	34%	
	0	1,020	
Deferred provision	$ 0	($ 680)	(680)

Effect of Use of NOL Carryforward			
Book NOL at 1/1/88	$9,000		
Book NOL at 12/31/88	5,000		
NOL used	4,000		
Tax rate	34%		
NOL benefit	$1,360		$1,360

Summary of Tax Provision	With NOL	Without NOL	Benefit of NOL
Current	$ 2,040		
Deferred	(680)		
NOL benefit	(1,360)		
Total	$ 0		

Balance Sheet Accounts

Taxes currently payable	$ 0		
Deferred taxes payable	0		
Total	$ 0		

Step 3(a)(i): Total Tax Expense Excluding All Losses

Current Provision	With NOL	Without NOL	Benefit of NOL
Pretax accounting income	$18,000	$18,000	
Permanent differences	1,000	1,000	
Capital loss not usable	0	0	
Change in temporary differences	(2,000)	(2,000)	
Taxable income before NOL	17,000	17,000	
Tax NOL used	(12,000)	0	
Taxable income	5,000	17,000	
Tax rate	34%	34%	
Current provision	$ 1,700	$ 5,780	$4,080

Deferred Provision

	With NOL	Without NOL	Benefit of NOL
Deferred tax balance at 12/31/88			
Temporary differences	$ 5,000	$ 5,000	
NOL used	0	0	
Future taxable income	5,000	5,000	
Tax rate	34%	34%	
	1,700	1,700	
Deferred tax balance at 1/1/88			
Temporary differences	3,000	3,000	
NOL used ($12,000 tax NOL)	(3,000)	0	
Future taxable income	0	3,000	
Tax rate	34%	34%	
	0	1,020	
Deferred provision	$ 1,700	$ 680	(1,020)

(continued)

EXHIBIT 7-2 *(cont'd)*

Effect of Use of NOL Carryforward	With NOL	Without NOL	Benefit of NOL
Book NOL at 1/1/88	$ 9,000		
Book NOL at 12/31/88	0		
NOL used	9,000		
Tax rate	34%		
NOL benefit	$ 3,060		$3,060

Summary of Tax Provision

Current	$ 5,780		
Deferred	680		
NOL benefit	(3,060)		
Total	$ 3,400		

Balance Sheet Accounts

Taxes currently payable	$ 1,700		
Deferred taxes payable	1,700		
Total	$ 3,400		

Incremental Effect

Total tax expense excluding all losses	$ 3,400		
Total tax expense	0		
Incremental effect of all losses	$ 3,400		

Step 3(a)(ii): Total Tax Expense Excluding Loss on Sale

Current Provision	With NOL	Without NOL	Benefit of NOL
Pretax accounting income	$5,000	$5,000	
Permanent differences	(1,000)	(1,000)	
Capital loss not usable	0	0	
Change in temporary differences	2,000	2,000	
Taxable income before NOL	6,000	6,000	
Tax NOL used ($12,000 tax NOL)	(6,000)	0	
Taxable income	0	6,000	
Tax rate	34%	34%	
Current provision	$ 0	$2,040	$2,040

Deferred Provision	With NOL	Without NOL	Benefit of NOL
Deferred tax balance at 12/31/88			
Temporary differences	$1,000	$1,000	
NOL used ($6,000 tax NOL)	(1,000)	0	
Future taxable income	0	1,000	
Tax rate	34%	34%	
	0	340	
Deferred tax balance at 1/1/88			
Temporary differences	3,000	3,000	
NOL used ($12,000 tax NOL)	(3,000)	0	
Future taxable income	0	3,000	
Tax rate	34%	34%	
	0	1,020	
Deferred provision	$ 0	($ 680)	(680)

Effect of Use of NOL Carryforward

Book NOL at 1/1/88	$9,000		
Book NOL at 12/31/88	5,000		
NOL used	4,000		
Tax rate	34%		
NOL benefit	$1,360		$1,360

Summary of Tax Provision

Current	$2,040
Deferred	(680)
NOL benefit	(1,360)
Total	$ 0

Balance Sheet Accounts

Taxes currently payable	$ 0
Deferred taxes payable	0
Total	$ 0

Incremental Effect

Total tax expense excluding loss on sale	$ 0
Total tax expense	0
Incremental effect of loss on sale	$ 0

(continued)

EXHIBIT 7-2 *(cont'd)*

Step 3(a)(iii): Total Tax Expense Excluding Loss From Discontinued Operations

Current Provision	With NOL	Without NOL	Benefit of NOL
Pretax accounting income	$16,000	$16,000	
Permanent differences	1,500	1,500	
Capital loss not usable	1,500	1,500	
Change in temporary differences	(2,000)	(2,000)	
Taxable income before NOL	17,000	17,000	
Tax NOL used	(12,000)	0	
Taxable income	5,000	17,000	
Tax rate	34%	34%	
Current provision	$ 1,700	$ 5,780	$4,080

Deferred Provision

Deferred tax balance at 12/31/88			
Temporary differences	$ 5,000	$ 5,000	
NOL used	0	0	
Future taxable income	5,000	5,000	
Tax rate	34%	34%	
	1,700	1,700	
Deferred tax balance at 1/1/88			
Temporary differences	3,000	3,000	
NOL used ($12,000 tax NOL)	(3,000)	0	
Future taxable income	0	3,000	
Tax rate	34%	34%	
	0	1,020	
Deferred provision	$ 1,700	$ 680	(1,020)

Effect of Use of NOL Carryforward

Book NOL at 1/1/88	$ 9,000		
Book NOL at 12/31/88	0		
NOL used	9,000		
Tax rate	34%		
NOL benefit	$ 3,060		$3,060

Summary of Tax Provision	With NOL	Without NOL	Benefit of NOL
Current	$ 5,780		
Deferred	680		
NOL benefit	(3,060)		
Total	$ 3,400		

Balance Sheet Accounts

	With NOL
Taxes currently payable	$ 1,700
Deferred taxes payable	1,700
Total	$ 3,400

Incremental Effect

	With NOL
Total tax expense excluding loss from discontinued operations	$ 3,400
Total tax expense	0
Incremental effect of loss from discontinued operations	$ 3,400

Step 3(a)(iv) and (v): Apportionment of the Total Tax Benefit

	Loss on sale	Loss from discontinued operations	Total
Incremental tax effects	$0	$3,400	$ 3,400
Percent	0%	100%	100%
Total tax benefit	$3,400	$3,400	$ 3,400
Allocated tax benefit	$0	$3,400	$ 3,400

Step 3(b): Tax Attributable to Net Gain Categories

Total tax expense	$ 0
Tax expense—continuing operations	2,040
Incremental effect of other categories	(2,040)
Less benefits attributable to loss categories	3,400
Tax attributable to extraordinary gain	$ 1,360

(continued)

EXHIBIT 7-2 *(cont'd)*

Summary Income Statement

	Loss on sale	Loss from discontinued operations	Total
Income from continuing operations			$14,000
Tax provision			(2,040)
			11,960
Discontinued operations			
Loss on sale	($2,000)		
Tax benefit	0		(2,000)
Loss from operations	(13,000)		
Tax benefit	3,400		(9,600)
			(11,600)
Gain on extinguishment of debt			4,000
Tax provision			(1,360)
			2,640
Net income			$ 3,000

A reconciliation between income tax expense from continuing operations and taxes computed by applying the statutory rate of 34 percent to pretax accounting income from continuing operations is as follows:

Expected tax at 34%	$4,760
Permanent differences	340
Benefit of NOL carryforward	(3,060)
Tax expense from continuing operations	$2,040

Note: This example has been simplified. It assumes that all the temporary differences from continuing operations and discontinued operations can offset in each deferred tax computation. In any particular situation, the question of whether, and the extent to which, offset would be appropriate in the various deferred tax computations would have to be considered. Moreover, alternative minimum tax as explained in Chapter 9, would generally operate to preclude complete elimination by an NOL of taxes currently payable; its effect in the deferred tax computation would also have to be considered. The effects of alternative minimum tax have been completely ignored in this example.

The analysis of the provision illustrated in this example follows the gross presentation discussed in Chapter 12. Chapter 12 discusses complications that arise when temporary differences increase taxable income (before NOL application) in the current provision and unused future net deductions in the deferred provision.

Do not be misled by the fact that in this illustration the tax effects resulting from the intraperiod allocation are the expected tax effects—that is, no tax benefit of a capital loss and the expected 34 percent rate applied to pretax income and to permanent differences. The focus in this example has been on illustrating the required mechanics; there has been no attempt to illustrate how unexpected tax effects could result.

CHAPTER **8**

Business Combinations

FAS 96 significantly changes the financial statement presentation and measurement of the tax effects associated with business combinations. The new rules will take getting used to but the end result usually will not be that difficult to understand. We will deal separately with the two types of business combinations—purchases and poolings.

¶ 8.01 PURCHASES

Prior to FAS 96, APB Opinion 16, *Business Combinations*, required, for purchase business combinations, the net-of-tax approach for allocating the aggregate purchase price to identifiable assets and liabilities acquired. In other words, the difference between the fair value of an asset or a liability, assuming equal tax basis, and its actual tax basis was considered an element in measuring its fair value; the tax effect of this difference increased or decreased the value assigned.

[1] New Approach

FAS 96 abandons the net-of-tax approach. Under the new approach, each identified asset and liability is assigned its respective fair value, assuming an equal tax basis. A deferred tax liability or asset is then established for the tax effects of the temporary differences resulting from the purchase price allocation (i.e., the differences between assigned fair values and tax bases).

[2] One Company Now

Although establishing a deferred tax balance at the acquisition date may be easier to understand than the old net-of-tax presentation, determining the appropriate balance may be difficult. Essentially, the deferred tax asset or liability arising from the acquisition is the difference between the combined company's deferred tax balance after the acquisition and the acquiror's balance immediately prior to it.

If, in the future, the combined company will file a consolidated tax return, the deferred tax balance should reflect that fact. FAS 96 requires that the acquiror's temporary differences "interact" with the target's temporary differences to determine the appropriate deferred tax asset or liability to record at the acquisition date. This is especially important when the target has future net deductions and the acquiror has a net deferred tax liability. Will the future deductions offset the future taxable income?

In order to answer this question, it is necessary to determine the temporary differences of both the target and the acquiror at date of acquisition. Temporary differences for the target should be identifiable either (1) as a result of valuations made in a taxable transaction or (2) from filing a short-period return prior to entering the consolidated group. Note, however, that, as discussed at ¶ 3.03[7], a question could arise in certain purchase business combinations (e.g., when equal amounts are assigned, for both book and tax purposes, to particular assets at date of acquisition) with respect to whether all future book and tax amounts for depreciable assets (and certain other items) should be included in the scheduling exercise at the date of acquisition.

A problem could arise with respect to the acquiror if the acquisition date is not on or about the acquiror's tax year-end, when temporary differences are computed in any event. Unfortunately, most acquisitions are not consummated on such a convenient date. The question then becomes how the acquiror's temporary differences should be computed as of an interim date. Three possibilities present themselves:

1. Assume that, as of the acquisition date, the acquiror files a short-period tax return. The tax laws govern how annual deductions are allowed in a short-period return. (Depreciation is one of them.) The existing book bases of the assets and liabilities would then be compared to these pro forma tax bases to determine the temporary differences.

2. Assume that temporary differences arise evenly throughout the year. That is, if the beginning temporary difference is $100 and the projected ending temporary difference is $220, the temporary difference increases by $10 a month as the year progresses.

3. Assume that temporary differences arise in the same pattern that pretax accounting income is earned. That is, if pretax income is earned 10 percent, 20 percent, 30 percent, and 40 percent in the first through fourth quarters, respectively, then temporary differences would increase or decrease on that basis as well. Mechanically, this could be achieved by separating the annual effective tax rate used in interim reporting into current and deferred components. Then the change in deferred taxes accrued through the interim date would be grossed up into the change in temporary differences through that date.

In terms of FAS 96, the first alternative might be viewed as the most supportable. But there are several difficulties with this approach. For starters, it is impractical. The mechanics of computing the appropriate tax attributes are complex for a short-period return. The second alternative would be a practical answer to this problem. But both alternatives are inconsistent with how a company estimates its quarterly tax provision and, thus, its deferred tax account. The temporary differences used to determine the acquisition accounting would yield an answer different from the amount recorded on the acquiror's interim balance sheet (see ¶ 10.08). The third alternative avoids the inconsistency and would be relatively easy to compute, at least for companies used to computing an effective tax rate for quarterly reporting.

¶ 8.02 ACQUIRED NET OPERATING LOSSES

FAS 96 also changes the accounting for a net operating loss (NOL) acquired in a purchase business combination. Under APB 11, when the benefit of an NOL was not recognized at the date of acquisition (the usual case), any benefit subsequently recognized was used to reduce goodwill and any noncurrent assets of the purchased company and then to establish negative goodwill, all on a retroactive basis. The only effect on the income statement was reduced depreciation and amortization charges and, perhaps, a credit from amortizing negative goodwill, and much of that impact might have been reflected in prior years through required restatement.

Under FAS 96, an acquired company's NOL may be recorded at the acquisition date if, under the laws of the applicable taxing jurisdiction, it can reduce the parent's deferred tax liability. As noted, calculating the deferred tax balance at the acquisition date usually will be determined on a combined company basis. Therefore, the acquired company's NOL carryforward must be considered in the scheduling exercise. Any benefit of using an acquired NOL carryforward would be recorded in the purchase price allocation and would not immediately affect net income (in effect, reducing the amount available to be allocated to other acquired net assets). Similarly, the parent's NOL carryforward may reduce the deferred tax liability resulting from the acquired company's temporary differences. In both cases, the benefit of the NOL carryforward recognized in this way is reflected in income in future years through reduced depreciation and amortization charges on the acquired assets.

As always, the tax laws must be followed, and not every jurisdiction permits the use of one entity's NOL against the combined future taxable income. The U.S. federal tax law limits the use of purchased NOL carryforwards according to the form of the purchase transaction. The Tax Reform Act of 1986 (TRA 1986) also introduced annual limitations on the use of carry-over tax benefits, including NOLs and excess tax bases of acquired assets, following a change in corporate ownership. All these restrictions must be reflected in applying acquired NOLs in the U.S. federal deferred tax calculation.

[1] Later Use of Acquired NOLs

FAS 96 has amended APB 16 to require that, if not recorded at the acquisition date, the benefit of a purchased NOL would first reduce goodwill and any other intangible assets (prospectively, not retroactively). Once those assets are reduced to zero, the benefit is included in income as a reduction of income tax expense. This procedure is illustrated in Exhibit 8-1. Similar treatment would be appropriate when the tax basis of net assets acquired exceeds the book basis at the acquisition date and no benefit could be recorded at that time.

This change could accelerate considerably the recognition of purchased NOL benefits. It also eliminates the need to restate (perhaps a number of times) prior financial statements; the effect of using an NOL is now entirely prospective, benefiting only current or future income statements.

FAS 96 does not explicitly specify the order of application of purchased NOLs (i.e., first goodwill, first other intangibles, or pro rata). Although the implication of the specific language in FAS 96 is pro rata, the FASB staff expressed a tentative conclusion at the March 31, 1988 meeting of the Implementation Group that goodwill should be completely eliminated before application of purchased NOL benefits to other intangibles. The rationale for this position is that goodwill is not valued separately as are the identified intangibles; it is a residual amount in the purchase price allocation, and if, at the date of acquisition, the purchased NOLs had been recognized, they would have reduced goodwill. The FASB staff has not taken a position with respect to any ordering of application among the other intangibles.

When preacquisition NOLs exist and the company anticipates using some or all of the NOLs in the current period, it raises a question as to how amortization of goodwill and other intangibles should be computed. Assume, first, a company that prepares financials only once a year. At the end of the year it has recognized a benefit from a purchased NOL. As discussed at ¶ 12.01, the company would have a tax provision that is a "charge equivalent" to the NOL benefit and a corresponding reduction in goodwill and other intangibles. Should its amortization for the year of goodwill and other intangibles be based on the beginning balance, that balance as reduced for the purchased NOL benefit, or the average of the two? Price Waterhouse believes that any of these approaches would be acceptable.

Now add in a necessity for interim reporting. If the company has elected to compute annual amortization after reduction of the beginning balance for half or all of the NOL benefit realized during the year, can it base its amortization on what it projects will be the reduction for the year from purchased NOL benefit? If so, what degree of assurance must there be that such benefit will be realized? There is an analogous situation in the FASI 18, *Accounting for Income Taxes in Interim Periods*, interim reporting rules after amendment by FAS 96. The benefit of an NOL can be reflected in the effective rate computation only if realization by "ordinary" income is assured beyond any reasonable doubt; otherwise recognition is based on year-to-date income. However, as discussed under at ¶ 10.08, upon examination, this rule does not appear to be particularly conservative. Moreover, there is a significant difference between an NOL benefit that is reflected immediately in income and one that is spread over several future years. It appears acceptable for interim reporting to estimate the annual reduction; of course, adjustment for estimate changes during the year and to actual at year-end would be required. Alternatively, interim year-to-date amortization could be based on year-to-date realization. This alternative would not be attractive when later loss quarters that will reverse the benefit are predictable.

No deferred taxes are provided with respect to goodwill, which typically does not have tax basis. However, under FAS 96, an intangible asset will either have tax basis equal to its carrying amount or a related temporary difference entering into the deferred tax computation. Because of the numerous restrictions on the use of preacquisition NOLs in the U.S. tax law, the existence of an unused preacquisition NOL does not necessarily indicate that temporary differences arising from the same acquisition will not give rise to deferred taxes. In any event, application of the benefits of a purchased NOL to reduce an intangible (creating or adjusting the temporary difference) potentially gives rise to a debit adjustment to balance sheet deferred taxes. The accounting firm of Price Waterhouse suggests that the resulting credit be applied to reduce any remaining balance of intangibles or goodwill. It should be reflected in income (as a reduction of deferred tax expense) only after any balances have been eliminated. Application to intangible assets could again give rise to a debit adjustment to deferred taxes and a credit to be applied to intangible assets, and so on (see ¶ 8.03 for discussion of a similar iterative process and a formula that could possibly be applied to this situation as well).

EXHIBIT 8-1
Use of an Acquired NOL Carryforward

On March 1, 1988, Gamma Corp. (a shell company) acquired the stock of Kappa Co. for $15,000. The allocation of the purchase price resulted in the assignment of $12,000 to tangible assets and $3,000 to goodwill. The tax basis of the net assets is $2,000 lower than the book basis. However, no deferred tax liability has been recorded as there is a tax NOL of $13,000 and the temporary differences reverse before the NOL expires.

During 1988, Gamma Corp. and Kappa Co. had pretax accounting income, before goodwill amortization of $125, of $12,000 and the accumulated temporary differences increased by $3,000 to $5,000. There is no current provision as the $9,000 of taxable income has been sheltered by the tax NOL. At December 31, 1988, there is a remaining tax NOL of $4,000. The acquired book NOL has been reduced from $11,000 ($13,000 less $2,000) to zero as the accumulated temporary differences of $5,000 can absorb the remaining tax NOL. The benefit from using the acquired NOL is allocated as follows:

	With NOL	Without NOL	Benefit of NOL
Current Provision			
1988 taxable income	$ 9,000	$ 9,000	
Tax NOL use	(9,000)	0	
	0	9,000	
Tax rate	34%	34%	
Current provision	$ 0	$ 3,060	$3,060
Deferred Provision			
Deferred tax balance at 12/21/88	$ 340	$ 1,700	
Deferred tax balance at 3/1/88	0	680	
Deferred provision	$ 340	$ 1,020	680
Recognition of NOL Benefit			
Acquired book NOL at 3/1	$11,000		
Acquired book NOL at 12/31	0		
Acquired NOL use	11,000		
Tax rate	34%		
NOL Benefit	3,740		$3,740
Goodwill balance, after $125 amortization, at 12/31/88	2,875		
NOL benefit to be recognized in the tax provision	$ 865		

Although Gamma Corp. and Kappa Co. would make separate journal entries reflecting their tax-sharing agreement, the sum of their entries would reflect the following debits and credits:

Debit:	Current tax expense	$ 3,060	
	Deferred tax expense	1,020	
Credit:	Goodwill		$ 2,875
	NOL benefit		865
	Deferred tax liability		340

The summarized consolidated income statment of Gamma Corp. will look like this:

Pretax accounting income		$11,875
Provision for income taxes		
Current	$ 3,060	
Deferred	1,020	
NOL benefit	(865)	
Net provision—charge equiva-lent to purchased NOL benefit		3,215
Net income		$ 8,660

Disclosure, similar to the following, would be appropriate in the notes to the financial statements in years when an acquired NOL is utilized:

> During 1988, the Company utilized the net operating loss of $11,000 that was acquired when Kappa Co. was purchased (see Note 2). The tax benefit of $3,740 was used, first to eliminate the balance of the goodwill that was recorded on the acquisition of Kappa Co. in the amount of $2,875, and then to reduce income tax expense in the amount of $865.

This example ignores, for simplicity of illustration, the effect of alternative minimum tax (AMT). AMT would generally operate to preclude total elimination by an NOL of taxes currently payable. Moreover, AMT provisions of the tax law would also have to be applied in the deferred tax computation. See Chapter 9.

The analysis of the provision in this example follows the gross method discussed in Chapter 12.

[2] Order of NOL Utilization

In some cases, NOLs will be both acquired and generated by the acquiror. In addition, NOLs may be generated after the acquisition. The order of precedence of recognition in financial statements has not previously been covered in authoritative literature. An Emerging Issues Task Force consensus in 1986 specified a particular ordering. Now FAS 96 has adopted a different ordering. Consistent with the view that the scheduling process consists of hypothetical future tax returns, the tax return ordering of the use of NOLs must be respected. That is, if the tax law mandates that the preacquisition NOLs must be used first, the deferred tax computation must respect this. For companies that have followed the EITF consensus or another ordering at variance with the tax return, the ordering mandated by FAS 96 may affect either retroactive or prospective application. The FAS 96 ordering must be followed with respect to any NOLs used either in initial application of FAS 96 or in subsequent periods.

¶ 8.03 "NEGATIVE GOODWILL" ALLOCATED TO NONCURRENT ASSETS

In a purchase business combination in which the fair value of the acquired net assets exceeds the purchase price, the excess is referred to as "negative goodwill." (See Exhibit 8-2.) APB 16 requires that the "negative goodwill" be applied first to reduce the value assigned to noncurrent assets (other than marketable securities). After the value of all noncurrent assets has been reduced to zero, unallocated negative goodwill (as defined in APB 16) would be reflected as a deferred credit in the balance sheet. The fair value (assuming equal tax basis) of a noncurrent asset less any allocated "negative goodwill" establishes its assigned value in the financial statements (net assigned value).

FAS 96 specifically prohibits recognizing deferred taxes for temporary differences arising from goodwill or negative goodwill, but it is silent with respect to temporary differences related to "negative goodwill" allocated to noncurrent assets. Assuming that the net assigned values exceed the tax bases of noncurrent assets at the date of acquisition, a deferred tax liability would be established.

Recognition of the liability, however, serves to reduce "negative goodwill." If all "negative goodwill" has been allocated, then its reduction increases the net assigned values of the noncurrent assets. This, in turn, increases the temporary difference amounts and the calculated deferred tax liability, which then reduces "negative goodwill" and so on.

The iterative process can be avoided by simply calculating the deferred tax liability and the addition to noncurrent assets (A in the formula shown) that will result in the appropriate deferred tax liability after the original temporary differences (B in the formula shown) have been adjusted for the addition. In formal terms:

Deferred tax liability (addition to noncurrent assets) = Tax rate $\times$ Original temporary differences + addition to noncurrent assets

$$A = 0.34\ (B + A)$$
$$A = 0.34B + 0.34A$$
$$0.66A = 0.34B$$
$$A = \frac{0.34B}{0.66}$$
$$A = 0.515B$$

This computation must be performed before it can be determined whether unallocated negative goodwill remains after the allocation.

Note that the formula requires use of the appropriate tax rate. When it is clear that all temporary differences arising in the purchase will be fully tax-effected at the statutory rate, there is no problem. But there may be situations where the temporary differences arising in the purchase would be tax-effected at some lower rate, whether the acquired company files in a separate tax jurisdiction or will file a separate return, or whether it will be consolidated in the parent's filing. Remember that the deferred tax liability arising in a purchase business combination is simply the change in the deferred tax liability of the acquiring company

EXHIBIT 8-2 _____
Purchase Business Combinations—Allocated "Negative Goodwill"

On December 31, 1987, Holding Co. was formed. On January 1, 1988, it acquired Target Inc. for $8 million in a nontaxable purchase business combination. The fair value of net assets acquired, assuming equal tax basis, was $11 million. Holding Co. will apply FAS 96 and establish deferred taxes at the acquisition date.

There is "negative goodwill" of $3 million before recognition of deferred taxes. In accordance with APB 16, the "negative goodwill" is recorded as a reduction in the amounts assigned to long-term, depreciable assets. Calculation of deferred taxes resulting from the purchase is outlined in the steps that follow. The reversal of temporary differences results in net taxable and deductible amounts that can be offset against each other. Holding Co. has no temporary differences.

Step 1: Measure Temporary Differences Based on Assigned Values Before Establishment of Deferred Taxes

	Assigned values before establishment of deferred taxes	Tax basis	Original temporary differences
Fair value of depreciable assets	$7,500,000	$4,050,000	$3,450,000
Less "negative goodwill"	(3,000,000)		(3,000,000)
Net value assigned to depreciable assets	4,500,000	4,050,000	450,000
Fair value of other net assets acquired	3,500,000	1,950,000	1,550,000
	$8,000,000	$6,000,000	$2,000,000

Step 2: Calculate Deferred Taxes to Be Recognized

Original temporary differences	$2,000,000
Tax rate	34%
Deferred tax liability on original temporary differences	$ 680,000

The deferred tax liability on original temporary differences ($680,000) reduces the amount of "negative goodwill" initially allocated to noncurrent assets from $3 million to $2,320,000. The reduction in "negative goodwill" then increases the amount assigned to depreciable assets and the related temporary differences that, in turn, increases the deferred tax liability. And the process would be repeated, and repeated, and repeated. To calculate the reduction in "negative goodwill" and the amount of deferred taxes to be recognized, the iterative process can be avoided by applying the formula shown below, which assumes a 34 percent tax rate.

$$\begin{bmatrix} \text{Deferred tax} \\ \text{liability (addition} \\ \text{to depreciable} \\ \text{assets) (A)} \end{bmatrix} = \text{Tax rate} \times \begin{bmatrix} \text{Original temporary} \\ \text{differences (B)} + \\ \text{addition to depreciable} \\ \text{assets (A)} \end{bmatrix}$$

$$A = 0.515B$$

Original temporary differences	$2,000,000
Factor to be applied	51.5%
Deferred taxes to be recognized	$1,030,000

The final purchase price allocation will reflect the following assigned values.

		Assigned value
Fair value of depreciable assets		$7,500,000
Less "negative goodwill" net of addition to depreciable assets	$3,000,000 (1,030,000)	(1,970,000)
Net value assigned to depreciable assets		5,530,000
Fair value of net assets acquired, excluding depreciable assets and deferred taxes		3,500,000
Deferred rax liability		(1,030,000)
		$8,000,000

before and after the temporary differences resulting from the purchase business combination have been included in its deferred tax computation. The appropriate tax rate would then have to be determined by a deferred tax computation before the prior "addition" is made and calculating the increment in the deferred tax liability from the "addition" described previously to the temporary differences. As the "addition" increases, the effective tax rate could change, which would in turn affect the actual "addition" computed. Some iteration may be necessary to establish the appropriate rate.

Note that not only federal tax effects but those in other jurisdictions must also be considered.

¶ 8.04　RATE CHANGES AND PURCHASE BUSINESS COMBINATIONS

Applying FAS 96 to purchase business combinations can yield some surprising results. For example, a company might be negotiating a purchase business combination at a time when it may be apparent that there will be a change in income tax rates. Both the buyer and the seller may be negotiating using the expected new rates.

After the Senate Finance Committee issued its report in March 1986, there was little doubt that substantial rate reductions would be enacted for future years. If a purchase business transaction was negotiated and consummated during the period before TRA 1986 was enacted, what would be the appropriate rate for providing deferred taxes at the acquisition date?

The Statement mandates that new rates be reflected in accounting only when enacted. Thus, under FAS 96, deferred taxes would be provided at the acquisition date at a 46 percent rate, resulting in "instant earnings" on enactment of TRA 1986. Alternatively, this mandate could create an "instant charge" if a purchase business combination was consummated shortly before an increase in corporate income tax rates. Keep in mind that this amount will enter into the effective rate reconciliation, a required disclosure under FAS 96 (see ¶ 12.01).

Although having to record instant earnings or an instant charge following a purchase business combination may be disconcerting, this provision does have a bright side: It treats all purchase business combinations consummated before the enactment date similarly by eliminating the need for trying to quantify the extent to which potential rate changes were actually reflected in negotiations. This is especially helpful given the current speculation concerning a tax rate increase in the United States in the next several years.

¶ 8.05 PRIOR PURCHASE BUSINESS COMBINATIONS

FAS 96 allows companies to choose the earliest application year. As noted, a company may elect to apply the new Statement's provisions retroactively by restating some or all prior years' financial statements. The discussion up to this point has focused on business combinations that occur after the date of earliest application. Special transition rules govern purchase business combinations that occurred before that date.

The two transition methods—restate and remeasure and take a shortcut—are outlined in Exhibit 8-3. The number of years a company opts to restate will dictate which method must be applied to purchase business combinations in the past. This transition rule is one of the few instances in which a transition election in adopting a mandated accounting principle change can significantly affect future financial statements. The implications of these provisions for implementation strategy are discussed in Chapter 11.

[1] Restatement Method

If the purchase price allocation is restated to comply with FAS 96, there will be, in the restated income statements for periods subsequent to the purchase, adjustments to depreciation or amortization of the acquired assets and to deferred tax expense. For

EXHIBIT 8-3 _____
Prior Purchase Business Combinations—Measuring Temporary Differences

Method 1: Restate and Remeasure

If the Statement is applied retroactively to a date *preceding* consummation of a purchase business combination, the net assets acquired are remeasured to their fair values, assuming equal tax bases, and deferred taxes are provided at the date of acquisition. In a purchase in which fair values of the acquired assets exceed their actual tax bases, the amounts assigned to the acquired assets will be increased and a deferred tax liability will be recorded at the consummation date.

Method 2: Take a Shortcut

When the earliest application of the Statement is to a year *after* the consummation date, the values previously assigned to net assets acquired are not adjusted, but deferred taxes are provided based on the difference between the carrying amounts of those net assets and their tax bases at the date of earliest application.

_____

a purchase in which fair values exceeded tax bases, pretax depreciation or amortization will be increased and income tax expense will be reduced.

Those effects will not exactly offset, however, and there will be an effect on net income. When purchases were recorded net-of-tax, the tax effects were not accounted for separately. The tax effects embodied in the amount assigned to a depreciable asset, for example, were simply depreciated over the remaining life. The actual incidence of the tax effects might have followed a completely different pattern and would usually have been reflected in income accordingly. Application of FAS 96 generally has the effect of "normalizing" the tax effects of acquired assets, that is, unless tax laws or rates change, pretax income effects of acquired assets and liabilities ordinarily will have tax effects at the statutory rates enacted at date of acquisition. Of course, factors such as operating losses or operative restrictions on recording the benefits of future tax deductions may preclude such normalization. In fact, a number of rate differentials that can occur in applying FAS 96 are listed at ¶ 6.08.

In the past, discounting of the tax effects in a purchase business combination was strongly encouraged. For simplicity, in Exhibit 8-4, discounting of the tax effects in the initial purchase price allocation (i.e., pre-FAS 96) has been ignored. However, restatement of a prior purchase business combination in which the tax effects had been discounted will result in adjustments to goodwill.

Restating prior financial statements and grossing up acquired assets will increase depreciation or amortization in future years. The AMT computation (discussed in Chapter 9) considers pretax accounting income a factor in determining the amount of AMT to be paid in 1987, 1988, and 1989. With the higher depreciation and amortization charges resulting from restatement, pretax accounting income will be reduced, potentially reducing the amount of AMT that might otherwise be payable.

[2] Shortcut Method

As noted, prior to FAS 96, APB 16 required the recording of the assigned values of assets and liabilities net of their tax effects. However, if FAS 96 is not applied retroactively to a preconsummation date, the value of net assets is not grossed up. Temporary differences relating to net assets acquired are measured by reference to the remaining net book value and the tax basis at the date of earliest application. Exhibit 8-4 illustrates this point.

It is interesting to note that the remaining net book value is already net of future tax effects; now deferred taxes are provided for the difference between that tax-effected carrying amount and actual tax basis. The FASB provided the special transition rule to accommodate companies that could not reallocate the purchase price of prior business combinations without incurring substantial cost. It is a purely pragmatic (certainly not conceptual) way to ensure that, after adoption of FAS 96, there will be deferred taxes for practically all book-tax bases differences.

Exhibit 8-4 also demonstrates another effect of the special transition provisions: The charge recorded on adopting FAS 96 to establish a deferred tax liability is offset by lower tax expense in the future. (To the extent that the charge establishes deferred taxes for LIFO inventories, however, there would be offsetting lower future tax expense only to the extent of liquidations.) On the other hand, any addition to goodwill resulting from retroactive restatement treatment generally is amortized to income. Given the typically long amortization period, the amounts are usually insignificant.

Applying the shortcut method to the remaining tax-effected carrying amount of a liability assumed in a prior purchase business combination could result in the recognition of a deferred tax debit. As previously noted, the carrying amount of the assumed liability would not be adjusted. Thus, if the assumed liability is settled at its original pretax estimate and if the original estimated tax effect is actually realized, a net loss could result in the year of settlement from writing off the tax debit recorded in the shortcut transition. Use of the shortcut transition method could result in a similar loss upon realization, subsequent to date of earliest application of FAS 96, of an asset whose tax basis exceeds its carrying amount. In most cases, the existence of a probable future loss would require an adjustment to the carrying amount of an asset or liability and immediate recognition of the loss. The FASB staff has taken the position that the shortcut method should be applied consistently to both assets acquired and liabilities assumed in prior years; permitting the loss to be reflected in future operations only reduces the usually favorable effect on future operations of the shortcut method.

[3] Shortcut Method and Higher Tax Bases

In accounting for certain purchase business combinations in prior years, the fair values assigned have not been increased to reflect the higher tax bases because of uncertainty about the realization of tax benefits from the higher tax bases. The FASB Emerging Issues Task Force considered the accounting under APB 11 for postacquisition realization of tax benefits from the higher tax bases in Issue 85-3. Under its consensus, if a transaction (e.g., the sale of some of the assets acquired) occurs within approximately one year after acquisition and results in eventual realization of previously unrecognized tax benefits, the tax benefits should be recognized as a purchase price adjustment similar to the accounting for the realization of purchased NOL carryforwards; if the transaction occurs after one year, the related tax benefits should be recognized in income.

When the shortcut transition method is applied, tax benefits would be ascribed to the higher tax bases to the extent permitted by the deferred tax liability computation, either as of the date of earliest application or subsequently. However, even if the date of earliest application is more than one year subsequent to the date of acquisition, it may not be appropriate to reflect the benefit directly in income. FAS 96 requires that excess tax basis for which tax benefit cannot be recognized at date of acquisition will be considered the equivalent of a purchased NOL carryforward. The FASB staff has indicated that this extends, effective with application of FAS 96, to remaining excess tax basis resulting from purchase business combinations which are not being remeasured, even when a portion of the excess tax basis has already been realized and has been credited directly to income based on the EITF consensus. Thus, adoption of FAS 96 may recharacterize book/tax basis differences as purchased NOL carryforwards. The treatment of purchased NOLs is discussed at ¶ 8.05[4].

When, in a prior purchase business combination, the higher tax bases have been fully recognized in assigning values at date of acquisition, the shortcut method will treat as temporary differences the remaining excess of tax bases over the book bases (the book bases in this case have already been increased once, at date of acquisition, to reflect the higher tax bases). In the view of the FASB staff, this excess also represents a purchased NOL carryforward. Note that this situation could also result, as discussed in the preceding section, in recognizing a loss when the tax debit, recorded in applying the shortcut transition method and perhaps

(continued on page 8-27)

EXHIBIT 8-4 —————————————————————————————
Purchase Business Combinations—Transition

Historical Facts

On January 1, 1985, ABC Company acquired the stock of XYZ Company for $10 million in a nontaxable purchase business combination. The tax rate at that time was 46 percent. The fair values, assuming equal tax bases, of the assets acquired and liabilities assumed and their actual tax bases at the date of acquisition are shown below.

In accordance with the provisions of APB 16, the future tax effects of the differences between the tax bases and the fair values of acquired net assets were taken into account when recording the business combination.

	Fair Value	Tax Basis	Recorded Value
LIFO inventories	$3,000,000	$ 950,000	$ 3,000,000
Depreciable assets	6,340,000	2,780,000	4,702,400
Goodwill			2,837,600
Loss accrual	(1,000,000)		(540,000)
Purchase price			$10,000,000

The tax effect arising from the basis difference of LIFO inventories has been discounted back to zero as it is not expected to reverse until the very distant future. For simplicity, discounting of the tax effects relating to depreciable assets and the loss accrual have been ignored.

Depreciable assets have a remaining three-year life for tax purposes and a six-year life for book purposes. The straight-line method is being applied in both cases. Goodwill is being amortized over 15 years. In 1985 and 1986, reported amounts relating to the acquisition were as follows:

	1985	1986
Depreciation expense	$783,733	$783,733
Goodwill amortization	189,173	189,173
Pretax expense	972,906	972,906
Current tax benefit*	(426,267)	(426,267)
Net expense	($546,639)	$546,639)

*The current tax benefit realized in 1985 and 1986 results from tax depreciation of $926,667 at a 46 percent tax rate. For simplicity, we have assumed that no new temporary or timing differences were generated after the acquisition. The difference between tax and book depreciation in each year was therefore a permanent difference.

Implementation Strategies

ABC Company has decided to adopt FAS 96 in 1987. Whether FAS 96 is first applied prior or subsequent to 1985 could affect not only amounts related to the acquisition that were reported in prior years, but also future results. In evaluating its adoption alternatives, management is assessing how amounts related to the 1985 acquisition of XYZ Company would be affected. It has been assumed that net taxable income will be reported in each future year, but, in order to focus on the effects of different transition accounting for the 1985 acquisition, taxable income earned from other sources has been omitted. In addition, it is assumed that the book tax basis difference of LIFO inventories remains constant.

Method 1: Restate and Remeasure

If ABC Company elects to restate prior years including 1985, the year in which the purchase business combination was consummated, FAS 96 requires that the assets acquired be recorded at fair value and that deferred taxes, calculated in accordance with the Statement, be established at the acquisition date. The business combination, on a restated basis, would be recorded at the acquisition date as follows:

LIFO inventories	$3,000,000
Depreciable assets	6,340,000
Goodwill	3,780,600
Current deferred tax liability**	(1,002,800)
Noncurrent deferred tax liability	(1,117,800)
Loss accrual	(1,000,000)
Purchase price	$10,000,000

**In this example, the future reversal of temporary differences results in net taxable and deductible amounts that will offset. The current deferred tax liability was based on the following schedule of temporary difference reversals.

(continued)

EXHIBIT 8-4 (cont'd)

	Temporary differences at 1/1/85	Future years				
		1985	1986	1987	1988	1989 and future
LIFO inventories	$2,050,000	$2,050,000				
Depreciable assets	3,560,000	130,000	$130,000	$130,000	$1,056,667	$2,113,333
Loss accrual	(1,000,000)					(1,000,000)
	$4,610,000	2,180,000	130,000	130,000	1,056,667	1,113,333
Tax rate		46%	46%	46%	46%	46%
		$1,002,800	$ 59,800	$ 59,800	$ 486,067	$ 512,133

The effect of restatement on the income statement for the years ended December 31, 1985 and 1986, is as follows:

	1985		1986	
	As reported	Restated	As reported	Restated
Depreciation expense	$783,733	$1,056,667	$783,733	$1,056,667
Goodwill amortization	189,173	252,040	189,173	252,040
Pretax expense	972,906	1,308,707	972,906	1,308,707
Current tax benefit	(426,267)	(426,267)	(426,267)	(426,267)
Deferred tax benefit		(59,800)		(59,800)
Reduction in tax rates				(391,200)
Total tax benefit	(426,267)	(486,067)	(426,267)	(877,267)
Net Expense	($546,639)	($ 822,640)	($546,639)	($ 431,440)

Reconciliation of income tax expense and taxes computed by applying the statutory rate of 46 percent to pretax expense demonstrates the impact of the restatement and FAS 96.

	1985		1986	
	As reported	Restated	As reported	Restated
Expected benefit at 46%	($447,537)	($602,005)	($447,537)	($602,005)
Permanent items Goodwill amortization	87,020	115,938	87,020	115,938
Depreciable asset basis difference	(65,750)		(65,750)	
Reduction in tax rates				(391,200)
Reported benefit	($426,267)	($486,067)	($426,267)	($877,267)

Method 2: The Shortcut

If ABC Company adopts FAS 96 in 1987 and applies it prospectively, the book bases of the assets acquired in 1985 would not be grossed up to their pretax values. A deferred tax balance would be established at January 1, 1987, as part of the effect of adopting the new Statement.

The temporary differences (excluding goodwill) at the date of earliest application (January 1, 1987) would be measured as the difference between the remaining book balance, net of tax, and the remaining tax basis.

	Book Balance	Tax Basis	Temporary Difference
LIFO inventories	$3,000,000	$ 950,000	$2,050,000
Depreciable assets	3,134,934	926,666	2,208,268
Loss accrual	(540,000)	0	(540,000)
	$5,594,934	$1,876,666	$3,718,268

(continued)

EXHIBIT 8-4 (cont'd)

A deferred tax liability of $1,378,634 would be provided on the scheduled reversals of temporary differences, as follows.

	Temporary Differences at 1/1/87	Future Years				
		1987	1988	1989	1990	1991
LIFO inventories	$2,050,000	$2,050,000				
Depreciable assets	2,208,268	(142,933)	$783,734	$783,734	$783,733	($540,000)
Loss accrual	(540,000)					(540,000)
	$3,718,268	1,907,067	783,734	738,734	783,733	(540,000)
Tax rate		40%	34%	34%	34%	34%
Deferred tax liability		$ 762,827	$266,469	$266,469	$266,469	($183,600)

Effect on Future Years

The following schedule demonstrates how each adoption method affects results of operations in 1987 and future years.

Method 1: Restate and Remeasure

	1987	1988	1989	1990	1991
Depreciation expense	$1,056,666	$1,056,667	$1,056,667	$1,056,666	
Goodwill amortization	252,040	252,040	252,040	252,040	$252,040
Loss accrual					0
Pretax expense	1,308,706	1,308,707	1,308,707	1,308,706	252,040

	1987	1988	1989	1990	1991
Current tax benefit	(370,666)	(359,266)	(359,267)	(359,267)	(340,000)
Deferred tax benefit	(175,000)				340,000
Total tax benefit	(545,666)	(359,266)	(359,267)	(359,267)	0
Net expense from operations (A)	$ 763,040	$ 949,441	$ 949,440	$ 949,440	$252,040
Effective tax rate, excluding goodwill	—52%	—34%	—34%	—34%	N/A

Method 2: The Shortcut

	1987	1988	1989	1990	1991
Depreciation expense	$ 783,733	$783,734	$783,734	$783,733	$189,173
Goodwill amortization	189,173	189,173	189,173	189,173	460,000
Loss accrual*					
Pretax expense	972,906	972,907	972,907	972,906	649,173
Current tax benefit	(370,666)	(266,469)	(266,470)	(266,469)	(340,000)
Deferred tax benefit	(65,826)				183,600
Total tax benefit	(436,492)	(266,469)	(266,470)	(266,469)	(156,400)
Net expense from operations (B)	536,414	706,438	706,437	706,437	492,773
Effect of adoption	1,378,634				
Net expense	$1,915,048	$706,438	$706,437	$706,437	$492,773
Effective tax rate, excluding goodwill	—56%	—34%	—34%	—34%	—34%

*In 1991 the previously accrued loss was settled. The difference between the $1 million settlement and the $540,000 accrual balance is reflected in pretax expense.

(continued)

EXHIBIT 8-4 *(cont'd)*

The effect of the two adoption alternatives on net expense from operations is as follows:

	1987	1988	1989	1990	1991
(A) Restate and remeasure	$763,040	$949,441	$949,440	$949,440	$252,040
(B) The Shortcut	536,414	706,438	706,437	706,437	492,773
Higher (lower) reported net expense from operations	$226,626	$243,003	$243,003	$243,003	($240,733)

Observations

The charge recorded on adoption of FAS 96 under the shortcut method is offset by a lower net tax expense in future years.

Under the shortcut method, the recognition of deferred tax benefits of loss accruals results in a net loss when the temporary difference reverses.

Under both methods, the effective rate in 1987 differs from the 1987 statutory rate of 40 percent. This results in both cases from the deferred tax liability related to LIFO inventories. At the beginning of 1987, the deferred tax liability was stated at the 40 percent statutory rate for 1987; at year-end 1987, the deferred tax liability was stated at the 34 percent statutory rate enacted for 1988.

treated as the benefit of a purchased NOL, is written off upon realization of the asset.

The FASB staff acknowledges that there may be difficulties in identifying separately the carrying amounts and tax bases of assets and liabilities acquired in a particular business combination and which still exist at date of earliest application of FAS 96. Further, the book/tax basis differences would have to be analyzed to determine the portion which remains from the book/tax differences at date of acquisition as opposed to the effect of post-acquisition originating timing/temporary differences. It would be the former that would be treated as a purchased NOL. The FASB staff is considering whether, notwithstanding conceptual issues, determination of the amount to be treated as a purchased NOL would be practicable.

[4] Shortcut Method and NOLs

After computing the deferred tax balance at the date of earliest application under the shortcut method, the company may be able to use NOLs carried forward to that date; as a consequence, the newly established deferred tax liability would be reduced. To the extent NOLs arising from prior years' operations can be used, the effect of adoption would be reduced.

In contrast, when purchased NOLs (whether actual tax NOLs or excess tax bases) are used, it would be expected that any tax benefit recognized in the effect of adoption of FAS 96 (or subsequently) would be credited to any remaining goodwill or other intangibles resulting from the acquisition rather than directly to income. However, the FASB staff is considering, in addition to the pragmatic concerns discussed in ¶ 8.05[3], whether this treatment must be required when the carryforward utilization is only a component of the effect of adoption, and the other components can significantly change the amount (and possibly the sign) of the aggregate (net) effect of adoption. It would, of course, be inconsistent to reflect the tax benefit recognized in the effect of adoption in income and to credit benefits recognized subsequently to goodwill and other intangibles.

[5] Implementation Strategies

A final word on this special transition provision is necessary. It can come into play whether a company elects retroactive or prospective treatment. The company may elect to restate—but not for all prior years. Unless restatement is to a date preceding all prior purchase business combinations, part of the effect of adoption that is recorded will contain an adjustment for those prior purchases. Note also that if the company elects to restate to a date earlier than October 22, 1986, the deferred tax liabilities created at 46 percent for prior business combinations, whether they arise through restatement or the shortcut method, will be reduced in 1986, when the new rates were enacted. (This topic is discussed in more detail in Chapter 11.)

¶ 8.06 POOLINGS

APB 16 requires combining the constituent companies' prior financial statements. Under APB 11, the NOL of a constituent company, existing at consummation date, would not have been recognized until it could be used in post-combination operations.

FAS 96 may require certain retroactive adjustments in a pooling. If one company has an NOL carryforward or unused future deductions, it may be possible, subject to tax rules allowing such utilization, to use the NOL against the deferred tax liability of the other company. The temporary differences must reverse in a period after the business combination but before the NOL carryforward expires. Further, there are rules in the Internal Revenue Code regarding NOLs in a combination and they must be respected in the calculation.

A question arises as to the application of this guidance while in the transition period of FAS 96. First, it seems obvious that each combining company, prior to the combination, can elect when and how it wishes to adopt FAS 96. Upon pooling, it is permissible but not required under APB 16 to conform accounting principles as part of the retroactive restatement. Second, the new rule can only be applied under FAS 96. Thus, in the pooled statements, FAS 96 may not have been applied to all prior years by all the combining companies. A question then arises with respect to the tax benefit of an NOL arising in a year prior to a year in which FAS 96 has been applied by both the loss company and the company whose deferred tax liability permits recognition of the NOL benefit.

Price Waterhouse believes that the FAS 96 rule for NOL treatment in poolings can only be applied to NOLs arising in years to which both companies have applied FAS 96. If the loss company has not applied FAS 96 to the loss year, the book loss may not be the same amount as would be measured under FAS 96. If the other company has not applied FAS 96 to that year, then it has deferred credits whose amount could well be different from the liability under FAS 96. If there are several companies in the pooling combination, probably all should have applied FAS 96 to the loss year for application of the new FAS 96 rule except when it can otherwise be demonstrated that their inclusion in post-combination scheduling of reversals would not preclude use of the NOL carryforward.

Exhibit 8-5 discusses NOLs in a pooling during the transition period of adopting FAS 96.

The retroactive review of NOL use is applicable to all computations for prior years in which all combined companies have applied FAS 96. The scheduling for each precombination year-end treats NOLs and temporary differences as includable in the separate returns of each company until combination date where-after they are includable in the consolidated return. This can result in significant recomputations.

The question arises whether tax-planning strategies should be applied at each restated year-end to compute a minimum tax liability, recognizing that a consolidated return will be filed after the combination. The pooling concept assumes that the pooled companies were always a single entity, and it is the postcombination filing of a consolidated return that requires the retroactive recomputations of deferred taxes in the pooled statements. Tax-

EXHIBIT 8-5
NOL in a Pooling

The appropriate accounting treatment of a net operating loss carryforward in a pooling situation during the transition period of adoption of FAS 96 is dictated by when and how each company adopted FAS 96. Assume the following facts:

- Company A and Company B are parties to a business combination in 1988. The transaction is accounted for as a pooling.
- Company A has a tax NOL carryforward which arose in 1985. Company B has net deferred tax credits which will reverse during the carryforward period.
- A consolidated tax return will be filed in future years.

Situation 1

Both Company A and Company B adopted FAS 96 in 1987 and applied its provisions prospectively.

To the extent permitted by the tax laws and the reversal pattern of temporary differences, the benefit of Company A's NOL carryforward would be reflected in the combined financial statements for 1987. To the extent that the NOL carryforward can be offset against the deferred tax liability of Company B at January 1, 1987, the benefit of the carryforward would be reflected as part of the effect of adoption of FAS 96.

Situation 2

Company A adopted FAS 96 in 1987 and restated prior years. Company B adopted it in 1988 and is applying it prospectively.

The benefit of the NOL, if it is recognized by Company A in 1986 and 1987, would be reflected in those years in the pooled financial statements, classified under FAS 96 rules. If any NOLs remain at January 1, 1988, any additional benefit would be reflected as part of the effect that could be recognized on adoption of FAS 96 by Company B.

Situation 3

Company A adopted FAS 96 in 1988 and restated prior years. Company B adopted FAS 96 in 1987 and restated prior years.

If, in 1985, the loss incurred by Company A could be used against Company B's temporary differences that reverse after the combination date, that benefit would be reflected, in 1985, in the intraperiod allocation process as part of the provision (benefit) for deferred taxes rather than as the benefit of an NOL. Whether or not used in 1985, the NOL would also enter into combined scheduling and deferred tax computations for later year-ends until actually used.

planning strategies should also recognize the postcombination consolidated return.

In the pooled statements, the benefit of the NOL carryforward would be recognized when it is first permitted in the combined scheduling process. This may significantly affect the earnings trend. For example, a deferred tax liability of one company, which in combined scheduling uses the loss of another, may have subsequently been released to precombination income in the separate statements of that company because of its own operating losses.

¶ 8.07 TAXABLE POOLINGS

Certain poolings are taxable events. That is, although the book bases of the assets and liabilities carry over to the combined entity, the tax basis of the acquired company is adjusted to reflect the purchase price. Assuming the tax bases of assets are stepped up, temporary differences will result for which deferred tax benefits may need to be recognized. As of the combination date, any tax benefits of the step-up that can be recognized by reducing the deferred tax liability should be credited to contributed capital. If tax benefits not recognizable at the combination date become recognizable later, the benefits should be credited to income tax expense.

CHAPTER **9**

Alternative Minimum Tax

The Tax Reform Act of 1986 (TRA 1986) ushered in a corporate alternative minimum tax (AMT). Essentially, AMT is a separate tax system that runs parallel to the regular one. For tax years beginning on or after January 1, 1987, a U.S. company's tax liability is the higher of the tax amount computed based on the regular tax or AMT.

Many companies will have little difficulty determining whether income taxes for the current year will be payable under the regular tax system or under AMT. But assessing AMT's impact on the calculation of deferred income taxes under FAS 96 may be a much tougher job. Sometimes a company is not subject to AMT in the current year (and does not expect to be in future years) but will have to provide for AMT in its deferred tax computation. The opposite scenario is also possible.

¶ 9.01 CALCULATING AN AMT LIABILITY

Calculating an AMT liability is discussed in detail in the Appendix, *Corporate Alternative Minimum Tax.* However, the Treasury Department has not issued final regulations for the AMT rules. Moreover, it is likely that revisions to the AMT computation will be proposed whenever tax legislation is considered by Congress. It is a good idea to consult with your tax adviser about the current status of the law.

Exhibit 9-1 summarizes the mechanics of the AMT calculation. Stated simply, AMT is the excess of tentative minimum tax (TMT) over the regular tax. Both the TMT and the regular tax are reduced by applicable foreign tax credits (FTCs) computed under their respective limitations.

¶ 9.02 ADJUSTMENTS AND PREFERENCES

The starting point of the TMT calculation is regular taxable income before the net operating loss (NOL) deduction. Adjustments are added to or subtracted from this amount (to reflect different treatment of certain items for AMT purposes), and preferences are added. AMT adjustments and preferences are summarized in Exhibits 9-2 and 9-3, respectively. The primary distinction between the two is that an adjustment item can increase or decrease AMT income, whereas a preference item always increases it.

EXHIBIT 9-1 ——————————————————
How to Calculate AMT

This example serves to illustrate the mechanics of the AMT calculation. Background information on how the amounts for each line item were derived can be found in Exhibit A-7 of the Appendix.

Regular taxable income	$12,226,000
Add (subtract) AMT adjustments	5,877,190
Add tax preference items	340,000
Pre-book alternative minimum taxable income	18,443,190
Add book income adjustment	2,395,405
Alternative minimum taxable income	20,838,595
Apply AMT rate	20%
Tentative minimum tax before AMT credits	4,167,719
Substract AMT foreign tax credits	(90,000)
Tentative minimum tax	4,077,719*
Subtract regular tax after credits	(4,056,840)
AMT	$ 20,879

* Tax liability paid.

¶ 9.03 BOOK INCOME ADJUSTMENT

The subtotal of regular taxable income, increased or decreased by adjustment items and increased by tax preferences, is called pre-book alternative minimum taxable income (pre-book AMTI). Added to this amount is the book income adjustment. For 1987, 1988, and 1989, this adjustment is defined as 50 percent of the amount by which adjusted pretax income exceeds pre-book AMTI. (There may be certain modifications for life insurance companies under the Revenue Act of 1987.) This adjustment can only increase AMTI.

For taxable years beginning after 1989, adjusted current earnings (ACE) will replace adjusted pretax income in the computation of the book income adjustment. ACE essentially represents an adjusted pre-book AMTI for a taxable year. Some of the dif-

EXHIBIT 9-2
AMT Adjustments

1. Depreciation on real and personal property placed in service after 1986. Add or subtract the net difference between the total modified accelerated cost recovery system (MACRS) depreciation deduction for regular tax purposes and the total depreciation deduction under the alternative method for AMT purposes. Under the alternative method, the recovery period generally is longer than under the MACRS used for regular tax purposes. Note that if the alternative method is elected for regular tax purposes, this adjustment would not be required.

2. Difference between gain on sale of assets placed in service after 1986 depreciated under AMT rules compared with the gain reported for regular tax purposes.

3. For AMT purposes, long-term contracts entered into after February 28, 1986, must be accounted for under the percentage-of-completion method. The amounts of revenue and expense recognized by using this method are substituted for the amounts recognized for regular tax purposes (if different).

4. Passive activity losses of certain corporations. However, any unused passive activity loss is carried forward indefinitely and treated as a deduction for computing AMTI to the extent there is net passive activity income in succeeding taxable years.

5. Dealer instalment sales in 1987 will be reported in full in 1987 for AMT purposes. Revenue recognized for these sales for regular tax purposes in post-1987 years must be adjusted to compute AMTI.

6. Amortization of certified pollution-control facilities. Add or subtract the net difference between the five-year amortization deduction for regular tax purposes and the amortization deduction under the alternative method for AMT purposes.

7. Expensing of mining exploration and development costs. Add or subtract the net difference between the deduction for regular tax purposes and the deduction computed under the 10-year straightline method for AMT purposes.

8. Amounts deposited in a capital construction fund established under the Merchant Marine Act of 1936 and earnings on such a fund.

9. Certain deductions for certain Blue Cross and Blue Shield organizations. (See ¶ 9.06 for a discussion.)

10. Deduction of circulation expenditures if a personal holding company. Add or subtract the net difference between the deduction for regular tax purposes and the deduction if circulation costs were amortized over a three-year period for AMT purposes.

EXHIBIT 9-3 _____
AMT Preferences

Deferral Preferences

1. Excess of intangible drilling costs (total amount incurred and deducted for regular tax purposes over the amount that would be deducted if amortized over 10 years) incurred in connection with productive oil and gas wells over 65 percent of net income from such oil and gas properties.

2. Reserves for losses on bad debts deducted for regular tax purposes in excess of an amount computed on the basis of actual experience for certain financial institutions.

3. Excess of accelerated depreciation over straight-line depreciation on real property and, if a personal holding company, on leased personal property placed in service before 1987.

Exclusion Preferences

1. Excess of percentage depletion allowed for regular tax purposes over the adjusted tax basis of the property.

2. Interest on certain "private activity" tax-exempt bonds issued generally after August 7, 1986. Generally, private activity bonds are debentures, the proceeds of which are used by nongovernmental persons (e.g., industrial-development bonds used by small businesses for plant and building needs).

3. Excess of the value of capital gain property contributed to a charitable organization and deducted for regular tax purposes over such property's basis.

See ¶ 9.06 for a discussion.

_____

ferences between ACE and pre-book AMTI are listed in Exhibit 9-4. In addition, the book income adjustment for years after 1989 is 75 percent of the difference between ACE and pre-book AMTI (as opposed to 50 percent in 1987, 1988, and 1989). The ACE adjustment can be a negative amount, although it cannot exceed the aggregate net positive amount of prior years.

EXHIBIT 9-4 _____
Adjustments Between Pre-Book AMTI and ACE

1. Interest on all tax-exempt instruments is included in ACE versus including interest only on specified private-activity bonds in computing AMTI.

2. The 70 percent dividends-received deduction (80 percent for some taxpayers) is not allowed in computing ACE but is recognized for AMTI purposes since it is allowed in determining regular taxable income, the starting point for AMTI.

3. Depreciation is computed using the slower of the method(s) used in the taxpayer's financial statements or the applicable method prescribed for ACE purposes. To determine which method is slower, compare the deductions computed under both methods and use the method that produces the smaller present value. This process involves depreciating the asset over its useful life using both methods, discounting (at an as yet unspecified rate) each year's amount back to the present, totaling the yearly present-value amounts, and comparing the two totals to determine which results in a smaller amount. The method yielding the smaller amount will be used in computing ACE.

Specific rules are provided for computing depreciation under the prescribed ACE method (i.e., the nonbook method) depending on when the property was placed in service. These rules are summarized as follows:

  • Post-1989 property: The alternative depreciation system.
  • Post-1986 to 1989 property: Adjusted alternative minimum tax basis over the remaining alternative recovery period (the ADR life or a prescribed period for certain property) using the straight-line method.
  • Post-1980 to pre-1987 property: Remaining adjusted regular tax basis over the remaining alternative recovery period using the straight-line method.
  • Pre-1981 property: Same as method used to compute regular taxable income.

The alternative method continues to be used to determine depreciation for AMTI.

4. Income from a life insurance contract will be included in ACE net of all premiums.

5. Charitable contributions exceeding the 10 percent regular tax limitation will be an allowable deduction in computing ACE, as will various penalties, including tax penalties.

6. There will be an increase or decrease to ACE for the change in the LIFO recapture amount at the close of each taxable year. The LIFO recapture amount represents the difference between inventory computed under FIFO and LIFO (i.e., the LIFO reserve).

7. The deduction for organizational expenditures incurred after 1989 and amortized over a 60-month period will not be allowed in computing ACE.

8. The depletion deduction will be determined under either the cost-depletion method or the method used for book purposes, depending on which method yields the deduction with the smaller present value. In determining AMTI, percentage depletion will be allowed and an amount is added as a tax preference to the extent the regular tax deduction exceeds the adjusted basis of the property.

9. If the present value of the intangible drilling cost (IDC) deduction for ACE purposes exceeds the present value of the deduction under the method used for book purposes, the amount deductible for ACE will be based on the method used for book purposes. (Amounts paid or incurred after 1989 are capitalized and amortized over the 60-month period beginning in the month in which production from the well begins.) For AMTI, the excess of the regular tax IDC deduction over a 10-year amortization period or a cost-depletion method, to the extent it exceeds 65 percent of the net oil and gas income, is a preference.

¶ 9.04 TENTATIVE MINIMUM TAX

After adding the book income adjustment, any AMT NOL is then deducted (limited to 90 percent of AMTI before the NOL deduction), and the resulting amount is AMTI.

AMTI is reduced by a standard exemption of $40,000. However, the exemption amount is phased out as AMTI increases and is eliminated completely if AMTI exceeds $310,000. For many companies, therefore, the standard exemption is irrelevant.

AMTI, net of the exemption amount, if any, is multiplied by 20 percent and then reduced by allowable foreign tax credits (limited to 90 percent of the calculated tax). The result is TMT. If TMT exceeds the corporation's regular tax, after FTC, the excess must be paid in addition to the regular tax.

¶ 9.05 MINIMUM TAX CREDIT

The minimum tax credit (MTC), or AMT credit, is available so that taxpayers will not lose all the benefits of certain tax preferences. MTC represents the total AMT paid, reduced by the amount of AMT that would have arisen if only exclusion preferences were present. This amount can be carried forward indefinitely to offset any future year's regular tax liability if it exceeds TMT in that year. The MTC cannot be carried back.

¶ 9.06 DEFERRALS AND EXCLUSIONS

An adjustment item may increase AMTI in one year but will ultimately reverse and decrease it in a subsequent year. Through the MTC, however, the AMT system recognizes that using most preferences also results in only a deferral of tax liability, not in a permanent reduction in the corporation's tax payments. These items are called deferral preferences. All AMT adjustments and preferences are deferral items except for the percentage depletion, the appreciated-property charitable contribution, the private-activity tax-exempt interest, and the special Blue Cross and Blue Shield deduction preference items. These four items are called exclusion preferences (see Exhibits 9-2 and 9-3).

The book income adjustment is also a deferral preference, at least in 1987, 1988, and 1989. For taxable years beginning after 1989, when ACE replaces adjusted pretax income, the book income adjustment will be either a deferral or an exclusion preference depending on the source of the ACE adjustment.

¶ 9.07 AMT AND THE LIABILITY METHOD

A basic premise of the FAS 96-mandated liability method is that measurement of a deferred tax liability or asset assumes that the only taxable or deductible amounts in future years are those that result from temporary differences at the end of the current year. Future years' pro forma tax returns are, in effect, prepared on that premise, following the tax laws of a given jurisdiction.

In the United States, since the tax law now includes AMT as well as regular tax, the deferred tax computation will entail both the regular tax and the AMT for each future year on the basis that only reversals of temporary differences at the balance sheet date would be reported. These computations would respect all applicable tax laws, including the book income preference and, beginning in 1990, the ACE adjustment.

Such a calculation would also have to respect the different reversal patterns for AMT. For fixed assets, for example, there can be three different patterns of reversals of temporary differences: one for regular tax, one for the pre-book AMTI adjustment, and yet another for the ACE preference. These alternative patterns for pre-book AMTI and ACE are effective, generally, for post-1986 acquisitions and for post-1989 ACE depreciation. Consequently, over time, as the three patterns diverge, fixed assets will have three different tax bases and thus there will be three different measures of temporary differences (the book/tax basis differences) at the balance sheet date. Exhibit 9-5 shows how to calculate AMTI, including the book income preference and the ACE adjustment, when determining the deferred tax balance.

With respect to the book income preference, it should be noted that FAS 96 mandates an assumption that future pretax income will be break-even. Thus, in the deferred tax computation, there will be a book income preference only when scheduled reversals give rise to net deductions (NOL) for AMTI in 1987, 1988, or 1989. It is likely that in such circumstances there will also be net deductions (NOL) for regular tax for the same year(s). When a regular tax NOL is carried back to a pre-1987 year, any AMTI NOL (which cannot be carried back to a pre-1987 year) is reduced to the extent of the regular tax NOL carried back but not below zero. Thus, if there is carryback availability for a scheduled regular tax NOL, there may be a book income preference that cuts in half the scheduled AMTI NOL but that has no ultimate effect in the deferred tax computation because the AMTI NOL is eliminated.

The calculation will determine whether AMT would be payable for any future year and whether any AMT actually paid or payable

EXHIBIT 9-5
Calculating AMTI Under the Liability Method

ABC Company adopted the liability method in 1987 and is applying its provisions prospectively. ABC Company has identified several temporary differences at December 31, 1987. The reversal pattern of only one temporary difference, depreciable assets, is affected by AMT. The identified temporary differences and their scheduled reversals for regular tax purposes (before considering NOL carrybacks/carryforwards) are as follows:

	Temporary Differences at 12/31/87	Future Years					
		1988	1989	1990	1991	1992	Indefinite
Regular Tax Calculation							
Depreciable assets	($1,200)	($300)	$300	$ 600	$600	($200)	$350
All other	(2,650)	(200)	(200)	(2,200)	(200)		
Net taxable income (deductions) resulting from the reversal of temporary differences	($1,450)	($500)	$100	($1,600)	$400	($200)	$350

Depreciation on assets placed in service after 1986 must be computed under the alternative method for purposes of computing pre-book AMTI. In addition, starting in 1990, a fourth pattern of depreciation will have to be calculated for purposes of calculating the ACE adjustment. For assets existing at December 31, 1987, the differences that will arise in future years as a result of the different methods of depreciation are shown below.

	1988	1989	1990	1991	1992
Pre-Book AMTI Depreciation Adjustment					
Depreciable assets	$200	($300)	$ 500	($200)	($200)
ACE Adjustment—Depreciation					
Depreciable assets	NA	NA	$ 200	($100)	($100)

9-10

When computing the deferred tax balance at December 31, 1987, AMT must be considered. The following schedule illustrates the mechanics of the AMTI calculation, based only on the future reversal of temporary differences existing at the balance sheet date.

	Future Years					
	1988	1989	1990	1991	1992	Indefinite
AMT Calculation						
Regular taxable income (loss) before NOL deductions	($500)	$100	($1,600)	$400	($200)	$350
Add (substract) pre-book AMTI depreciation adjustment	200	(300)	(500)	(200)	(200)	0
Pre-book AMTI	(300)	(200)	(2,100)	200	(400)	350
Book income preference	150	100	NA	NA	NA	NA
ACE adjustment	NA	NA	150	(75)	(75)	0
Alternative minimum taxable income	($150)	($100)	($1,950)	$125	($475)	$350

TRA 1986 defines the book income adjustment in 1988 and 1989 as 50 percent of the difference between adjusted pretax income and pre-book AMTI. Under the liability method, adjusted pretax income is assumed to be zero. Pre-book AMTI in this calculation considers only the reversal of temporary differences existing at the balance sheet date. Therefore, the starting point of the calculation is "Regular taxable income (loss)" resulting from the reversals of temporary differences." In 1988, for example, the book income preference would be:

Adjusted pretax income	$0
Less pre-book AMTI	(300)
	300
Multiplied by 50%	50%
Book Income preference	$150

(continued)

EXHIBIT 9-5 *(cont'd)*

A similar calculation would be made for the ACE adjustment, required by the tax law starting in 1990.

Pre-book AMTI	($2,100)	
ACE depreciation adjustment	200	
Adjusted current earnings		($1,900)
Less pre-book AMTI		(2,100)
		200
Multiplied by 75%		75%
ACE adjustment		$ 150

Note: The amounts used in this Exhibit are not necessarily representative and are for illustrative purposes only.

in the deferred tax calculation could be recovered as MTC in the deferred tax calculation against regular tax in subsequent years. Like other potential tax benefits that cannot be carried back, MTC would be recognized only if it can be appropriately offset against a regular tax liability in the deferred tax computation. Exhibit 9-6 illustrates MTC in the deferred tax calculation.

¶ 9.08 IS THERE A SHORTCUT?

The complexity of the AMT computation and the mechanics of the liability method are sure to mean more extensive record keeping. Moreover, even if a company has no reasonable expectation of paying AMT, it must still accrue for any AMT (net of MTC recoveries) payable in the deferred tax computation because the expectation that AMT will not be paid includes an assumption about future sources of taxable income (losses) other than reversals of temporary differences. As noted, FAS 96 does not permit anticipation of future events.

Perhaps it would sometimes be possible to take a shortcut—an aggregate computation. Companies should keep in mind, however, that a tax-planning strategy used for regular tax purposes must be consistently applied in the AMT calculation as well. A strategy that will offset all years of net deductions against years of taxable income for regular tax may not achieve a similar offset for AMT because of the different reversal patterns for pre-book AMTI and for ACE and the limitation on the use of NOLs and FTCs.

Commencing with year-end 1987, the amount of some temporary differences for regular tax and for AMT will vary and, commencing with year-end 1990, the amount of temporary differences for pre-book AMTI and for ACE (both in the AMTI calculation) will also vary. The divergence will increase with the passage of time. A strategy that appears to reduce the deferred tax liability when only the regular tax is considered may not have that effect after the same strategy is employed in the AMT computation.

Some other problems are: (1) preferences—perhaps most notably the book income preference—that can represent permanent in-

EXHIBIT 9-6
MTC Under the Liability Method

As described in Exhibit 9-5, ABC Company has scheduled the reversal of temporary differences identified at December 31, 1987, and has also calculated AMTI for future years on that basis. ABC Company can now complete its deferred tax calculation. ABC Company did not pay taxes in 1985 or 1986 but will report $1,000 of regular taxable income on its 1987 tax return. AMTI for 1987 was $1,300.

	Current Year	Future Years					
	1987	1988	1989	1990	1991	1992	Indefinite
Regular Tax Calculation							
Taxable income to be reported on the tax return	$1,000						
Enacted tax rate	40%						
Current taxes payable	$ 400						
Net taxable income (deductions) resulting from the reversal of temporary differences	($1,000)	($500)	$100	($1,600)	$400	($200)	$350
Carryback to 1987		500		500			
Carryback to 1989			(100)	100			
Carryforward to 1991				400	(400)		
Taxable income (loss)	(1,000)	0	0	(600)*	0	(200)*	350
Enacted tax rate	40%						34%
Deferred tax (asset) liability	($ 400)	$ 0	$ 0	$ 0	$ 0	$ 0	$119

*These amounts represent NOL carryforwards for which no benefit can be ascribed.

AMT Calculation

Current year's AMTI	$1,300					
AMT rate	20%					
Tentative minimum tax	$260					
AMTI based on reversals of temporary differences	($150)	($100)	($1,950)	$125	($475)	$350
Carryback to 1987 (limited to 90% of 1987 AMTI) ($1,170)	150	100	920			
Carryforward to 1991 (limited to 90% of 1991 AMTI)			112	(112)		
AMTI	(1,170)	0	(918)	13	(475)	350
AMT rate	20%		20%	20%		20%
Tentative minimum tax	($234)	$0	$0	$3	$0	$70

For 1987 current tax purposes, ABC Company is not in an AMT position since the $400 currently payable under the regular tax system exceeds the $260 of tentative minimum tax. In the deferred tax calculation, the $400 of regular tax paid in 1987 would be recoverable by carrying back net deductions scheduled to occur in 1988 and 1990. However, since the AMT carry back to 1987 is limited to 90 percent of AMTI, the TMT for 1987 after carryback would be $26 ($260 less $234). In the deferred tax calculation, then, the refund of 1987 tax would be the $400 paid less the $26 tax remaining after carryback, or $374.

The $26 of AMT liability that would accrue after carryback and the $3 of AMT liability scheduled to occur in 1991 represent a minimum tax credit that can be carried forward indefinitely. Therefore, the $119 regular tax liability scheduled to occur in the indefinite future would be reduced by the MTC carryforward to $90 (which still exceeds the $70 TMT which would arise in the same period).

(continued)

9-15

EXHIBIT 9-6 *(cont'd)*

At December 31, 1987, ABC Company's balance sheet would reflect a net deferred tax asset of $281 computed as follows:

Refund of 1987 regular tax ($400) less TMT after carryback ($26)	$374
TMT payable in 1991	(3)
Regular tax payable in the indefinite future	(90)
Net deferred tax asset	$281

The current portion of the deferred tax asset is determined based on temporary difference reversals scheduled in the following year (1988) and is derived as follows:

Regular tax liability after 1988 carryback ($500 at 40%)	$200
TMT liability after 1988 carryback ($1,150 at 20%)	$230
Higher of regular tax or TMT liability after carryback of temporary difference reversals scheduled in 1988	$230
Taxes paid in 1987	(400)
Current deferred tax asset	$170

In this example, there is no net effect of AMT on the amount of deferred tax. However, if the example did not include temporary difference reversals of $350 scheduled in the indefinite future, the $26 of AMT generated in the carryback to 1987 and the $3 AMT liability scheduled to occur in 1991 would have to be expensed.

creases in AMTI versus regular taxable income; (2) the fact that usage of NOLs and foreign tax credits against, respectively, AMTI and TMT before credits is limited to 90 percent; and (3) the fact that MTCs can be carried forward but cannot be carried back.

Because of the complexity of AMT and of the FAS 96 methodology, it is probably wise to perform full-fledged scheduling and computations, including AMT, until greater familiarity with both is achieved.

S Corps, ESOPs, and Other Provisions

Because of all the furor about several of the core issues of FAS 96 when it was still in the exposure draft stage, other provisions have received scant attention. Some of them are responsive to questions that have cropped up since 1967, when APB 11 was issued. However narrow a provision may be, the impact on an affected company's tax provision can be substantial. Here are some of these less-heralded FAS 96 changes.

¶ 10.01 CHANGE IN TAX STATUS

Many businesses change tax status, and a large number of C corporations played beat the clock by converting to S corporations because of adverse Tax Reform Act of 1986 (TRA 1986) provisions that would apply unless the S corporation election was made by December 31, 1986.

Before FAS 96, no authoritative guidance covered a change in tax status. Switching from a taxable to a nontaxable entity and vice versa could be handled in a number of ways.

FAS 96 eliminates the freedom of choice on this issue. Now, the cumulative tax effect of a change in tax status is computed as of the date of change and is included in the tax provision for continuing operations.

[1] Date of Change

FAS 96 states that the new tax status should be reflected on the date of change in status. The question of when the date of change occurs was discussed by the Implementation Group on January 29, 1988. The FASB staff expressed the view that, when a company properly files an election to change tax status (and, when necessary, permission from the IRS has been received), the change in tax status has occurred, even though the change may not be effective for several months or may be effective retroactively to an earlier date.

The rationale for the FASB staff view is the analogy to enacted tax law changes whose cumulative effects are, under FAS 96, recognized in the financial statements as of the enactment date rather than as of an earlier or later effective date. However, Price Waterhouse has stated that they do not find this analogy compelling because a change in tax status may be completely within the control of the reporting entity, whereas the enactment of tax law changes is completely outside its control.

In most changes between C corporation and S corporation status, permission from the IRS is unnecessary. In these cases, the timing of the proper filing of the election is largely, perhaps entirely, at the discretion of the corporation, and the election can be made either before or after the effective date of the change. The date chosen by the corporation can, under the FASB staff's view, dramatically affect the financial statements. For example, assume that the effective date of a change in tax status is January 1, 1989, one day after the year-end balance sheet date. The December 31, 1988 balance sheet would reflect the effect of the change in tax status if the election was filed before the year-end date. If the election was filed after January 1, 1989, the effect of the change would not be reflected in the December 31, 1988 balance sheet.

Price Waterhouse believes that, when there is no requirement for IRS approval and the timing of the election is completely discretionary, the effective date should be treated as the date of change in status. Furthermore, when the effective date is one day after the year-end date, the change in status should be reflected in the year-end financial statements (i.e., treated as a Type I subsequent event). This assumes, of course, that, when the election is retroactive, the proper filing is made before the financial statements are issued.

The FASB staff's view is still tentative.

[2] Switching to and From S Corp Status

An election to change to an S corporation can be effective as of the beginning of the enterprise's next fiscal year, or retroactively to the beginning of the current year if the election is filed within two and one-half months of the beginning of the year.

S corporation status may be terminated by revocation or by the corporation's ceasing to qualify as an S corporation. An election to revoke S corporation status can be effective either retroactively to the beginning of the year, if the election is filed within two and one-half months of the beginning of the fiscal year, or for a specified prospective date. S corporation status automatically terminates effective on the first day that the corporation ceases to qualify as an S corporation.

Under the FASB staff view, when a corporation is switching to S corporation status and the date of filing (the date of change in tax status, according to the FASB staff) precedes the effective date, the deferred taxes that will not be required after the effective date should be released to income at the date of change. Similarly, no tax will be provided for subsequent originations during the remainder of the year that will not require deferred taxes after the effective date. In other respects, the financial statements for the remainder of the year will continue to reflect the corporation as a taxable entity. The required disclosure of the effect of the change in tax status would be measured as the amount of deferred taxes released as of the date of change; but the amount of deferred taxes not provided subsequent to the date of change because of the change in status should be disclosed as well in order to indicate the total effect of the change.

Under the FASB staff view, when S corporation status is retroactively revoked, the change in status should be reflected as of the date the filing is made and, if necessary, approved.

Price Waterhouse finds the FASB staff approach particularly troubling when retroactive changes are involved. An S corporation electing C corporation status would have *no* tax provision, either current or deferred, for the period prior to the date of filing the election even though its results for that period will in fact be taxed. Conversely, a C corporation electing S corporation status retroactive to the beginning of the year would provide taxes, both current and deferred, for the period prior to the date of filing the election. These answers would be generated by applying the FASB staff's approach even when the election, which retroactively changes status, has been filed prior to the issuance of the financial statements for the period preceding the filing.

Exhibit 10-1 illustrates application of FAS 96 under the FASB staff's view when a change to taxable status occurs at an interim date.

[3] Post-1986 S Corp Elections

TRA 1986 and the Revenue Act of 1987 contain provisions that may cause some corporations to pause before electing S corporation status. In general, under TRA 1986, corporations making the election after December 31, 1986 will be subject to a corporate-level tax on the net unrealized built-in gain recognized for tax purposes during the 10-year period after the conversion. (There are transition exceptions through December 31, 1988 for certain corporations with a value of less than $10 million.) For this purpose, net unrealized built-in gain is the amount by which, in the aggregate, the fair market values of the corporation's assets exceed their tax bases. Gain on the disposition of any asset with unrealized built-in gain at date of conversion is considered recognized to the extent the corporation cannot establish that some or all of the gain exceeds the gain inherent in the asset on the conversion date. Recognized built-in gains are subject to tax during the 10-year period until gain has been recognized in an amount equal to the amount of the net unrealized built-in gain at the date of conversion. The tax is determined by applying the maximum corporate tax rate applicable to the particular type of income for the year in which the disposition occurs to the lesser of (1) the recognized built-in gain for the year or (2) the amount that would be taxable income for the year if the corporation were not an S corporation. Clearly, when there is net unrealized built-in gain at date of conversion, the question arises whether the S corporation is a nontaxable entity and whether, and to what extent, recorded deferred tax liabilities are still necessary.

The calculation of the deferred tax liability to be retained or recorded will be extremely complex. (No deferred tax asset could be recorded since carryback is not available to an S corporation.) The FASB staff may in the future provide guidance that clarifies, or conflicts with, the procedures set forth in the following text.

According to Price Waterhouse's view of the date of change, the computation would initially be made and recorded as of the effective date of the change in status (or, as discussed previously, as of the preceding day), assuming the election has been made

EXHIBIT 10-1
Change to Taxable Status

The following situations both involve a change to taxable status at an interim date. As discussed at ¶ 10.08, measuring temporary differences at an interim date can be complicated. For simplicity of illustration, those complications have been ignored in this example. Further, these examples illustrate the accounting that would result under the FASB staff's tentative position, with which Price Waterhouse disagrees, in determination of the date of change in status.

Situation 1: To Taxable Status in Subsequent Year

On September 30, 1989, Epsilon Corp., an S corporation, revoked its S corporation election thereby changing to C corporation status effective January 1, 1990. The information below relates to temporary differences that exist at September 30, 1989 and that will reverse after January 1, 1990.

	Net Book Value	Tax Basis	Temporary Difference
Accounts receivable	$2,200	$2,500	($ 300)
Land	600	500	100
Machinery and equipment	3,000	800	2,200
Warranty reserve	(1,000)	0	(1,000)
Totals	$4,800	$3,800	$1,000

The future reversal of temporary differences will result in net taxable and deductible amounts that will offset. As a result, the following entry would be recorded as of September 30, 1989:

Debit:	Deferred tax provision	$340	
Credit:	Deferred tax liability		$340

The following information relates to temporary differences at December 31, 1989:

	Net Book Value	Tax Basis	Temporary Difference
Accounts receivable	$2,500	$2,800	($ 300)
Land	600	500	100
Machinery and equipment	2,900	600	2,300
Warranty reserve	(1,000)	0	(1,000)
Totals	$5,000	$3,900	$1,100

A deferred tax liability of $374 ($1,100 at 34 percent) results. Because the deferred tax liability increased from September 30 to December 31, a deferred tax provision is required even though Epsilon remained during that period, in terms of actual tax status, an S corporation. The following journal entry would be recorded at December 31, 1989:

Debit:	Deferred tax provision	$34	
Credit:	Deferred tax liability		$34

Note that there would be a total tax provision of $374 (all deferred) for the year ended December 31, 1989. The $340 provision at September 30, 1989 would be disclosed as the effect of the change in tax status.

Situation 2: To Taxable Status During the Year

On February 28, 1990, Omega Corp., an S corporation, revoked its S corporation election, changing to C corporation status effective January 1, 1990. The following information relates to temporary differences at February 28, 1990:

	Net Book Value	Tax Basis	Temporary Difference
Accounts receivable	$2,500	$2,800	($ 300)
Land	600	500	100
Machinery and equipment	2,900	600	2,300
Warranty reserve	(1,000)	0	(1,000)
Totals	$5,000	$3,900	$1,100

At February 28, 1990, Omega Corp. would record a deferred tax liability of $374 ($1,100 at 34 percent) as follows:

Debit:	Deferred tax provision	$374	
Credit:	Deferred tax liability		$374

Further, a current tax provision for the taxable income for the two months ended February 28, 1990 would be accrued at February 28, 1990. That current tax provision together with the $374 deferred tax provision would be disclosed as the effect of the change to taxable status in any financial statements that include the two-month period ended February 28, 1990.

and, when necessary, approved by the IRS prior to the issuance of financial statements. Under the FASB staff view of date of change, the calculation would initially be made and reflected in the financial statements as of the date the election is made. When the election precedes the effective date of the change, projections of assets on hand and estimates of their fair market values at the effective date would be necessary, and the scheduling would have to be updated through the effective date for changes in temporary differences and in estimates of assets and market values.

Because the actual tax liability is based on the lower of the built-in gain for the year and C corporation taxable income, it appears that calculation of the deferred tax liability will require two scheduling exercises. The first would consider only reversals of conversion-date temporary differences related to assets with un-recognized built-in gains at conversion date, and only built-in gains would be scheduled. In performing this scheduling, the following points should be noted:

- Even though the actual built-in gain is based on fair market value at date of conversion, no consideration in this scheduling would be given to any appreciation above the book value as of the conversion date. Any actual tax resulting from such appreciation would be expensed when the appreciation itself is recognized upon disposition. FAS 96 assumes recovery of assets at their carrying amounts and gives no effect to actual values in excess of carrying amounts.

- When it can be assumed that a fair market value at date of conversion lower than book basis at that date can be established to the satisfaction of the IRS, computation of any scheduled built-in gains would be based on the excess over the tax basis of the lower fair value. Similarly, built-in gains would be scheduled only to the extent that realization of an asset is expected to result from sale (or other taxable disposition) and when it is anticipated that the carrying amount at date of sale will exceed the conversion-date tax basis. To the extent that recovery of a depreciable asset is expected from use in operations (i.e., to the extent that future book depreciation is anticipated), there would be no effect on built-in gains.

- Because the actual liability for tax is based on excess of fair market value over conversion-date tax basis, subsequent originations (as for existing depreciable assets) would be ignored. Further, in reassessing the liability at a future balance-sheet date, any scheduled built-in gains would only include any remaining excess of book value at that date (assuming equal or higher fair value at conversion date) over the conversion-date tax basis. When the book value is equal to or less than the tax basis at the date of conversion, recovery of the asset at its carrying amount (the assumption made by FAS 96) will yield no built-in gain, regardless of the tax basis at the future balance sheet date.

Because the corporate-level tax is limited to the amount of taxable income that would be reported as a C corporation, a second scheduling exercise would include all book/tax basis differences. Price Waterhouse believes that this computation would include not only reversals of conversion-date book/tax basis differences but that rather it would be the same scheduling that would be performed for a C corporation. Thus, it would include future originations for existing depreciable assets, and it would include temporary differences related to liabilities as well as to assets. And the calculation at each balance sheet date would include all book/tax basis differences at that date, including those arising after conversion to S corporation status.

The results of the two scheduling exercises would be compared to determine the tax that would result under the tax law. Qualified tax-planning strategies would be utilized to minimize the deferred tax liability. However, in assessing whether a strategy is prudent, its effects on taxable income (loss) to be reported by shareholders would have to be considered. Also, any tax-planning strategy would have to be employed in both scheduling exercises.

There would be two obvious limitations on the computation of the deferred tax liability:

1. No deferred tax would be required for years after those in which the scheduled built-in gains accumulate, together with

built-in gains which have already been actually recognized on post-conversion tax returns, to the net unrealized gain existing at conversion date.

2. No deferred tax would be required for years after the 10-year post-conversion period.

These limitations may make it possible to abbreviate the scheduling exercises if scheduled amounts for subsequent years are not important in evaluating tax-planning strategies.

The deferred tax liability will have to be recomputed at each balance sheet date. As in other FAS 96 computations, the computed deferred tax liability can vary considerably from actual taxes expected to be paid. But that results from anticipated future events other than recovery of assets and settlement of liabilities at their carrying amounts.

There may be some surprising results. If the only net unrealized built-in gain at the conversion date relates to inventory for which there is no related temporary difference, no deferred tax liability will be required at date of conversion. If post-conversion sale of the inventory results in a tax payable, it would be charged to income tax expense in the period of the sale. Alternatively, if there are other assets with built-in gains, there may be a deferred tax provided at date of conversion based on the computations described previously. Tax payable on sale of the inventory will be charged to expense, but because the recognized built-in gain on the inventory applies toward the conversion-date net unrealized built-in gain that provides a limitation on the deferred tax liability, there could be some release of the deferred tax liability previously recorded.

[4] LIFO Recapture

Under the Revenue Act of 1987, a corporation with LIFO inventories electing S status after December 17, 1987 will include its LIFO reserve in its last return filed as a C corporation. The tax is payable in equal amounts over four years with the first payment due by the due date (not including extensions) of the last return filed as a C corporation. Under the FASB staff view of determining the date of change in status, the total liability would be accrued and expensed in the financial statements at the date of change. When the change in status precedes the effective date of the change, presumably the accrual as of the date of change would be based on the LIFO reserve at the date of change. (Because LIFO is an annual computation, determining the appropriate accrual at an interim date could be very complicated.) Under the view preferred by Price Waterhouse, the tax on the LIFO reserve and the release of deferred taxes in excess of that required for built-in gains would both be reflected in the balance sheet prepared for the last day in C corporation status.

¶ 10.02 INTERCORPORATE INCOME TAX ALLOCATION

The FASB has formalized certain disclosures regarding the method and results of intercorporate tax allocation policies. Pre-FAS 96, these disclosures generally had been made under FAS 57, *Related Party Disclosures*. The FASB, however, missed an opportunity to resolve an issue lacking current formal guidance—the measurement of intercorporate income tax allocations.

The variety of intercorporate tax allocation agreements and the absence of any guidance for determining deferred tax provisions for members of a consolidated group have given rise in the past to tax provisions in separate financial statements that have no relation to pretax income. As a result, the reported amounts of deferred taxes may have little to do with the difference between the financial statement and tax bases of an entity's assets and liabilities.

In adopting the liability method, the FASB had a golden opportunity to eliminate this problem. The liability method focuses on the future tax effects of the differences between the financial statement and tax bases, and it would seem appropriate that the deferred taxes of any entity included in a consolidated return should, in its separate statements, be based on this difference. This is especially true since a subsidiary must compute its temporary differences so that its parent can use the figures in computing the consolidated tax provision. However, because the FASB did not resolve this matter, intercorporate tax allocation policies that are not based on a particular subsidiary's temporary differences will continue to be acceptable with appropriate disclosure.

¶ 10.03 ESOP DIVIDENDS

Under an employee stock ownership plan (ESOP), the sponsoring corporation receives tax deductions for dividends paid on shares held by an ESOP trust, subject to certain restrictions. In current practice, tax benefits are credited to equity and cannot become a component of income tax expense. FAS 96 changes that.

When a company adopts the new Statement, tax benefits related to ESOP dividends reduce income tax expense. This will create a rate differential that will be included when reconciling the statutory and effective tax rates. It is interesting to note that an enterprise that can deduct dividends on ESOP shares may increase its net income (through reduced tax expense) merely by paying a dividend that is, of course, charged to equity.

¶ 10.04 NONTAXABLE PUBLICLY HELD ENTITIES

Certain publicly held entities, such as general and limited partnerships (except for those affected by the Revenue Act of 1987), are not subject to tax because their earnings and losses are taxed directly to their owners. Other publicly held entities, such as regulated investment companies (RICs) and real estate investment trusts (REITs), also are not subject to tax if distribution and other requirements are met. FAS 96 requires these entities to disclose this fact. In addition, the net temporary differences at the balance sheet date must be disclosed. As RICs and REITs cannot pass through tax losses to owners (as partnerships can), they must disclose the amount of any NOL or capital loss carryforward.

¶ 10.05 MASTER LIMITED PARTNERSHIPS

Under the Revenue Act of 1987, publicly traded limited partnerships, formed after December 17, 1987, will be taxable as corporations for post-1987 years. Those that existed at December 17, 1987 will become taxable as corporations for years beginning after 1997. There are exemptions from both these rules for certain limited partnerships, for example, those engaged in real estate or oil and gas.

For entities that become taxable after 1997, FAS 96 requires that, at the enactment date, any net deferred tax liability required for post-1997 reversals of current temporary differences be recorded. There may be available tax-planning strategies that can avoid or reduce the liability. For example, the general partner might be able to cause acceleration of most temporary differences into the pre-1998 period in order to avoid taxation at the partnership level. Another possibility lies in certain partnership agreements that specify that, if the partnership becomes taxable because it is public, the general partner can suspend trading in partnership units and avoid meeting the public criterion; what steps must be taken to avoid the public criterion will be subject to IRS regulations and to legal interpretation. As for many tax-planning strategies, determination of whether one of these strategies would be "prudent" and "feasible" could be difficult.

¶ 10.06 QUASI REORGANIZATIONS

Before FAS 96, companies that had been involved in a quasi reorganization were precluded from reflecting the post-quasi benefit of a pre-quasi NOL carryforward in the income statement, even as an extraordinary item. Instead, the benefit was credited directly to equity. Under FAS 96, if all losses are charged to the income statement and the quasi reorganization involves only the reclassification of the accumulated deficit to additional paid-in capital, the post-quasi reorganization use of the NOL would be reflected in the income statement as a benefit. An adjustment reclassifying the benefit from retained earnings to additional paid-in capital is then required.

FAS 96 requires a different treatment when charges have been made directly to equity in connection with the quasi reorganization. In the view of Price Waterhouse, FAS 96 requires that the tax benefits of such charges, when recognized subsequent to the quasi reorganization, must also be credited directly to equity. The FASB staff, however, has taken the position that, when a charge (*or* credit) is made directly to equity in connection with a quasi reorganization, then the tax benefit of all NOL carryforwards existing at the date of the quasi reorganization, including those previously charged to income, must, when recognized, be credited directly to equity.

A pre-quasi NOL for purposes of applying FAS 96 includes (is reduced by) temporary differences at the quasi reorganization date that will result in net future deductions (taxable income). FAS 96 requires the same treatment for tax credit carryforwards arising before but used after a quasi reorganization.

¶ 10.07 STOCK OF A SUBSIDIARY

When a corporation acquires another company, it often acquires stock rather than purchasing assets directly. Unless an election is made under the Internal Revenue Code, the assets' tax bases will carry over from the predecessor company and the stock's tax basis will equal the purchase price. These amounts are rarely the same.

Such a difference can also arise when a holding company is created. If the holding company shares are exchanged for shares of the operating company, the holding company's basis in the operating company's stock is the aggregate of the bases of its former holders.

If the stock's tax basis is higher than the assets' tax bases at any balance sheet date, the parent company may have a potential benefit. The parent can elect to sell the subsidiary's stock, as opposed to the assets, and thereby minimize its tax liability.

This future tax deduction cannot be considered in the scheduling process except to offset a future liability that would become payable when the subsidiary is sold or liquidated. Some temporary differences are long-lived, for example, basis differences relating to land. Just because a temporary difference is long-lived, it does not make the related deferred tax a "future liability that would become payable upon sale or liquidation of the subsidiary."

To recognize the benefit, one might consider selling the stock with a concurrent leaseback of the operating assets rather than selling the underlying assets. It will likely be difficult, however, to demonstrate that this strategy is feasible.

A parent cannot use this provision with respect to a subsidiary that uses an APB 23 exception. Keep in mind, too, that if selling a subsidiary's stock would generate a capital loss, it may be used only to offset capital gains. Further, the parent's tax basis would have to be adjusted for reversals of the subsidiary's temporary differences scheduled to occur before the sale or liquidation.

On balance it appears that this potential tax benefit cannot be recognized except when APB 23 taxes for that subsidiary are being provided, if applicable, or when taxes are provided for an increase in equity in net assets resulting from a subsidiary's capital transactions.

¶ 10.08 ACCOUNTING FOR TAXES IN INTERIM PERIODS

Previously, when estimating the effective tax rate under APB 11, companies estimated their pretax accounting income (actually, "ordinary" income as defined by FASI 18) and adjusted that number for permanent differences. As noted in ¶ 1.07, extraordinary precision was not necessary when determining timing differences. On an interim basis, generally there was no requirement to identify the current and deferred components of the income tax provision. Accordingly, unless it was necessary to adjust the balance sheet captions of taxes currently payable and deferred taxes, timing differences were not identified or quantified until it was time to prepare the annual provision at year-end.

All that has changed under FAS 96. It is now necessary to identify and estimate the year-end temporary differences when computing the tax provision for all quarters. The process must be updated quarterly. This requirement harks back to an earlier point: There is no shortcut to determining the total tax provision. The current and deferred provisions are computed under separate systems.

Many companies now need to do quarterly what they previously did annually. Once the total estimated tax provision is computed, an effective rate can be determined; it will be used for computing the interim tax provision and making quarterly adjustments to the balance sheet accounts.

As companies become more familiar with FAS 96, especially as it relates to the specific company and its temporary differences, shortcuts may be developed for identifying and quantifying the principal rate differentials that cause the effective tax rate to change.

While FAS 96 dramatically changes the manner in which the annual deferred tax computation is made, it maintains the general principles of APB Opinion 28, *Interim Financial Reporting*, and FASI 18 with respect to the assignment of annual amounts to interim periods. Because recognition of use of NOL carryforwards in income is no longer always classified as extraordinary, the question arises whether use of NOLs—specifically that portion that will be recognized in income (some purchased NOLs, certain pre-quasi reorganization NOLs, and certain stock compensation deductions would not be)—can now be anticipated in the effective annual tax rate. FAS 96 amends paragraph 20 of FASI 18 to specify that the benefit can be so anticipated only "if realization as a result of 'ordinary' income in the current year is assured beyond any reasonable doubt." Otherwise, the NOL benefit is recognized to the extent that income in the period and for the year to date is available; the benefit is classified according to the source of income.

This rule could give rise to situations where NOL benefits not includable in the effective rate computation are reflected in early interim periods against gains from discontinued operations or extraordinary gains and in later periods reclassified to continuing operations when "ordinary" income for the year to date is sufficient to absorb the entire NOL available.

Establishing a high threshold for including NOL benefit in the effective rate does not seem to be particularly conservative; if recognition is based on year-to-date income, then any income for the year to date, whether "ordinary" or not, will have no tax except effects of AMT until the NOL is completely recognized. Inclusion in the effective rate could only delay its recognition, for example, if not enough NOL is available to offset the entire anticipated "ordinary" income for the year or if there is other than "ordinary" income that is recognized in early periods and that could utilize the NOL absent its deduction through the effective rate for use against future "ordinary" income.

[1] Tax Law Changes

In the past, considerable controversy has surrounded the accounting in interim statements for new tax laws enacted with retroactive effective dates. FAS 96 has tried to resolve the problems in this area by precluding retroactive restatement of prior interim periods.

The effect of a change in tax law or rates on a deferred tax liability or asset must be reflected in the interim period of enactment. This effect must also be disclosed as a separate component of tax expense (see ¶ 12.01). Computing this effect, however, will require measuring temporary differences and the related deferred taxes at an interim date. This problem has already been discussed in connection with business combinations (see ¶ 8.01[2]).

Implementation Strategies

FAS 96 must be adopted for fiscal years beginning after December 15, 1988. But management has leeway in selecting the year of initial application. Retroactive application, for example, is permitted but not required, and it can be to the beginning of any selected prior year. The new Statement can also be applied prospectively, and there is a three-year window (1987, 1988, or 1989) for choosing the most desirable method of adoption.

This important decision should be made in the context of a company's specific facts and circumstances. Exhibit 11-1 highlights some of the key questions to ask. Companies should keep in mind that if they apply FAS 96 retroactively to 1986 or any prior year, the effect of the Tax Reform Act of 1986 (TRA 1986) will be reflected in the 1986 ordinary tax provision; otherwise it will be a component of the effect of adoption.

When these questions have been answered, the company is ready to pick the best method. If the retroactive method is selected, the company must decide how many years to restate. For example, if the annual report includes a 10-year financial summary, the company may wish to restate all years to improve comparability.

¶ 11.01   COST/BENEFIT

As with any business decision a company makes, determining whether or not to restate prior years' financial statements will involve some cost/benefit considerations. For example, a major purchase business combination consummated in the sixth prior year may be costly to restate. The company could avail itself of the option to restate to the first year after the acquisition, that is, only the last five years. By using the shortcut method FAS 96 permits for determining the effect of adopting the Statement on prior business combinations, the company will avoid the costly recalculation of the acquisition.

¶ 11.02   DISCONTINUED OPERATIONS

If, in a prior year, a subsidiary had been sold, the information needed to restate may not be readily available. Obviously, if the company wishes to restate, it will have to make reasonable estimates using information from all available sources—accounting records, tax returns, independent accountants' workpapers and the new owners. At the January 29, 1988 meeting of the Implementation Group, the FASB staff stated that restatement would not be permitted unless the company is able to determine that the tax effects computed using available information would not be materially different from the effects computed if all relevant information were available.

Adopting FAS 96: How and When?

1. Do you want to report good news—for example, benefits of TRA 1986 rate reductions—in the current year?

2. Have you considered the potential for tax rate increases before mandatory adoption in 1989? If Congress moves in this direction, it could reverse some or all of the benefits of TRA 1986.

3. Do you want to deemphasize, through restatement, any bad news that could result from using the new method?

4. What options were selected by companies to which your company's results are compared?

5. Is it preferable to maintain the historical record, or to make prior years comparable to the current and future years?

6. How will FAS 96 effect working capital and equity, and ratios and debt covenants?

7. Will much additional effort be required for restating one or more prior years? This would entail restating interim periods of those years and recomputing taxes allocated to discontinued operations or extraordinary items.

8. How much time will it take to quantify the Statement's effects, especially if foreign operations are large and/or complex?

9. Have you assessed the difficulty of restating prior purchase business combinations and considered the different effects that would result?

10. If there have been purchase business combinations with higher tax bases, what will be the effects of the shortcut method?

11. How will various provisions of the new Statement affect prior financial statements if you select restatement?

12. Which adoption method and year will minimize the effect of recording deferred tax assets at 46 percent that will be recovered at 34 percent?

¶ 11.03 ADOPTION BY SUBSIDIARIES

Another factor to consider before selecting the method and year of adoption is the reporting requirements of subsidiaries. For example, to avoid technical default under existing debt covenants, it may be advantageous for a subsidiary, in its separate financial statements, to adopt FAS 96 and restate prior years. On the other hand, the parent, in its consolidated financial statements, may decide to adopt and apply the Statement prospectively. Or the parent may decide to wait until 1989 to adopt for purposes of the consolidated financial statements although the subsidiary would like to adopt in 1987. The parent may decide to restate three years while the subsidiary would prefer to restate 10 years.

There may be valid reasons why the method and year of adoption reflected in a subsidiary's separate financial statements would not be the same as in the parent's consolidated financial statements. However, the FASB staff indicated at the January 29, 1988 meeting of the Implementation Group that, in its view, if the subsidiary is included in the parent's consolidated tax return, the method and year of adoption should be consistent with the method used by the parent. The staff supported this position by reference to footnote 12 of FAS 96, which requires that the sum of the tax amounts allocated to members of a consolidated tax group (net of consolidation eliminations) shall equal the amount reported in the consolidated financial statements. (Obviously the staff did not read "consolidation eliminations" to include differences that could arise from different years or methods of adoption of FAS 96.) A majority of the Implementation Group members disagreed with the staff's view and the FASB staff agreed to reconsider the issue.

In any event, it is important to keep in mind that the consolidated financial statements must contain only one method. If a parent and a subsidiary adopt FAS 96 differently, some consolidation adjustments will be necessary to conform the method of accounting.

¶ 11.04 ADOPTION BY EQUITY INVESTEES

One of the basic concepts underlying the equity method is that the results of operations should be the same whether an investee is accounted for by the equity method or consolidated. That may not be the case under FAS 96. As noted previously in ¶ 11.03, there may be some differences in the year and method of application among subsidiaries in their separate financial statements. That same situation could also apply to the equity investees of a company. However, unlike consolidated subsidiaries over which the parent company has control and can force the subsidiaries to conform to one year and method of application of FAS 96 (at least in consolidation), the investor only has significant influence, not control, over the equity investees. It therefore cannot force the equity investees to provide information to permit the investor to conform its equity accounting for the investee to the investor's year and method of application of FAS 96.

This situation can cause some unusual presentations in the financial statements of the investor. Consider the following example of an investor with five equity investees. The investor and one investee adopt in 1987, two investees adopt in 1988, and two in 1989. In 1987, the investor adopts prospectively and the investee adopts retroactively. In both 1988 and 1989, one investee adopts prospectively and the other adopts retroactively. The investor's income statement will include the effect of adopting FAS 96 in each year, 1987, 1988, and 1989. In addition, 1986 and prior years will have been restated three times, 1987 will have been restated twice, and 1988 once.

This is clearly a situation that should be avoided, if at all possible. It is difficult enough to expect readers of the financial statements to understand the impact of an accounting change without subjecting them to repeated restatements and effects of adoption for piecemeal adoption of the same accounting change.

¶ 11.05 AMT PAYABLE

The method of adoption may also affect the amount of federal income tax that a company will pay. As discussed at ¶ 8.05, a company that was a party to a prior purchase business combination may elect to restate prior years and the purchase price allocation, or it may take a shortcut. If the fair value of net assets acquired exceeded the tax bases, depreciation expense in future years will be higher if the entity elects restatement.

Under present law, for taxable years through 1989, pretax income enters into the computation of the book income adjustment in the alternative minimum tax (AMT) computation. If pretax income is lowered by higher depreciation expense, it reduces the likelihood that alternative minimum tax will be payable. Accordingly, the FAS 96 adoption election could affect the amount of AMT paid currently. Over the long haul, there may be no net cash outflow as there is an unlimited carryforward period on AMT credits. However, the cash will be unavailable until the credits are used.

¶ 11.06 FOREIGN SUBSIDIARIES AND BRANCHES

As stated at ¶ 1.01, *all* subsidiaries must adopt FAS 96. As a result, there will be an effect of adopting the Statement recorded in the foreign-currency financial statements prepared in conformity with U.S. generally accepted accounting principles. The effect will be reflected in the U.S. dollar financial statements when they are translated.

For a subsidiary or branch that has the foreign currency as the functional currency, any change in its net assets will affect the translated accounts. If prior years are restated, translation of the restated foreign currency net assets into U.S. dollars at different exchange rates will give rise to annual adjustments to the currency translation adjustment (CTA) account in the restated consolidated financials. In the year to which the Statement is first applied, some portion of the effect of adoption of FAS 96 could theoretically be allocated to the CTA account as the accumulated effect of rate changes on the prior years' differences between APB 11 and FAS 96 deferred taxes. However, as indicated in ¶ 7.04, adoption of FAS 96 does not require retroactive computations. Determination of the adjustment that would have been made to the CTA account if FAS 96 had been applied to prior years could only be determined by such retroactive computations.

Consequently, Price Waterhouse maintains that under FAS 96 none of the effect of adoption resulting from initial application of FAS 96 to deferred foreign taxes would be reflected in the CTA account.

If the foreign operation is a branch or if a foreign subsidiary generates subpart F income (as defined in the Internal Revenue Code), then it could have one set of temporary differences for purposes of the U.S. return (reversals would be included in the scheduling for the U.S. consolidated tax group) and another set for foreign tax purposes. The foreign deferred tax asset or liability resulting from application of FAS 96 will affect the deferred provision for U.S. tax. The foreign deferred tax asset or liability would have to be included in the U.S. deferred tax computation as deductions or credits in the appropriate reversal years.

¶ 11.07 ASSESSING THE IMPACT

A practical way to assess the effect of FAS 96 on a company is to break down the net effect into these components:

- The effect of TRA 1986's reduction of U.S. tax rates
- The effect of AMT
- The effect of "washing out" prior U.S. rate changes
- The effect of rate and other changes in other jurisdictions
- The effect on prior purchase business combinations
- The effect of lost tax benefits that cannot be used currently but may be used in future years as the computation permits
- The effect of applying FAS 96 to the current year

It is also a good idea to break out this information for each subsidiary, especially if one or more of the subsidiaries has separate reporting requirements.

Financial Statement Disclosures

Many FAS 96 disclosure requirements should be familiar because they continue requirements of APB 11 or SEC regulations. The disclosure requirements that follow apply to a public company. They are the same for a nonpublic company with two exceptions: a nonpublic company does not have to numerically reconcile the statutory and effective rates, although it must disclose the nature of significant reconciling items, and a nonpublic, nontaxable entity need not disclose the difference between book and tax bases.

¶ 12.01 FAS 96 REQUIRED DISCLOSURES

Financial statements must disclose the following:

- Current and noncurrent deferred tax assets and liabilities.
- The amount of income tax expense or benefit allocated to continuing operations, discontinued operations, extraordinary items, the cumulative effect of accounting changes, prior period adjustments, gains and losses included in comprehensive income but excluded from net income, and capital transactions. (Except for the amount of income tax expense or benefit allocated to continuing operations, all other information may be presented in the notes rather than on the face of the financial statements.)
- Certain components of income tax expense attributable to continuing operations (this information may be presented in the notes rather than on the face of the financial statements):
  — Current tax expense or benefit
  — Deferred tax expense or benefit, exclusive of the last item in this list
  — Investment tax credits
  — Government grants (to the extent recognized as a reduction of income tax expense)
  — The benefits from using operating loss carryforwards
  — Adjustments of a deferred tax liability or asset for enacted changes in tax laws or rates or a change in tax status

[It is not clear whether it is intended that components of income tax expense should add to the total (or net) income tax provision. If so, then the amounts of current tax expense and deferred tax expense disclosed would be before application of investment credits and net operating loss (NOL) carryforwards. However, the definition of deferred tax expense provided both in the text of FAS 96 and in its glossary is clearly the amount computed *after* application of those items; the language with respect to current tax expense is ambiguous, at best, with respect to loss carryforwards applied in the current year. Unless and until clarification is provided, it appears that disclosure of either the gross or the net amount would be acceptable. Price Waterhouse suggests that, whichever option is elected, separate disclosures be made for both investment credits and NOL carryforwards of the amounts used against current and against deferred expense; this would give the reader enough information to derive the other figure.

The gross presentation is illustrated in Exhibits 7-2 and 8-1. The exhibits illustrate determination of the benefit of usage of NOL carryforwards by computations of current and deferred provisions with and without the NOL. But care must be taken when there are unused NOL carryforward benefits in the deferred computation and there are originating temporary differences that increase current taxable income (before NOL application). Paragraph 51 of FAS 96 observes that, when a tax NOL carryforward is applied to taxable income that is deferred for book purposes, there is no usage of book NOL carryforward; the same is true for taxable income resulting from deferral for tax purposes of book expenses. In these cases, the benefit of NOL carryforwards in the current provision must be reversed in the deferred provision, reflecting an increase in the amount of unused deductions in the deferred tax computation.

It should also be noted that paragraph 27 of FAS 96 does not mention benefits of purchased NOLs that are applied to reduce goodwill and intangible assets, rather than applied to reduce tax expense. In past practice, this has been generally referred to as a charge equivalent to the NOL benefit. If the gross presentation is followed, as illustrated in Exhibit 7-2, it appears that both current and deferred expense could include portions of the charge equivalent, and there would have to be disclosure either in the income statement or in its notes that the amounts are charges equivalent rather than current or deferred payables. If the net presentation is used, a separate charge equivalent caption in the analysis of the tax provision would be necessary.

While it is not repeated in FAS 96, companies must remember that APB Opinion 4, *Accounting for the "Investment Credit,"* continues to require disclosures about the method of accounting for investment credit and the amounts involved, when material.]

Notes to the financial statements must disclose the following:

- The nature or type of temporary differences that give rise to significant portions of the deferred tax liability or asset.
- A reconciliation of the income tax expense attributable to continuing operations to the statutory rate applied to pretax income from continuing operations.

[If alternative minimum tax (AMT) has affected the amount of tax expense charged to continuing operations, it would presumably be one of the rate differentials included in this disclosure.]

- The amounts and expiration dates of NOL and tax credit carryforwards for tax purposes and the amounts and expiration dates for financial reporting purposes.
- Significant amounts of acquired NOLs or investment tax credits that, if realized, will be used to reduce positive goodwill or other intangible assets rather than credited directly to income.

[Paragraph 29 of FAS 96 discusses the requirement for the disclosure of the amounts and expiration dates of the book and tax NOLs and credit carryforwards. Given that the definitions of the book NOL and credit carryforwards include future tax deductions and, perhaps, future credits, it does not appear meaningful to disclose, for example, that a tax deduction to be claimed in the year 2030 will expire in the year 2045, if unutilized. Rather, the years and amounts should be specified for each of the next 15 years (as is current practice) with any future tax deductions aggregated to one amount. In certain circumstances, it may be appropriate to provide more than one aggregate amount, such as when a significant amount of the book NOLs will expire in years 16 through 20.

Remember that NOLs and credit carryforwards may be different for regular tax and for AMT. If AMT is a significant factor in computing either the current or the deferred provision, consideration should be given to disclosure of the AMT carryforward amounts. Indeed, a company that expects to be subject to AMT rather than regular tax should, in disclosing regular tax carryforwards, indicate that AMT amounts are those expected to be actually relevant. Any minimum tax credit carryforwards should be disclosed.

When there has been a cumulative change in ownership, as defined, of more than 50 percent within a three-year period, the Tax Reform Act of 1986 (TRA 1986) places an annual limitation on the use, for both regular tax and AMT, of NOL and other carryforwards and of "built-in losses," the excess of tax bases over fair values of assets. The limitation applies to built-in losses realized in the five-year period beginning with the ownership change if, when ownership changes, the net unrealized built-in losses exceed 25 percent of the assets' fair values. If the annual limitation is triggered, it may delay utilization of the carryforwards or built-in losses, or it could result in a permanent loss, for example, if an entire carryforward cannot be utilized prior to its expiration because of the annual limitation. When such limitations are operative for NOLs and built-in losses arising in a purchase business combination, disclosure would be appropriate, similar to disclosure of limitations on use of NOLs to income of the acquired company.

The rules for computing a change in ownership are complex, but it is possible for the limitation to apply to a company that is not an acquired company in a business combination. The limitation could be triggered, among other events, by exercises of stock options, conversions of convertible debt or preferred stock, new common stock offerings, or treasury share purchases. Price Waterhouse recommends disclosure of the potential limitation in all circumstances (except if the prospect of such a change in ownership is remote) by a brief statement such as: "If certain substantial changes in the Company's ownership should occur, there would be an annual limitation on the amount of the carryforward(s) that can be utilized." If there are circumstances (e.g., convertible debt, the exercise price of which is below the market, or a planned public offering) that make the change in ownership reasonably possible, general description of those circumstances may be warranted. More specific disclosures concerning the limitation should be made if its triggering is probable and, if it is in fact triggered, disclosure of the amount of the annual limitation is required.

TRA 1986 continues the "continuity of business" requirement. If there is an indication that carryforwards could be lost because of failure to meet this test, disclosure is necessary.]

- For the temporary differences identified in and meeting the criteria of APB 23 and those related to the statutory reserve funds of U.S. steamship companies:
  - A description of the nature of the temporary differences and the types of events that could trigger a tax liability
  - The cumulative amount of each type of temporary difference
  - Except for unremitted earnings of subsidiaries, the amount of any unrecognized deferred tax liability for each type of temporary difference
  - For unremitted earnings of subsidiaries, the amount of unrecorded deferred tax liability if determining that amount is practical or, if not practical, the amount of withholding taxes that would be payable when those earnings are remitted

[With respect to foreign subsidiaries, this requirement runs only to unremitted earnings. Although not required, it would seem appropriate to make similar disclosures with respect to cumulative translation adjustments for which deferred taxes have not been provided—see Exhibit 2-2.]

- If the enterprise is included in the consolidated tax return of its parent:
  - The current and deferred tax expense for each income statement presented and the amount of any tax-related balances due to or from affiliates as of the date of each balance sheet
  - The principal provisions of the method of allocating the consolidated current and deferred tax provision to the members of the consolidated group

> — The nature and effect of any changes in the method of allocating the consolidated provision or in determining the amount of any balance due to or from affiliates for each year that an income statement is presented

- An enterprise that is not subject to tax because its income is taxed directly to its owners shall disclose that fact as well as the net difference between the tax bases and book bases of its assets and liabilities.

Exhibit 12-1 offers sample wording for a typical footnote on income taxes.

¶ 12.02 SEC DISCLOSURES

In addition to disclosure items required by FAS 96, public companies must also follow the SEC's disclosure rules. Rule 4-08(h) of Regulation S-X, for example, contains specific guidance for income taxes.

The FAS 96 disclosures cover those in Rule 4-08(h) with certain exceptions. For example, FAS 96 requires disclosure of "the types of temporary differences," while Rule 4-08(h) requires disclosure of "the net tax effects of timing differences" by major categories. When translating that requirement to temporary differences, public companies will have to attribute the deferred tax provision to major categories of temporary differences. It should be noted that, with respect to disclosures about temporary/timing differences, the FAS 96 requirement runs to the composition of the balance sheet deferred tax liability or asset, and the Rule 4-08(h) requirement runs to the composition of deferred tax expense. At the March 31, 1988 meeting of the Implementation Group, the SEC Observer noted that the Rule 4-08(h) requirement contemplates a "gross" presentation; that is, tax effects of timing/ temporary differences should be before application of investment tax credits (ITCs), NOLs, and so forth, and the effects of ITCs, NOLs, and the like would be shown separately. The SEC staff has observed that it will be necessary to include in this disclosure

EXHIBIT 12-1 ——————————————————————————————
Sample Footnote Disclosures

The following sample disclosure is based on the retroactive application of FAS 96 to or before 1984:

Note X—INCOME TAXES

The components of earnings before income taxes and extraordinary item (Note Y) for the years ended December 31 were taxed under the following jurisdictions:

	In thousands		
	1987	1986	1985
Domestic	$100,000	$ 90,000	$ 80,000
Foreign	30,000	20,000	25,000
Total	$130,000	$110,000	$105,000

The provision for income taxes on those earnings was as follows:

	1987	1986	1985
Current tax expense			
United States	$ 28,000	$ 40,480	$ 29,900
Foreign	3,420	2,700	4,320
State and local	5,600	6,600	770
Total current	37,020	49,780	34,990
Deferred tax expense			
United States	13,600	3,400	9,200
Foreign	2,160	1,620	720
State and local	3,200	750	1,540
Total deferred	18,960	5,770	11,460
Investment tax credits		(1,000)	(3,000)
Benefits of operating loss carryforwards			(11,500)
Adjustment for changes in tax laws or rates		(6,000)	
		(7,000)	(14,500)
Total provision for income taxes	$ 55,980	$ 48,550	$ 31,950

Investment tax credits were applied in 1985 and 1986 to reduce U.S. current tax expense.

The U.S. current tax expense was reduced in 1985 by $25,300, reflecting the use of a tax operating loss carryforward. Of the tax carryforward, $13,800 had previously been recognized by reduction of the U.S. deferred tax liability and was accordingly applied to reinstate the deferred tax liability. The balance of $11,500 was recognized in 1985 income.

The Company reduced its U.S. deferred tax liability in 1986 as a result of the reduction in corporate tax rates from 46 percent to 34 percent and certain other provisions enacted by TRA 1986.

Deferred income taxes are provided for the temporary differences between the financial reporting basis and the tax basis of the Company's assets and liabilities. The major temporary differences that give rise to the deferred tax liability and asset and the effect that changes in those temporary differences had on the provision for deferred tax expense are as follows:

	1987	1986	1985
Inventory reserves	($ 3,000)	($2,000)	($ 5,000)
Plant-closing costs	8,000	(8,000)	
Depreciation	8,000	7,000	6,000
Pensions	2,000	3,500	3,000
Income on long-term contracts	1,000	2,000	3,000
Deferred income	2,000	4,000	5,000
Other	960	(730)	(540)
Deferred tax expense	$18,960	$5,770	$11,460

The deferred tax liabilities (assets) are reflected in the consolidated balance sheet as follows:

	1987	1986	1985
Current assets	($ 3,310)	($ 1,000)	($ 2,040)
Noncurrent assets		(1,870)	
Current liabilities	19,000	14,000	12,000
Noncurrent liabilities	31,000	16,600	18,000
Net liability	$46,690	$27,730	$27,960

The provision for income taxes is less than the amount of income tax determined by applying the applicable U.S. statutory income tax rate to pretax income before extraordinary item as a result of the following differences:

	Percent of pretax income		
	1987	1986	1985
Statutory U.S. tax rates	40.0%	46.0%	46.0%
Increase (decrease) in rates resulting from:			
Lower rates on earnings of foreign operations	(5.1)	(5.1)	(6.7)
Nondeductible items	3.4	5.0	3.5
Tax credits		(0.9)	(2.9)
State and local taxes, net	4.1	3.6	1.2
Enacted future rate changes		(5.5)	
Benefits of operating loss carryforwards			(11.0)
Other	0.7	1.0	0.3
Effective tax rates	43.1%	44.1%	30.4%

(continued)

EXHIBIT 12-1 *(cont'd)*

Provision has not been made for U.S. or additional foreign taxes on undistributed earnings of international subsidiaries as those earnings have been and will continue to be reinvested. It is not practical to estimate the amount of tax that might be payable on the eventual remittance of such earnings. On remittance, certain foreign countries impose withholding taxes that are then available for use as credits against a U.S. tax liability, if any, subject to certain limitations. The amount of withholding tax that would be payable on remittance of the entire amount of undistributed earnings would approximate $42 million.

The tax effect related to the extraordinary item (Note Y) is a currently payable U.S. tax, and it approximates the statutory U.S. tax rate.

---

certain reconciling items specifically arising from the application of FAS 96. Examples include:

- The change in the amount of net deductions to which a tax benefit cannot be ascribed.
- The write-off in the deferred tax provision of benefits ascribed to scheduled net deductions at 46 percent or 40 percent because of carryback availability but actually realized at a lower rate. (For 1987 adoption, the tax provision charged to continuing operations potentially could reflect a write-off of a 6 percent differential from this effect.)

These items would presumably also be included as rate differentials in the reconciliation of the statutory to the effective rate.

There are two other disclosures that are required by the SEC that are not specifically required by FAS 96. These disclosures are included in Exhibit 12-1. They are:

1. The source of income (loss) before tax expense (benefit) as either foreign or domestic
2. The amounts applicable to U.S. federal income taxes, foreign income taxes, and to other income taxes stated separately for each major component of income tax expense (i.e., current and deferred)

When the gross presentation is made, it may be necessary, to comply with Rule 4-08(h), to identify, as domestic, foreign or other and as current or deferred, investment credits and NOL benefits recognized.

In addition, the SEC staff has stated that, when a corporation has recorded a deferred tax asset at an amount higher than it expects to realize that asset as a result of the requirements of FAS 96 (see Exhibit 4-2), the management's discussion and analysis section must contain a discussion of how future taxable income will affect the recovery of the asset.

The SEC has often withdrawn specific disclosure requirements when the FASB has given comprehensive consideration to a particular area and promulgated its own requirements. The SEC staff is evaluating the need for adjustments to its rules and regulations. It is unclear when the SEC will take action on this issue.

¶ 12.03   PRO FORMA INFORMATION NOT REQUIRED

Paragraphs 32 to 36 of FAS 96 specify the effective date of and transition rules for adopting FAS 96. The transition rules, in addition to the unusual treatment accorded business combinations, are unusual in one other respect.

APB 20 is the authoritative guidance on accounting for and reporting of accounting changes unless otherwise specified in a newly issued pronouncement. One of APB 20's requirements is that, if a change in accounting is reported using the cumulative effect method (the usual case), the pro forma effect on income for prior periods must be shown on the face of the income statement for all periods presented.

This requirement is absent in FAS 96, presumably for two reasons. Because of the Statement's special transition provisions for purchase business combinations, pro forma information may not be meaningful if a company has elected the shortcut method. Also, because of the difficulties that can be encountered when applying the new requirements to prior years, no retroactive computations are required.

¶ 12.04 EARLY ADOPTION IN AN INTERIM PERIOD

In the case of early adoption, there is no explicit requirement for adopting FAS 96 in the first quarter. But if FAS 96 is adopted in other than the first quarter, prior quarters should be restated to conform to the Statement.

Given the mechanics of quantifying temporary differences and calculating the estimated annual effective tax rate for the year, information about the effect at the beginning of the year in which the Statement is adopted should be readily available. Companies must keep in mind, however, that if they restate prior years, they must also restate the interim periods presented for such years. Such restatements should reflect the estimates made in computing the interim provisions originally reported; changes should be only for differences between the APB 11 and FAS 96 computations. The effect of adoption in the earliest year restated would be reported in the first quarter of that year if quarterly results for that year are presented.

¶ 12.05 POSTPONED ADOPTION

Although FAS 96 permits retroactive or prospective application, a company does not have to make the decision until fiscal years beginning after December 15, 1988. If it elects restatement at that time, it may restate 1987 and 1988 financial statements that were prepared under APB 11 rules after FAS 96 was issued. This is an undesirable effect of FAS 96 that often cannot be avoided.

The staff of the Securities and Exchange Commission issued Staff Accounting Bulletin (SAB) 74 on December 30, 1987. The SAB deals with the appropriate disclosure for public companies in their annual financial statements in situations where an accounting change is mandated but there will be a delay in the actual adoption.

Public companies that do not elect to adopt FAS 96 in 1987 will have to reflect the provisions of SAB 74 in their 1987 annual reports.

Specifically, public companies will be required to include a discussion of FAS 96 both in the management's discussion and analysis section and in the notes to the financial statements "unless the impact on its financial position and results of operations is not expected to be material." SAB 74 states that the following disclosures should be considered:

- A brief description of the new Statement, the date of required adoption, and the date the company intends to adopt.
- A description of the methods of adoption allowed (prospective versus retroactive) and the method expected to be used by the company, if determined.
- A discussion of the impact of the new Statement on the company unless not known or reasonably estimable. In that case, a statement to that effect should be made.
- Disclosure of any other effects that adoption of the new Statement might have, such as violations of debt covenants.

These disclosures are required for public companies. We believe that generally accepted accounting principles require that these same disclosures be made by nonpublic companies in order to fully inform the readers of the financial statements.

Exhibit 12-2 offers sample wording for a footnote to satisfy the minimum disclosure requirements when adoption of FAS 96 has been postponed. Of course, actual disclosure should be tailored to each company's specific facts and circumstances.

EXHIBIT 12-2 _____
Sample Footnote Disclosures—Adoption Postponed

The following sample disclosure would be appropriate when adoption of FAS 96 has been postponed. The first and second paragraphs, which briefly describe FAS 96 and the adoption alternatives offered by the Statement, would be appropriate in most circumstances. The third paragraph should be tailored to the company's specific facts and circumstances.

Note X—INCOME TAXES

In December 1987, the Financial Accounting Standards Board issued Statement of Financial Accounting Standards No. 96, *Accounting for Income Taxes*. FAS 96 mandates the liability method for computing deferred income taxes. [*Optional*: Under the liability method, total tax expense is the amount of income taxes expected to be payable for the current year plus (or minus) the change from the beginning of the year in a deferred tax liability or asset established for the expected future tax consequences resulting from differences in the financial reporting and tax bases of assets and liabilities.] One of the principal differences from the deferred method used in these financial statements is that changes in tax rates and laws will be reflected in income from continuing operations in the period such changes are enacted; under the deferred method such changes were reflected over time, if at all.

Adoption of FAS 96 is required no later than the first quarter of 1989; earlier adoption is permitted. Upon adoption, the principles of the Statement may be applied retroactively through restatement of previously issued financial statements, or on a prospective basis.

The Company will adopt FAS 96 in 1989. However, due to the complexities of the calculations that will be required to implement the Statement, the effect on the Company's financial statements is not known nor reasonably estimable at this time.

[*alternate third paragraph*]
The Company intends to adopt FAS 96 in 1989. Adoption of the new Statement will not have a significant effect on the Company's financial position or results of operations.

[*or*]
The Company intends to adopt FAS 96 in 1989 and to apply it retroactively to 1986. As a result of applying FAS 96, it is expected that the deferred income tax liability at December 31, 1986 will be reduced by approximately

(continued)

EXHIBIT 12-2 *(cont'd)*

$800,000 and that 1986 net income and shareholders' equity will be increased by the same amount, primarily as a result of reduced U.S. federal income tax rates enacted in 1986. Earnings per share for 1986 will be increased approximately $0.03 per share. FAS 96 is expected to have no significant effect on 1987 or 1988 net income.

[*or*]

The Company intends to adopt FAS 96 in 1989 and to apply it prospectively. Adoption of FAS 96 is expected to have a one time, unfavorable effect on 1989 net income of approximately $2 million primarily as a result of recognizing the deferred tax consequences of net assets acquired in the 1982 purchase of ABC Company.

[*or*]

Adoption of the new Statement is also expected to place the Company in technical default of its loan agreement with Payme Bank (see Note Y). However, management believes that the loan covenants will be revised, at no cost to the Company, to accommodate the requirements of FAS 96.

Questions and Answers

Listed in this chapter are questions that will most likely arise during the implementation of FAS 96, with a cross-reference to the chapter where the topic being addressed is discussed in detail. No book can possibly anticipate each and every implementation question or "wrinkle" that may crop up—especially in view of FAS 96's complexities and length.

¶ 13.01 TEMPORARY DIFFERENCES

■ *Must deferred taxes be provided on all temporary differences?*

No. FAS 96 provides an exception for temporary differences addressed by APB 23 that meet the indefinite reversal criteria, and for deposits in statutory reserve funds by U.S. steamship enterprises. In addition, providing deferred taxes on goodwill, negative goodwill, and leveraged leases in a purchase business combination is prohibited (see Exhibit 2-2).

■ *My company owns several foreign subsidiaries located in countries where indexing of fixed assets for foreign tax purposes is permitted. Does FAS 96 change the financial statement effect of indexing?*

Yes. In the past, the tax benefit of indexing was recognized only as the resulting higher depreciation was claimed on the tax return. Under FAS 96, however, it is possible to recognize the benefit each year of that year's increase in the index on the entire tax basis of the asset (see Exhibit 2-3 for an example).

■ *We sell a significant amount of our products to overseas subsidiaries who then resell to the end user. In consolidation, we eliminate the profit in inventory at the end of each year. Is this a temporary difference?*

Yes. But there's a change from APB 11, which measured the deferred tax effect as the tax paid by the seller on the intercompany profit. Under FAS 96, the temporary difference is the excess tax basis of the buying company over the book amount reflected in consolidation. Deferred taxes should be provided on the elimination entry, assuming the future "tax deduction" can be realized through offset of future taxable income or through carryback (see ¶ 3.07).

■ *Is the excess cash surrender value of life insurance over cumulative premiums paid a temporary difference for which deferred taxes must be provided? If so, how should the reversal be scheduled?*

Yes. The reversal will usually be scheduled in the year that minimizes the deferred tax liability (see ¶ 3.13).

■ *Must deferred taxes be provided on the difference between book and tax bases of LIFO inventories? My company has no intention of invading low-value, base-year LIFO layers, and our ability to maintain inventory levels is evident from historical performance.*

Deferred taxes must be provided in this situation. The timing of reversal depends on your inventory movement. For example, if inventories "turn over" at least once a year, then the amount of LIFO inventories would be recoverable next year (see ¶ 3.05).

■ *We had a business combination in which net assets exceeded our purchase price. We reduced our noncurrent assets by the amount of the excess. How do we compute temporary differences when "negative goodwill" has been allocated to noncurrent assets?*

Deferred taxes are, in effect, provided on "negative goodwill" allocated to noncurrent assets. Accordingly, the net balance, after reduction by the excess, must be used to determine the temporary differences and thus the deferred tax balance. However, the amount of deferred taxes will affect the amount of the "negative goodwill" to be applied to the noncurrent assets. This is a circular process (see ¶ 8.03 for a formula to determine the appropriate adjustment).

■ *We have adopted FAS 87 and FAS 88 on pension accounting. Are there any temporary differences related to these new balance sheet accounts for pensions?*

Yes. However, determining the reversal pattern of temporary differences relating to pension balances can be quite complicated (see ¶ 3.06).

■ *How do I identify my company's temporary differences?*

Many of the temporary differences were timing differences under APB 11. However, there are some new ones with purchase business combinations being the major new temporary difference (see ¶ 2.01).

■ *As a lessor, we have certain leases that are direct-financing leases for financial reporting purposes but are operating leases for tax purposes. How is the temporary difference computed?*

The book basis is represented by the rents receivable, the residual value, unearned income, and deferred investment tax credit (ITC). The net of these amounts is the book basis. The tax basis is represented by the depreciable asset. The difference is, of course, the temporary difference. The reversal pattern of these temporary differences will generate both originating and reversing temporary differences (see ¶¶ 2.05[2], 3.03[2]).

¶ 13.02 SCHEDULING

■ *My company has operations in a number of tax jurisdictions. Is a detailed scheduling exercise always necessary?*

No. If the deferred tax balance (in any jurisdiction) computed by the aggregate method is not materially different from the balance calculated by scheduling, you may use the aggregate method. However, it may be difficult to assess the materiality of the difference between the two methods without actually performing both for a number of years (see ¶ 3.01).

■ *FAS 96 states that some temporary differences may accumulate over several years and then eliminate over several years. We have accrued a liability for deferred compensation that is increased by an annual interest accrual. It will be paid and deductible over the 10 years after retirement. Does that mean that interest expected to accrete in future years would be considered in the scheduling process?*

No. The accretion of interest is a result of the passage of time, a future event, and it would result in book expense, contrary to FAS 96's assumption of future break-even income. FAS 96 prohibits the consideration of future events (see ¶ 3.03[6]).

■ *How should the reversal of temporary differences arising from inventory reserves be scheduled?*

Reversal should be scheduled as the related inventory is expected to turn on a flow-of-goods basis (see "Inventory reserves, excluding LIFO reserves" in Exhibit 3-6).

■ *One of our subsidiaries sold some of its stock at a price per share that was greater than our carrying amount per share and we recorded a so-called "change-in-interest" credit. We didn't provide deferred taxes under APB 11. Will we have to provide deferred taxes under FAS 96?*

Yes, if it's a foreign subsidiary. Perhaps not, if the subsidiary is domestic (see ¶ 3.14).

■ *When providing taxes at an interim date, must I calculate my company's temporary differences and perform a scheduling exercise at each quarter end?*

No. However, you will need to identify and estimate the year-end temporary differences when computing the tax provision for the first and subsequent quarters (see ¶ 10.08).

■ *What does FAS 96 mean by "all tax jurisdictions?"*

The deferred tax calculation under FAS 96 is tantamount to preparing future years' tax returns based on the reversal of temporary differences. Therefore, a separate calculation must be performed for each jurisdiction in which an income tax return is filed (see ¶ 1.01).

■ *We have to change our tax accounting as a result of the Tax Reform Act of 1986. How does this affect my scheduling?*

You will have to schedule both the reporting of the transition date amount as well as the reversal of any temporary difference that is now either created or changed by the tax accounting change (see ¶ 3.08).

¶ 13.03 TAX-PLANNING STRATEGIES

■ *Would an election to forgo a loss carryback constitute an acceptable tax-planning strategy?*

Yes, but only if it minimizes a deferred tax liability (see ¶¶ 4.04, 5.07).

■ *Can different tax-planning strategies be used for federal and state tax purposes or for a parent and its subsidiaries?*

Tax-planning strategies that assume transactions that affect the timing of deductions and taxable income must be used consistently. However, different tax filing elections may be assumed for different jurisdictions when allowable (see ¶ 5.08).

■ *Is the company obligated to actually carry out a selected tax-planning strategy?*

No. These tax-planning strategies are hypothetical; actual strategies will be dictated by actual future events (see ¶¶ 5.06, 5.07).

■ *If I estimate that the temporary difference related to a litigation accrual will reverse in 1990 but believe that I can settle the litigation in 1989 at a higher cost, can I shift the reversal in my deferred tax calculation in order to decrease deferred taxes?*

Not if the additional cost is "significant" (see ¶ 5.09).

■ *We have thought up a number of tax-planning strategies. There is some element of "cost" involved in each of them, but the tax benefits would clearly more than offset the cost. Can we apply these strategies?*

No. The tax savings from entering into a transaction cannot reduce the cost of the transaction (see ¶ 5.09).

¶ 13.04 COMPUTATION

■ *Our company is not subject to alternative minimum tax (AMT) currently and does not expect to be in the future. Do we need to consider AMT in the deferred tax computation?*

Yes. FAS 96 requires that the deferred tax calculation consider all aspects of the enacted tax laws including alternative tax systems (see ¶ 9.07).

■ *The state that we do business in provides for a tax that is the highest of three computations: one based on income, one based on capital, and the third being a fixed minimum tax. We have historically paid a tax based on capital. How should we compute the tax based on capital for the future years?*

You don't. It is impossible to predict (and precluded under FAS 96) what the capital base will be in each of the future years. Accordingly, the current year's provision should be the higher of the tax based on income or the minimum amount (see ¶ 6.05).

■ *We are a relatively small company but generally have sufficient taxable income in the United States such that the effect of the graduated rates is completely phased out. If the sum of the temporary differences in any year is such that the graduated rates apply, should these lower rates be used?*

Yes. You may not anticipate the future income (see ¶ 6.06).

¶ 13.05 DEFERRED TAX ASSET

■ *When is it appropriate to recognize a deferred tax asset under FAS 96?*

A deferred tax asset can only be recognized if future net deductions can be carried back to recover taxes actually paid or currently payable or to reduce a deferred tax liability classified as current (see ¶ 4.05).

■ *My company has completed the scheduling of temporary difference reversals. In year one, we have net deductible amounts that cannot be carried back but can be carried forward to offset future taxable income. Should we record a current deferred tax asset?*

No. The net deductible amounts in year one reduce the noncurrent deferred tax liability so the benefit will not be realized within the next 12 months (see ¶ 7.01[1]).

■ *Is there any way to avoid the carryback of a hypothetical loss to recover taxes paid at 46 percent when I know that we will have sufficient taxable income so that there will be no carryback?*

The carryback may be avoided only if, by not carrying the loss back, a lower deferred tax liability or higher deferred tax asset results (see ¶ 4.04). Further, you may need to search for tax-planning strategies to record the maximum benefit from the higher carryback rates (see ¶ 5.06).

¶ 13.06 CLASSIFICATION

■ *Under APB 11, we always recognized the tax benefit of a net operating loss (NOL) carryforward as an extraordinary item. Does FAS 96 require the same treatment?*

No. Under FAS 96, recognition of the tax benefit from an NOL carryforward is generally classified in the same manner as the source of income that gives rise to its recognition. There are three exceptions—purchased NOLs, certain pre-quasi reorganization NOLs, and certain stock compensation deductions (see ¶ 6.02).

■ *We have a number of subsidiaries that file tax returns in other tax jurisdictions. May we net the deferred tax balances so that the consolidated accounts show one current deferred tax balance and one noncurrent deferred tax balance?*

No. Netting of deferred tax balances arising from different tax jurisdictions is not permitted (see ¶ 7.01[3]).

■ *My company expects to elect S corporation status before the end of the year. How should the cumulative tax effect of the change in tax status be reflected in the financial statements?*

All deferred taxes that will not be required after the date of change in tax status will be released and the effect will be included in the tax provision for continuing operations. However, the question arises as to when the date of change occurs (see ¶ 10.01). (Significant questions also arise as to the extent to which deferred taxes can be eliminated by post-1986 S corporation elections. See ¶ 10.01[3].)

■ *Some of the captions in my equity section are tax-effected. How does FAS 96 compute the tax effect?*

The tax to be allocated to components of the equity section is computed in the same manner as intraperiod tax allocation to components of the income statement. However, if the tax effect should be computed by reference to prior years (e.g., the cumulative effect of an accounting change or an error correction), a separate computation would have to be made (see ¶ 7.05).

■ *We have a debit in stockholders' equity related to a reduction in the value of our portfolio of nonmarketable equity securities. Beginning in 1990, we may have another debit related to our minimum pension liability under FAS 87. Should these amounts be tax-effected?*

Yes. They should be considered in the intraperiod tax allocation process (see ¶ 7.05).

¶ 13.07 BUSINESS COMBINATIONS

■ *I understand that FAS 96 will end the net-of-tax recording of purchase business combinations. Two years ago, my company was party to a business combination accounted for as a purchase. Upon adoption of FAS 96, must that prior purchase business combination be remeasured?*

Not necessarily. Whether a prior purchase business combination is remeasured will depend upon whether FAS 96 is applied retroactively to the year the purchase was consummated (see ¶ 8.05 for a description of the two transition methods).

■ *Our company is considering purchasing a company with considerable NOL carryforwards. At the date of acquisition, can we recognize the benefit of the target's NOLs? Should our own temporary differences "interact" with the target's temporary differences to determine the appropriate deferred tax asset or liability to record at the acquisition date?*

If, in the future, the combined company will file a consolidated tax return and, based on the enacted tax law, the acquired NOLs could be used in the computation to reduce the deferred tax liability of the acquiring company, then the deferred tax balance at the acquisition date should reflect that fact (see ¶ 8.02).

■ *How should we measure temporary differences at the acquisition date if the acquisition date is at any time other than our year-end?*

FAS 96 does not specify how the acquiring company should measure its temporary differences at the acquisition date. We believe that an effective rate computation is the most appropriate method but there are other approaches (see ¶ 8.01[2]).

■ *If not recorded at the acquisition date, how is the benefit from a purchased NOL later accounted for?*

The benefit would reduce goodwill and any other intangible assets (prospectively not retroactively). Once those assets are reduced to zero, the benefit is included in income as a reduction of income tax expense (see ¶ 8.02[1]).

■ *My company consummated a purchase business combination on September 30, 1986, just before the Tax Reform Act of 1986 was enacted. If I restate 1986, what tax rate should be used when providing deferred taxes at the acquisition date?*

The enacted tax rate at September 30, 1986 was 46 percent and, therefore, that rate should be used, just as it was for your other deferred taxes. On October 22, 1986, the deferred tax balance should be adjusted as a reduction of income tax expense to reflect the lower rates enacted on that date (see ¶ 8.04).

■ *We have acquired NOLs and our own NOLs. Has anything changed with respect to the order of utilization?*

Yes. NOLs must now be used in the same order as that determined by applying the tax law. Prior to FAS 96, a different ordering may have been used (see ¶ 8.02[2]).

¶ 13.08 IMPLEMENTATION

■ *My company owns one subsidiary that issues separate financial statements. Must the subsidiary's separate financial statements reflect adoption of FAS 96 in the same year as its parent?*

Price Waterhouse does not believe that a parent and its subsidiaries have to conform their adoption elections in separate financial statements. The FASB staff have a different view in circumstances where the subsidiary is included in the consolidated tax return of its parent. Of course, the consolidated financial statements must contain only one method (see ¶ 11.03).

■ *We haven't decided whether to adopt FAS 96 prospectively or retroactively. Is it possible that the method of adoption could affect the amount of tax we will actually have to pay?*

Yes, if you have had prior purchase business combinations. The amount of future book income may affect the amount of AMT that you will have to pay (see ¶¶ 8.05[1], 11.05).

■ *We have a currency translation adjustment (CTA) account, and we're applying FAS 96 prospectively. Should some portion of the effect of adoption of FAS 96 be allocated to the CTA account?*

No (see ¶ 11.06).

■ *When we have had accounting changes in the past, we had to spend a lot of time computing the pro forma effect of the change. If FAS 96 is applied prospectively, is pro forma disclosure required for prior years?*

No (see ¶ 12.03).

■ *If I elect to restate, must all years presented be restated?*

No. FAS 96 allows you to choose the earliest year of restatement (see Chapter 11).

■ *We have two significant investees that we carry at equity. Must our equity accounting for these investees adopt FAS 96 at the same time and in the same way as our consolidated companies?*

No. The investor does not control the investees (see ¶ 11.04).

■ *In the past, my company was a party to a number of purchase business combinations. As restatement would require a significant amount of work, we have elected to apply FAS 96 prospectively and thus the shortcut transition rule for prior purchase business combinations. As there was higher book than tax basis in each purchase, we'll have to increase our deferred tax liability significantly. Will there be any major effects from this?*

Application of the shortcut transition rule should improve the measurement of operating results in the future. Otherwise, the major effect is on the adjustment recorded upon adoption of FAS 96. You also forgo a potential reduction of AMT (see ¶ 8.05[2]).

■ *In a prior purchase business combination, my company discounted the future tax effects of the higher assigned book basis over tax basis. What is the effect of FAS 96 if we adopt prospectively? What if we apply FAS 96 to a date prior to the purchase business combination?*

If you elect prospective application, the fact that you discounted the future tax effects will cause the charge from the effect of adoption to be higher than if you had not discounted. If you apply FAS 96 to a date preceding the acquisition, the discounting effect will increase goodwill at the date of the acquisition (see ¶ 8.05).

■ *Will adoption of FAS 96 affect any important ratios that are included as debt covenants?*

Probably. Retained earnings will be affected to some degree. Therefore, the debt to net worth ratio and any net worth requirement will be affected. As well, working capital may be positively or negatively affected by the new classification rules and by the more stringent rules on recording deferred tax assets. Because of the revised method of recording prior purchase business combinations, there could also be an effect on tangible net worth tests (see ¶ 7.01[4]).

¶ 13.09 DISCLOSURE

■ *Are there any new disclosures required by FAS 96?*

Yes. The major new requirements relate to certain information when deferred taxes have not been recorded because of the APB 23 exceptions (see ¶ 12.01).

■ *We will not adopt FAS 96 in 1987. Are there any special disclosures required?*

Yes. The SEC staff issued Staff Accounting Bulletin No. 74, which describes the disclosure requirements for the management's discussion and analysis section and for the notes to the financial statements of a public company. Price Waterhouse believes the same footnote disclosures are required for nonpublic companies (see ¶ 12.05).

¶ 13.10 OTHER

■ *Five years ago, my company provided cushion for a gain that we treated as a capital gain but expect the IRS to reclassify to ordinary income. (The year is still an open year.) We have increased the cushion each year to cover interest. Is that practice affected by FAS 96?*

Yes. FAS 96 states that "interest and penalties assessed on income tax deficiencies" shall not be reported as income tax expense (see ¶ 7.03).

■ *We have a tax-sharing agreement with our subsidiaries. What guidance does FAS 96 provide regarding accounting for intercorporate income tax allocation?*

The new Statement formalizes certain disclosures regarding the method and results of intercorporate tax allocation policies. The only measurement requirement is that the sum of the amounts allocated to members of the group, net of consolidating eliminations, must equal the consolidated amount. Various methods will continue to be acceptable with appropriate disclosure (see ¶ 10.02).

■ *Our employee stock option plan owns a number of shares of our stock. How are tax benefits related to dividends paid to the ESOP accounted for under FAS 96?*

The tax benefits are credited to income tax expense (see ¶ 10.03).

■ *How does FAS 96 affect foreign operations?*

First, for financial statements issued in conformity with U.S. generally accepted accounting principles, foreign operations included in the consolidated financial statements must apply FAS 96 to the computation of the foreign deferred tax balance (see ¶ 1.01).

Second, if the U.S. dollar is the functional currency, a new temporary difference is created related to the remeasurement of the foreign currency financial statements into the U.S. dollar (see ¶ 2.04).

■ *If we record a deferred tax liability for the undistributed earnings of our foreign subsidiaries, may the liability be discounted to its net present value?*

No. The question of discounting of deferred taxes was excluded from the scope of FAS 96. Until the FASB considers the question, discounting is prohibited (see ¶1.02).

■ *My company traditionally takes aggressive tax positions, and invariably the IRS proposes substantial adjustments to defer deductions to later years. Of course, the assessments have been charged to our deferred tax reserve and to interest accruals that we've made separately. Do we need to be concerned about open years in adopting FAS 96?*

Yes. You may not write down deferred tax balances from 46 percent to 34 percent if the tax deferrals are going to be reclassified to 46 percent return years. Your calculation of refund availability and your scheduling of reversals should reflect the positions expected to be ultimately sustained (see ¶¶ 3.18, 4.06).

■ *I've read through FAS 96, and I don't recall any reference to permanent differences. Isn't that term used any more?*

You will find several references in this book to permanent differences because there is a general understanding, from its use under APB 11, that it indicates tax-exempt income or nondeductible expense. However, FAS 96 doesn't use the term, and it changes the treatment of some items that were permanent differences under APB 11—for example, differences arising in a purchase business combination and from indexation. The term "permanent difference" will probably continue to be used for several years by preparers and auditors, if not by standards-setters. Note that this use is in the context of regular tax. Given the AMT enacted by the Tax Reform Act of 1986, there may be few, if any, items of financial reporting income or expense that do not potentially have some tax effect.

Corporate Alternative Minimum Tax— Why All Corporations Will Be Affected

Prior to the Tax Reform Act of 1986 (TRA 1986), many perceived that large corporations often did not pay their fair share of federal income tax, although they reported impressive earnings to shareholders and the public and regularly paid dividends. Public interest group studies confirmed this perception; indeed, many major U.S. corporations paid little or no federal income tax despite impressive financial statement earnings.

Though a minimum tax system existed for corporations prior to TRA 1986, it was an add-on tax. This system did not attempt to tax a corporation's economic income. Rather, it was an excise tax on the use of certain exclusions, deductions, and credits available under the law (i.e., tax preferences).

The political pressure to ensure that every corporate taxpayer paid its fair share of federal income tax led to the repeal of the add-on minimum tax and the adoption of the alternative minimum tax (AMT) system for corporations for tax years beginning after December 31, 1986.

The AMT has one main objective—to ensure that every corporation with substantial economic income pays federal income tax, despite using tax preferences. The AMT is a separate tax system that corporate taxpayers must address yearly, in addition to the regular tax system. More complicated than the add-on minimum tax, it requires intensive planning to minimize its impact.

The corporate AMT system was adapted from the AMT system in place for individuals. Congress, however, believed that this AMT system was insufficient to counter the perception that corporations were not being taxed on their true economic income. Therefore, the corporate AMT system also requires corporations to treat half the excess of financial statement income over AMT income as a tax preference when computing AMT for tax years beginning in 1987, 1988, and 1989. After 1989, TRA 1986 replaces the use of book income with an earnings and profits (E&P) approach.

The new book income item adds complexity to the AMT process. When subject to AMT, corporations now pay tax indirectly on income that was never subject to federal income tax (for example, tax-exempt interest and dividend income excluded by the dividends received deduction).

In addition to the book income item, other AMT wrinkles include the treatment of net operating losses (NOLs), foreign tax credits (FTCs), and transitional or carryover investment tax credits (ITCs). To further toughen the AMT bite, a corporation may not use an NOL, FTC, and/or ITC to completely eliminate its AMT liability.

While not every corporation will pay AMT in a given year, all will be affected by the new AMT system. Although not subject to AMT, corporations must maintain AMT records (that is, keep track of items computed differently for AMT versus regular tax purposes). These items include NOL, FTC, ITC, depreciation deduction, installment sales income, and long-term contracts results. In addition, corporations must compute AMT income to compute the environmental tax liability, if any (see ¶A.08).

Now, the good news. Since most tax preferences only defer taxation—and do not afford a permanent avoidance of tax—the AMT system enables taxpayers to recoup AMT paid on certain tax preferences. This device is called the minimum tax credit (MTC).

¶ A.01 OVERVIEW OF THE CORPORATE AMT SYSTEM

A corporation calculates the AMT separately from its regular tax. The AMT consists of a flat rate applied to a broader tax base. It is defined as the excess of the tentative minimum tax (TMT) over the regular tax. Both the TMT and the regular tax are reduced by FTCs computed under applicable limitations.

With the exception of the transitional or carryover investment credit, nonrefundable credits (e.g., the targeted jobs tax credit and research credit) cannot reduce the regular tax to an amount lower than the TMT amount. Amounts limited, however, can be carried forward 15 years or carried back three years and used, when available, against regular tax in such years.

[1] Determination of the Tentative Minimum Tax

TMT is determined by applying the AMT rate of 20 percent to alternative minimum taxable income (AMTI) (net of the exemption amount, if any) and reducing such product by any AMT FTC allowed.

AMTI is regular taxable income (before NOL deduction) *increased or decreased* to reflect different AMT treatment of adjustment items and *increased* by items of tax preference. AMT adjustments and preferences are outlined in Exhibits 9-2 and 9-3.

The subtotal of regular taxable income, increased or decreased to reflect adjustment items and increased by items of tax preference, is called pre-book AMTI. Added—though never subtracted for pre-1990 years—to this amount is the book income adjustment. This adjustment is 50 percent of the amount that adjusted net book income exceeds pre-book AMTI.

After adding the book income adjustment to pre-book AMTI, a final deduction is made for the AMT NOL (if any). The resulting sum is AMTI.

AMTI is then reduced by the exemption amount of $40,000. However, the exemption amount is reduced by 25 percent of the amount that AMTI exceeds $150,000. So, when AMTI exceeds $310,000, the exemption amount is completely phased out.

When AMTI has been reduced by the exemption amount (if any), and multiplied by 20 percent, the resulting gross tax is then reduced by allowable AMT foreign tax credits. This amount is the TMT. To the extent that TMT exceeds the corporation's regular tax (after FTC), such excess (defined as the AMT) must be paid in addition to the regular tax.

Exhibit A-1 outlines the corporate AMT system.

EXHIBIT A-1 ————————————————————————————
Outline of the AMT System

Regular taxable income (before NOL)
+/— Adjustments
    Post-1986 depreciation
    Sale of depreciable assets
    Long-term contracts
    Passive activity losses—offset against portfolio income—certain
        corporations
    Dealer installment sales
    Certified pollution control facilities
    Mining exploration and development costs
    Circulation expenditures (if a personal holding company)
    Capital construction funds—Shipping Co.
    Special deduction—Blue Cross/Blue Shield Co.
+   Preferences
    Percentage depletion
    Intangible drilling costs
    Bad debts—financial institutions
    Pre-1987 depreciation
    "Private activity" tax-exempt interest
    Appreciated property contributions

Subtotal
+   Book income adjustment (50% of excess of adjusted net book
    income over the above subtotal)
—   AMT NOL

Alternative minimum taxable income
—   Exemption amount (phased-out by 25% of amount by which AMTI
    exceeds $150,000)

Subtotal
×   20%

Tentative minimum tax (before credits)
—   AMT FTC

Tentative minimum tax
—   Regular tax after FTC

Alternative minimum tax

¶ A.02 DISCUSSION OF CERTAIN ADJUSTMENTS AND PREFERENCES

The principal difference between adjustment and tax preference items is that an adjustment item—with the exception of the pre-1990 book income adjustment—either increases or decreases AMT income (referred to as netting), while a preference item always increases AMT income.

For example, the AMT depreciation adjustment for property placed in service after 1986 reduces the depreciation deduction in computing AMT income in the early years of the asset's life. However, a greater depreciation deduction for AMT purposes will be available in the later years of the asset's life.

In contrast, a tax preference item, such as accelerated depreciation on real property placed in service before 1987, includes in the AMT base the excess of the accelerated depreciation over straight-line depreciation in the early years of the asset's service. However, it does not reduce the AMT base in later years when straight-line depreciation is greater than accelerated depreciation.

[1] Depreciation

Depreciation on all real estate and personal property placed in service after 1986 will be computed under the alternative method for purposes of computing AMTI. Under this depreciation system, the recovery period equals the property's useful life determined under the asset depreciation range (ADR) system or a certain prescribed period, both of which are generally longer than the periods available under the modified accelerated cost recovery system (MACRS) used for regular tax purposes.

For example, real estate will be depreciated over a 40-year period, and most personal property over 12 years (five years for automobiles and trucks), under the AMT system. The straight-line method will be used for real estate and the 150 percent declining balance method (switching to straight-line at the optimum point) for personal property.

Regular taxable income will either be increased or decreased by the net difference between the total MACRS depreciation deduction for regular tax purposes and the total depreciation deduction under the alternative method for AMT purposes for post-1986 depreciable property. However, should a company elect the alternative method for regular tax purposes for a class of property in a particular year, no adjustment would be required.

Since a corporation must use the alternative depreciation method for AMT purposes, its accounting system is required to compute another method of depreciation. So, at least three different depreciation systems will have to be used—assuming the alternative method is not elected for regular tax purposes (i.e., one for the books, one for regular tax, and one for AMT). This is in addition to the previous depreciation systems that a company might be using under prior law, such as the accelerated cost recovery system (ACRS) and ADR. Depreciation for state income tax purposes often will add more computations.

[2] Long-Term Contracts

To compute AMTI, a corporation must use the percentage-of-completion method for long-term contracts entered into after February 28, 1986. The percentage-of-completion-capitalized-cost method (PCM), previously known as the completed-contract method, used for regular tax purposes may not be used to compute AMTI.

Similar to the depreciation adjustment treatment, the amount of revenue and expenses recognized by using the percentage-of-completion method is substituted for the amount recognized for regular tax purposes using the PCM.

For taxpayers that have used the completed-contract method, the adjustment for new contracts results in income bunching in the AMT base in the first few years under new tax law. Amounts recognized on prior-year contracts for regular tax purposes (after the effective date) under the completed-contract method will be included in regular taxable income and, therefore, included in the starting point for computing AMTI. Also, amounts deferred for regular tax purposes from new contracts under the new PCM are included under the percentage-of-completion method for AMT purposes.

[3] Passive Activities of Closely Held Corporations

Losses from passive activities, which are allowed to offset portfolio income (e.g., interest, dividends after dividends received deduction, and so forth) of a closely held corporation (five or fewer share-holders own more than 50 percent of the stock) or any personal service corporation during the four-year phase-in period for regular tax purposes, are denied in computing AMTI. Passive activity losses denied, however, are carried forward indefinitely and treated as deductions for purposes of computing AMTI to the extent that there is net passive activity income or business activity income in succeeding taxable years. In addition, in the year the entire interest in the activity is disposed of in a taxable event, any carryforwards resulting from the denial of the phase-in losses will be allowed in computing AMTI.

Though passive activity losses can offset a corporation's passive activity income and active business income, they cannot offset portfolio income.

The AMT adjustment for denial of the passive activity loss is computed after all other AMT preferences and adjustments related to the passive activity have been made.

The AMT passive activity loss rules apply to any loss incurred after 1986. Investments purchased before 1987 are not grandfa-thered. Losses generated by these investments, as well as invest-ments purchased after 1986, are subject to the new AMT rules.

[4] Installment Sales

Both TRA 1986 and the Revenue Act of 1987 made dramatic changes to the installment sale rules. These changes affect both regular tax and AMT. The changes and their effective dates are complicated. Companies affected by these changes should consult a tax advisor.

TRA 1986 required income from dealer sales of inventory (either real or personal property) made after March 1, 1986 to be reported in full in the year of sale for AMT purposes. This rule also applied to nondealer sales of property made after August 16, 1986, which were also subject to the proportionate disallowance rules. The law was effective in taxable years beginning after 1986 for dispositions after the preceding dates. Accordingly, dispositions that met this criterion could not be reported using the installment method in the computation of AMTI.

The Revenue Act of 1987 retroactively repealed the tax preference for use of the installment method to compute AMT for nondealer dispositions of property as described previously. The net impact of these two laws is that the prohibition on the use of the installment method for AMT purposes applies only to dealer dispositions of inventory made after March 1, 1986. The installment method has always been available for nondealer dispositions of property in the determination of the AMT.

The AMT installment sale prohibition, which applies only to dealers because of the Revenue Act of 1987, is effective in tax years beginning after 1986 for dispositions of inventory after March 1, 1986. A special rule applies to installment sales made after March 1, 1986 and before the tax year beginning after 1986 (the year beginning January 1, 1987 for calendar year taxpayers). All of the income related to these sales is treated as if it had been recognized in the 1986 tax year for AMT purposes. Accordingly, the income on these sales that is recognized under the regular tax rules in tax years beginning after 1986 must be subtracted from taxable income in the computation of AMTI. This subtraction is necessary since all of the income is treated as if it had been recognized in the 1986 tax year for AMT.

The Revenue Act of 1987 repealed the installment method for dealer dispositions occurring after December 31, 1987 for regular tax purposes (exceptions exist for dealer dispositions for residential lots or timeshares and for certain farm property). Separate consideration must be given to dealer sales of inventory made before March 1, 1986; sales made between March 1, 1986 and December 31, 1986 (for calendar year taxpayers); sales made between January 1, 1987 and December 31, 1987 (for calendar year taxpayers); and those sales made after December 31, 1987.

Any installment sale made before March 1, 1986 is not affected by any of the changes made in the computation of the regular tax or the AMT. Accordingly, the gross profit related to these sales will continue to be recognized on the installment method for both regular tax and AMT.

Installment sales of inventory made between March 1, 1986 and December 31, 1986 continue to be subject to the installment sale provisions (proportionate disallowance rules are applied) for regular tax purposes until the tax year beginning after 1987. Any gain remaining to be recognized on the first day of the tax year beginning after 1987 is required to be taken into taxable income over a period not to exceed four years. A subtraction from taxable income in the computation of AMTI will be allowed to exclude the taxable income related to these sales from AMTI. This adjustment will be allowed in tax years beginning after 1986.

Installment sales of inventory made between January 1, 1987 and December 31, 1987 are eligible to use the installment sale provisions for regular tax purposes (proportionate disallowance rules are applied) but are not allowed to use them for AMT. Accordingly, all income from these sales is taken into consideration in the 1987 tax year for AMT purposes. An adjustment is allowed in years subsequent to 1987 to exclude the taxable income related to these sales from AMTI.

An installment sale of inventory made after December 31, 1987 will not require an adjustment in the computation of AMTI since all of the income related to these sales will be recognized for both regular tax and AMT in the year of sale.

[5] Book Income

All corporations will have to address the book income adjustment when determining if AMT applies in any given year. Congress enacted this item to ensure that no corporation will report profits to shareholders and creditors and simultaneously pay little or no federal income tax. Unfortunately, the book income item may tax timing and permanent differences between financial statement income and taxable income.

Any provision that reduces taxable income but not financial statement income (e.g., plant closing costs incurred that were previously accrued for book purposes) or increases financial statement income but not taxable income (e.g., tax-exempt interest on state and local bonds), will increase the book income adjustment. Conversely, any item that reduces financial statement income more than taxable income (e.g., amortization of goodwill) or increases taxable income more than financial statement income (e.g., gains recognized for tax purposes on sale/leaseback transactions that are deferred and amortized for financial statement purposes) will reduce the book income adjustment, but not below zero.

Corporations will use book income to compute the adjustment through tax years beginning in 1989. After 1989, adjusted current earnings (ACE) replaces book income to calculate the adjustment. A Treasury study is to be completed by January 1, 1989, presumably to implement the transition to an E&P approach.

Net income from a company's financial statements provides the starting point for determining its book income adjustment. Net income should come from an income statement that is part of a package that includes a balance sheet. The income statement and, more importantly, net income (loss) should reconcile to the balance sheet.

Net income can be obtained from the following sources, in order of priority:

1. Financial statements filed with the Securities and Exchange Commission.

2. Financial statements used as a report or statement for credit purposes, issued to shareholders, or used for any other substantial nontax purposes that have been audited and certified by a CPA. This includes a financial statement where the CPA has issued a qualified "subject to" opinion, a

qualified "except for" opinion because of a departure from generally accepted accounting principles (GAAP), or an adverse opinion where the accountant discloses the amount of the departure from GAAP.

3. Financial statements provided to the federal government or agency thereof, a state government or agency thereof, or a political subdivision.

4. Noncertified reports or financial statements actually used for credit purposes, sent to shareholders, or used for any other substantial nontax purposes.

If a corporation has none of these sources, or only has a report or financial statement of the type mentioned in the fourth category, it may elect to treat net income (loss) equal to tax E&P for the taxable year. Once this election is made, however, the determination of net income (loss) must continue under this method, as long as the corporation is eligible for the election, or until IRS approval is obtained to revoke the election.

Broadly conceived, a corporation's E&P represents its undistributed earnings for income tax purposes. The calculation of E&P, both for the current year and on an accumulated basis, is usually associated with a corporation's determination as to whether or not a distribution is afforded dividend treatment.

Generally, a corporation's E&P differs from both accounting income and taxable income. These differences, however, are not of a magnitude to preclude using either as a starting point in determining E&P. From this starting point, the corporation makes adjustments to equate E&P with the net amount of income actually realized and expenses or losses sustained on an economic basis, as opposed to a tax or financial accounting basis.

The adjustments, which have been developed by statute, judicial determinations, and proclamations by the IRS, include items in E&P that are excluded from taxable income (e.g., interest on tax-exempt bonds), allow deductions for E&P purposes that are not deductible for tax purposes (e.g., charitable contributions in excess of the 10 percent limitation), or disallow deductions taken in computing taxable income (e.g., excess ACRS depreciation on real property).

Many adjustments necessary to transform taxable income into E&P are similar to adjustments now required to compute AMTI. For example, corporations must use the percentage-of-completion method and may not use the installment sales provisions. One major concern with using the E&P approach is the requirement that the LIFO reserve be recaptured.

The main disadvantage with using E&P to determine the book income adjustment is that most corporate taxpayers do not regularly calculate E&P.

When a corporation establishes the applicable financial statement, it must make certain adjustments to conform the applicable financial statement net income with taxable income. The adjustments that follow must be made:

- The net income must be from companies that are included in the consolidated tax return. Therefore, the taxpayer must remove net income from companies consolidated for book, but not for tax (e.g., controlled foreign corporations, Puerto Rican subsidiaries, and subsidiaries whose ownership by the parent is greater than 50 percent—where control is exercised—but less than 80 percent).

  However, dividends or deemed distributions received from a corporation consolidated for book, but not for tax, must be added to net income for the year. So, 100 percent of any dividend is included in net income (loss) for purposes of the AMT book income adjustment; for regular tax purposes dividends from domestic corporations would be subject to the 80 percent dividends received deduction.

  In essence, this may represent the third level of taxation on the dividend, assuming the company receiving the dividend is in an AMT position—that is, first by the payor corporation on the taxable income that was the source of the dividend, a second time by the recipient when 20 percent of the dividend (100 percent less the 80 percent dividends received deduction assuming between 20 percent and 80 percent ownership) is subject to the regular tax, and finally when the AMT tax is imposed on 50 percent of 80 percent of the dividend included in the book income adjustment at the AMT rate of 20 percent.

A group of related corporations may want to elect to file a consolidated tax return to avoid the third level of tax on the dividend component of the book income adjustment.

Controlled foreign subsidiaries' earnings do not have to be included in net income unless currently repatriated. Subpart F income or a dividend gross-up under Internal Revenue Code Section 78 for a deemed paid foreign tax credit must be added to net book income. However, if the earnings are repatriated as dividends, the dividend would have to be reflected at a gross amount if the company is claiming a foreign tax credit.

- Income from companies consolidated for tax, but carried at cost for book (foreign or insignificant subsidiaries), must be added to net income in a manner consistent with the company's normal financial statement consolidating process. Dividends reflected in net income received from a subsidiary not consolidated for book purposes must be eliminated.

- A corporation must remove from its net income the equity income for a subsidiary not consolidated for book or tax purposes where the net income is recorded by the parent under the equity method of accounting (generally ownership between 20 and 50 percent, where the ability to exercise significant influence is present). It must include, however, in net income dividends received from these subsidiaries.

- Since the adjusted net book income represents a pre-tax number, companies must add back all federal and foreign taxes. Conversely, since state and local taxes are deductible, they remain as expenses; no adjustment to net income is required. If a corporation deducts foreign taxes rather than taking a foreign tax credit, the current foreign provision is treated the same as state and local taxes.

- All intercompany transactions between a parent and its subsidiaries must be scrutinized for their impact on net income. Transactions eliminated in consolidation for financial statement purposes may have to be restored if the two companies in question do not file a consolidated tax return.

- Adjustments to net book income resulting from different book and tax year ends and short taxable years are required.

- Extraordinary items must be included in net book income, unless they are tax benefit items (e.g., an NOL utilization).

- If net book income includes a cumulative adjustment from an accounting method change, and the amount of the cumulative adjustment may be determined upon review of the financial statement (including footnotes or other supplementary disclosure), a company must adjust its net book income to exclude that portion of the cumulative adjustment related to taxable years beginning before 1987. If an accounting method change results in a restatement of a financial statement, other rules may apply.

- Footnote disclosure or other supplemental information may require an adjustment to net book income. If the disclosure is specifically authorized by GAAP or is in accordance with the taxpayer's historic practice (defined in the proposed regulations as used by the taxpayer in the previous two years prior to 1987), no adjustment to net book income is allowed. However, if the disclosure is not authorized by GAAP or is not in accordance with historic practice, net book income is adjusted—if the disclosure results in adjusted net book income greater than the amount reported on the taxpayer's financial statement.

  A corporation must increase its book income if its financial statements include disclosure that reflects the difference between GAAP income and income determined using tax accounting principles or disclosure that reconciles income determined under the accrual method to cash-basis income. However, the corporation makes the adjustment only when such a disclosure reflects more income than that reported on the financial statements.

- A corporation will increase book income when it has differences between ending and beginning equity accounts. Generally, no adjustment to net book income is allowed if the equity adjustment is specifically authorized by GAAP or is in accordance with the taxpayer's historic practice. The proposed regulations provide examples (for example, the equity adjustment required by FAS 52 regarding foreign translation gains). However, if GAAP does not authorize the adjustment, or the adjustment is not in accordance with historic practice, net book income will be increased by the amount that an equity adjustment increases shareholders' equity (as reported on the financial statement). The increase must relate to the taxpayer or a member of the taxpayer's consolidated group.

- A company must adjust consolidated net book income to include income or loss allocated to minority interests of consolidated tax group members.

- Special rules provide guidelines for financial statement amendments. For example, if because of an accounting error (1) a taxpayer restates net book income prior to the extended due date of its federal income tax return in what would have been its financial statement and (2) the restated financial statement has equal priority with the original financial statement, the restated financial statement is the taxpayer's applicable financial statement in computing the book income adjustment.

   However, if the financial statement is restated for reasons other than an accounting error, the taxpayer's applicable financial statement is the one with the greater amount of adjusted net book income. This rule is intended to prevent taxpayers from manipulating book income.

- If a taxpayer restates its financial statement after the last date that it could have filed its federal income tax return for the taxable year, it must adjust its net book income for the first succeeding year to reflect the cumulative effect of the restatement. Such an adjustment is required, however, only to the extent that it may be attributed to post-1986 taxable years.

When financial statement net income is adjusted to reflect these items, it is then compared to the pre-book AMTI before NOL. The tax preference item is 50 percent of the excess. Companies must calculate this excess even if one amount is negative. In other words, an excess will exist if there is adjusted book income compared to a pre-book alternative minimum taxable loss before NOL, or if there is an adjusted net book loss less than the pre-book alternative minimum taxable loss before NOL.

Exhibit A-2 illustrates the adjustments necessary to convert financial statement income into adjusted net book income.

[6] Adjusted Current Earnings

For taxable years beginning after 1989, ACE will replace adjusted net book income in the adjustment computations.

Adjusted current earnings essentially represents an adjusted AMTI—determined without the AMT NOL deduction.

Some of the adjustments (i.e., differences between ACE and AMTI) are outlined in Exhibit 9-4.

To compute the book income adjustment for years after 1989, a corporation will use 75 percent (increased from 50 percent) of excess ACE over AMTI —a positive adjustment.

When AMTI exceeds ACE, a corporation will use 75 percent of the excess to compute the adjustment—a negative adjustment. This negative amount, however, cannot exceed the aggregate net positive amount from prior years.

Finally, unlike the adjustment for 1987-1989, after 1989, when the adjustment is computed using ACE, the AMT resulting from the adjustment will not automatically qualify as a MTC. Instead, the taxpayer must classify each ACE adjustment item as a deferral or an exclusion item (see *Deferral Items*, ¶ A.03).

[7] Net Operating Losses

The final step in determining AMTI is the AMT NOL deduction. A corporation uses its current year AMT NOL deduction, if any,

EXHIBIT A-2
Computation of Adjusted Net Book Income for the Book Income Adjustment

Facts:

Company *P* is a calendar year, closely held corporation whose financial statements are audited annually, with ownership interests in the following corporations:

Company *A*	85%
Company *B*	53%
Company *C* (controlled foreign corporation)	95%
Company *D*	28%

A is included in *P*'s consolidated financial statement and tax return, with *B* and *C* consolidated for book purposes only, and *D* accounted for under the equity method.

The pretax income of each company and dividends paid to the parent company are as follows:

	Income (loss)	Dividends paid to P
Company *P* (consolidated)	$25,000,000 (1)	—
Company *A* (separate company)	2,000,000	$100,000
Company *B* (separate company)	(500,000)	50,000 (2)
Company *C* (separate company)	700,000	80,000 (3)
Company *D* (separate company)	4,000,000	200,000

(1) Net of minority interest.
(2) Assume sufficient accumulated E&P to afford the distribution dividend treatment.
(3) Net of foreign taxes withheld of $10,000.

Assume that intercompany profit was eliminated in consolidation on the sale of inventory from *P* to *B* totaling $14,000. Finally, the total tax provision reflected on the consolidated income statement was as follows:

Federal		
Current	$6,000,000	
Deferred	4,000,000	
Foreign	400,000	(4)
State and local	600,000	(5)
	$11,000,000	

(4) *P* expects to claim a foreign tax credit for the taxes paid and accrued during the year.
(5) For purposes of our example, assume all state and local tax is attributable to *P* and *A*.

Given these facts and assumptions, the transformation of financial statement net income to adjusted net book income for the book income adjustment is as follows:

Consolidated book net income	$14,000,000
Add:	
Federal tax provision	
Current	6,000,000
Deferred	4,000,000
Foreign tax provision	400,000
Less:	
C's separate company net income, net of 5% minority	
interest ($700,000 × 0.95)	(665,000)
D's separate company earnings reflected under the	
equity method ($4,000,000 × 0.28)	(1,120,000)
Add:	
A's minority interest ($2,000,000 × 0.15)	300,000
B's separate company net loss, net of 47% minority	
interest ($500,000 × 0.53)	265,000
Dividends	
Company *B*	50,000
Company *C* (grossed-up for $10,000 of foreign taxes	
withheld and $5,000 Section 78 gross-up)	95,000
Company *D*	200,000
Add:	
Recognition by *P* of intercompany profit	14,000
Adjusted net book income	$23,539,000

in lieu of its regular tax NOL deduction. However, the AMT NOL cannot offset more than 90 percent of AMTI before the NOL deduction.

Exhibit A-3 illustrates the AMT NOL deduction.

Generally, the AMT NOL for any post-1986 tax year is calculated in the same manner as for regular tax purposes. There are, however, two important exceptions. First, a company must make the normal adjustments to regular taxable income (loss) to compute AMTI. Second, the taxpayer reduces the regular tax NOL

EXHIBIT **A-3** _____
AMT NOL Deduction

	000's
Assumptions:	
AMTI before AMT NOL and book income adjustment	$ 7,000
Book income adjustment	$ 3,000
Pre-1987 AMT NOL carryover	$ 4,000
Post-1986 AMT NOL	$ 8,000
A. 90% limitation	
AMTI before NOL	$10,000
	× 90%
AMTI NOL limitation	$ 9,000
B. AMTI	
AMTI before AMT NOL and book income adjustment	$ 7,000
Book income adjustment	3,000
	10,000
NOL utilization (limited to $9,000):	
Pre-1987 NOL	4,000
Post-1986 AMT NOL	5,000 (9,000)
AMTI	$ 1,000

for all tax preference items (except for the charitable property preference).

EXAMPLE: In 1987, Company T had $20,000 of income and $35,000 of deductions and losses, resulting in a regular tax NOL of $15,000. If T had $10,000 of tax preference items included in the NOL amount, the AMT NOL for the year would be $5,000. Company T could carry over the $5,000 to reduce up to 90 percent of AMTI. If, in 1988, Company T had $20,000 of income subject to AMT before the NOL carryover, AMTI would be $15,000 (the 90 percent limitation would not apply).

A transitional rule allows a corporation to carry forward regular tax NOLs generated before enactment of TRA 1986 as AMT NOLs. It may use the NOLs (until fully utilized) in years in which it is subject to the AMT. An exception to this general rule applies, however, to corporations that had a deferred add-on minimum tax liability as a result of an NOL. Under a transitional rule, a corporate taxpayer will be forgiven the deferred add-on minimum tax liability. However, it must reduce the AMT NOL carried forward by the amount of the tax preferences that generated the deferred add-on minimum tax liability.

Conversely, if a regular tax NOL and AMT NOL are generated in a year beginning after 1986, and the regular tax NOL is carried back and used in a pre-AMT year, the AMT NOL is reduced by the amount of regular tax NOL utilized.

Finally, if a corporate taxpayer elects to forgo the carryback period, and carries forward the regular tax NOL, it must also carry forward the AMT NOL.

The transitional rule allowing forgiveness of a deferred add-on minimum tax liability, with the tax preferences that generated the liability reducing the AMT NOL, may present interesting opportunities. In this situation, the regular tax NOL will be greater than the AMT NOL. The company may be exposed to the AMT; if so, the tax preferences that generated a 15 percent add-on minimum tax may generate a 20 percent AMT. This may be desirable, however, if the AMT paid related to the NOL differential generates MTC, which is then eventually recouped as an offset against regular tax.

Also, if the potential AMT on the NOL differential never occurs (i.e., the AMT is avoided in the year(s) the NOL is utilized), the existing 1986 deferred add-on minimum tax is permanently forgiven.

¶ A.03 DEFERRAL PREFERENCES

The AMT adjustments represent part of the good news in the AMT system. The other good news is the MTC, which is discussed in detail later. The AMT system recognizes that most adjustments and tax preferences result in only a deferral of tax liability and not a permanent reduction in a corporation's tax payment. These are deferral items.

With deferral items, an increase in AMTI in an earlier year will ultimately reverse and result in a decrease in AMTI in a subsequent year. For example, when an asset depreciated under the MACRS method for regular tax purposes becomes fully depreciated, the alternative depreciation method will still produce a depreciation deduction for AMTI purposes. Also, when income is still recognized for regular tax purposes under the PCM, little or no income will be left to be recognized under the percentage-of-completion method in computing AMTI for that particular year. This is a "netting concept" because the adjustments represent *both* additions to and subtractions from regular taxable income.

The concept of adjustments and tax preferences only deferring tax is present in all AMT adjustments and tax preference items, except for the percentage depletion, appreciated property charitable contribution, private activity tax-exempt interest, and the special insurance company deduction items. These four items are exclusion items. Even the book income adjustment for pre-1990 years is considered a deferral item, although some of the differences between financial statement income and pre-book AMTI will not reverse (e.g., nonpreference tax-exempt interest and goodwill amortization).

¶ A.04 MINIMUM TAX CREDIT

Along with the netting concept, the MTC ensures that taxpayers do not entirely lose the benefit of certain adjustments and tax preferences. MTC is the total AMT paid, minus the AMT that

EXHIBIT A-4 _____
Minimum Tax Credit

	19X1 000's	19X2 000's
Book income	$8,000	$3,000
Schedule M's	(6,000)	3,000
A. Taxable income	$2,000	$6,000
Adjustments	2,000	(2,000)
Preferences (Deferral)	1,500	0
AMTI before book income adjustment	$5,500	$4,000
B. Book income adjustment		
($8,000—$5,500) × 0.50	1,250	
($3,000—$4,000) × 0.50		0
C. AMTI	$6,750	$4,000
Tax on taxable income (A) @ 34%	$ 680	$1,370*
TMT on AMTI (C) @ 20%	$1,350	$ 800
AMT	$ 670	$ 0
*Regular tax		$2,040
Minimum tax credit		(670)
Net regular tax		$1,370
PROOF:		
Cumulative taxable income	$8,000	
Cumulative tax liability	$2,720	
Effective tax rate	34%	

would have arisen if only exclusion items were present. In other words, MTC is allowed only for the AMT resulting from deferral items. This amount is carried forward indefinitely—although it cannot be carried back—as an offset against future years' regular tax. A company, however, can only reduce the regular tax to the TMT amount in the respective carryforward year.

Exhibit A-4 illustrates the MTC.

¶ A.05 AMT FOREIGN TAX CREDITS

Foreign taxes accrued or paid during the year may offset up to 90 percent of the TMT. Foreign taxes exceeding this 90 percent limitation are carried over or, in the case of an excess incurred after 1987, carried back, and may offset future (prior) years' TMT.

The ratio of foreign source AMTI to total AMTI determines the extent to which foreign taxes accrued or paid can offset TMT. The formula used in determining the AMT foreign tax credit is:

(A) Total foreign source AMTI / Total AMTI × Tentative
    Minimum tax = Tentative FTC
(B) TMT before FTC × 90% = FTC limitation
(C) AMT FTC = lesser of (A) or (B)

To determine foreign source AMTI, a corporate taxpayer must classify all adjustments and tax preferences reflected in AMTI as either foreign or U.S. source. This is based on the sourcing and allocation rules under the regular tax system. In most instances, taxpayers will compute different ratios of foreign source income to total income for AMT and regular tax purposes. This will result in different levels of FTC utilization and carryforwards for AMT and regular tax purposes.

TRA 1986 provides a special sourcing rule for the pre-1990 book income adjustment. That is, the ratio of foreign source pre-book AMTI to total pre-book alternative minimum taxable income will be used to determine the foreign sourcing of the book income adjustment. Post 1989 years, the elements of ACE will have to be distinguished as U.S. or foreign source for AMT FTC purposes.

Taxpayers may treat regular tax FTC carryovers from pre-1987 years as AMT FTC carryovers. However, post-1986 regular tax FTC carried back and used in pre-1987 years will reduce available post-1986 AMT FTC.

Exhibit A-5 illustrates the computation of the AMT FTC.

EXHIBIT A-5 _____
AMT FTC Offset

	000's
Assumptions:	
Regular tax (before FTC)	$ 3,000
FTC	(2,900)
Net regular tax	$ 100
TMT before FTC	$ 4,000
AMTI	$20,000
AMT foreign source income	$18,500
Available FTC	$ 5,000
No regular tax or AMT NOL	

A. Tentative FTC

$$\frac{\text{AMT foreign source income}}{\text{AMT Income}} \times \text{TMT}$$

$$\frac{\$18,500}{\$20,000} \times \$4,000 \qquad \$ \ 3,700$$

B. AMT before 10% limitation

TMT before FTC	$ 4,000
AMT FTC	(3,700)
	$ 300

C. 10% limitation

TMT before FTC	$ 4,000
	× 10%
	$ 400

D. TMT: Greater of B or C $ 400

E. AMT: TMT of $400 less regular tax of $100 $ 300

¶ A.06 AMT AND THE INVESTMENT TAX CREDIT

Although TRA 1986 repealed the ITC for years after 1985, investment credit allowed under the transitional rules and ITC carryover affect AMT computations.

The transitional and carryover ITCs, after the 35 percent reduction, are part of the general business credit. After the regular tax and the AMT have been computed, a total tax liability is determined. The general business credit is offset against this total tax liability. A special calculation is used to determine the ITC that can offset either the regular tax or the AMT.

When the regular tax exceeds the TMT, the investment credit will be allowed against the regular tax to the extent of the lesser of (1) $25,000 plus 75 percent of the excess of the regular tax over $25,000 or (2) the excess of regular tax over 75 percent of the TMT.

The ITC is the only credit allowed to offset regular tax lower than TMT.

When the TMT exceeds the regular tax, a company can use the ITC to offset up to 25 percent of the TMT. However, any resulting minimum tax credit carryforward is not affected by the ITC reduction.

Exhibit A-6 illustrates the investment credit offset against regular tax and AMT.

Note: This discussion is based on statute changes proposed in the Technical Correction Bills. This language provides a statute that correctly interprets Congress' intent with respect to ITC and the AMT.

¶ A.07 OTHER CONSIDERATIONS

As previously discussed, the AMT NOL, FTC, and ITC may not reduce the TMT below 10 percent of what it would be without

EXHIBIT A-6 _____
AMT and ITC

	1	2
Regular tax	$10,000,000	$ 0
TMT	$ 4,000,000	$ 4,000,000
ITC	$ 8,000,000	$ 2,000,000
ITC allowed		
$10,000,000—($4,000,000 × 0.75)	$ 7,000,000	
$4,000,000 × 0.25		$ 1,000,000

	3	4
AMTI (before NOL)	$10,000,000	$10,000,000
AMT NOL	0	$11,000,000 .
TMT (before credits)	$ 2,000,000	$ 200,000
FTC	$ 1,800,000	$ 0
TMT	$ 200,000	$ 200,000
Regular Tax	$10,000,000	$ 0
ITC	$ 8,000,000	$ 200,000
ITC allowed ($25,000 + 0.75 ($10,000,000 — $25,000))	$ 7,506,000	$ 0*

*No ITC allowed since TMT equals 2% (i.e., 20% × 10%) of AMTI before AMT NOL ($10,000,000 × 0.20 × 10).

Note: Based on proposed language in the Technical Correction Bills.

_____

consideration for these losses and credits. To calculate the limitation, the NOL is applied first, then FTC, and finally ITC.

In certain circumstances, a corporation can avoid tax preference treatment of a particular item by making a "normative election." For example, the tax preference for intangible drilling costs is the excess of intangible drilling or development costs over 65 percent of the net income from gas, oil, and geothermal properties. Excess intangible drilling costs is the excess of costs paid or incurred and deductible for regular tax purposes over the amount that would be allowable if such costs were capitalized and amortized over a 120-month period. A taxpayer making the normative election, which may be revoked only with the consent of the IRS, could deduct all or a part of the intangible drilling costs so elected over the 120-month period for regular tax purposes. This would eliminate the related AMT tax preference. This provision provides some flexibility to companies planning for the AMT.

The final change corporations need to address is that the AMT is subject to the estimated tax payment provisions. Since most corporations must pay at least 90 percent of their total tax liability via estimated tax payments to avoid the nondeductible underpayment penalty, this could prove troublesome.

AMT is a complex calculation, dependent on the regular tax and book income. Corporations must monitor their exposure to the AMT to avoid the underpayment penalty. Subjecting the AMT each quarter to the estimated tax provisions again establishes the AMT as a clear and definitive tax system that corporations will have to continually address.

¶ A.08 ENVIRONMENTAL TAX

Corporations with AMTI exceeding $2 million will pay a tax at the rate of 0.12 percent on AMTI above the $2 million threshold.

This tax is intended to apply only to corporations to which the new corporate AMT applies. A corporation, however, may be liable for the environmental tax, though not liable for the regular tax or AMT. The tax is effective for years beginning after 1986 and before 1992. As an excise tax, it is deductible for regular and alternative tax purposes, but not for environmental tax computations.

A corporation may not deduct a regular or AMT NOL to compute income subject to the environmental tax. Nor may it use tax credits to reduce the tax. In the case of a controlled group of corporations, only one $2 million threshold is allowed. The rules for estimated tax payments, penalties, and refunds applicable to corporate income taxes also apply to the environmental tax.

¶ A.09 PLANNING OBSERVATIONS

Corporations that can manage the timing of income, deductions, and occurrences of originating and reversing AMT adjustments and preferences will be in the best position to deal with the AMT. Except for AMT on exclusion items, the AMT cost is the time value of money. Accordingly, corporations must develop multiyear projections to identify the best way to manage the AMT.

Corporations with widely fluctuating income may be in a regular tax position in one year and subject to the AMT in the subsequent year. For instance, if book income remains constant while taxable income falls, a preference may result and lead to an AMT position. So, in many instances, the timing of a transaction or the recognition of income or deductions is critical to minimizing the AMT impact.

For example, if a company expects to be in an AMT position next year, the deferral of taxable income and acceleration of deductions (especially those that would be denied or reduced by the AMT system) is a planning strategy for the current year because of the rate differential between the regular tax rate and the AMT rate.

A company should consider what potential effect available alternatives within GAAP (for recognizing income and expenses for book purposes) might have on the book income adjustment. From a tax strategy standpoint, book and tax conformity should be a company's goal for AMT purposes. The closer book income is to taxable income, the less likely a book income adjustment will occur. Where available, refinement or change of accounting methods (e.g., revising the asset capitalization policy and/or depreciation methods/lives, or changing the LIFO pool mix or method of computation) may be the answer.

Companies must remember, however, that GAAP must be followed when planning to minimize the book income adjustment exposure. A company must justify a change in accounting principles as preferable. Before making a change in principle, a company should consider the long-term effect. If a change in principle can be currently justified as preferable, it may not be possible to justify a change back when ACE (instead of book income) is used to compute the adjustment.

When a company has a "priority four" financial statement (i.e., no SEC, audited or federal/state regulatory financial statement), it should consider whether the E&P alternative would be advantageous. Early election of the E&P approach will minimize the impact in 1990 when the adjusted current earnings concept takes effect.

With the top corporate rate higher than the top individual rate, many closely held corporations should consider the S corporation election. What is more, S corporations escape the "backstop" clutches of the book income adjustment. Partnerships and master limited partnerships also escape the book income adjustment.

Finally, a corporation should review the impact leasing may have on its AMT situation. It should make the traditional economic-based analysis of the lease-versus-buy decision (a comparison of the present values of the costs associated with buying and the after-tax lease payments). Though AMT complicates the decision, it does not offer a new loophole. However, because owning equipment will generally cost more for a corporation with AMT liability versus a corporation that only pays regular tax, the former may decide to lease new equipment.

The key to tax-oriented leasing is to maximize tax benefits by matching a lessor and lessee with appropriate facts and circumstances. For example, it may make sense to match a lessee that is subject to AMT with a lessor that is not. In such cases, companies subject to AMT may lease equipment from lessors who are able to use the depreciation writeoffs. The lessor may then pass a portion of the tax benefits on to the lessee in the form of lower rental rates.

¶ A.10 SUMMARY

The AMT is devised to tax a company's economic income. The AMT system further strikes several "hall of fame" tax deferral techniques, including the installment sales and completed contract methods of accounting. Also, by limiting the use of FTCs to offset the entire TMT, the corporate taxpayer may no longer fully use the double taxation shield to avoid U.S. tax.

Finally, the book income adjustment will force corporate taxpayers that report earnings to stockholders, creditors, and the public to pay a minimum level of federal income tax on such earnings. Corporations must exercise caution, however, when planning to minimize the book income adjustment item. The acceleration or deferral of book income must be within the constraints of GAAP.

The AMT system is now on equal footing with the regular tax system as a force to be reckoned with by corporate taxpayers. The separate determination of income (installment sales and long-term contracts) and deductions (depreciation), along with the "backstop" book income adjustment, will force every corporate taxpayer to address the AMT computation, if not pay the tax.

The introduction of the MTC, concurrent with the netting concept, will take some of the sting out of the AMT. These provisions, however, are small consolation. To take advantage of them acknowledges that either: (1) an AMT was remitted in a prior year with the MTC only getting the taxpayer even with Uncle Sam or (2) a reversal of a prior increase in AMTI is occurring, signaling that once again the taxpayer is only catching up.

A company in an AMT situation year after year will benefit little from the MTC. It should structure its affairs so that it will be in a regular tax paying position and utilize available MTCs. Exhibit A-7 illustrates how a closely held corporation should handle an AMT situation.

EXHIBIT A-7 _____
AMT Illustration

The following example will further assist in understanding the new AMT.

MN Company is a calendar year, closely held corporation that files a consolidated tax return with one other 85 percent owned domestic subsidiary. The company has a foreign subsidiary that remits a small dividend each year, net of foreign tax withheld. MN, the parent company, also has an exporting business that currently is not operated through a foreign sales corporation, which generates foreign sourse income.

The 85 percent owned subsidiary had three long-term contracts commencing early in 1988 with completion occurring late in 1989. No new contracts were started in 1989. The subsidiary utilized the PCM method for regular tax purposes. The AMT adjustment in 1988 recognizes the percentage-of-completion income on the contracts, while the 1989 adjustment reflects the netting of the smaller percentage of completion income for AMT purposes against the larger PCM income for regular tax purposes.

In 1988, financial statement income was higher than taxable income because of the Company's significant investment in municipal bonds and adjustable rate preferred stock, whose dividends were afforded the 80 percent dividends received deduction for tax purposes and the recognition for tax purposes of the loss and expenses associated with the disposal of an unprofitable division that was reserved for and expensed in 1987 for financial statement purposes.

In 1989, taxable income was greater than financial statement income because of the switch from municipal bonds and adjustable rate preferred stock to U.S. government instruments, the establishment for financial statement purposes of a sizeable reserve for contingencies associated with the three contracts started in 1988, and the goodwill amortization recognized for financial statements associated with the acquisition of stock of a new company on January 1.

	1988	1989
AMT computation		
Regular taxable income	$12,226,000	$23,236,000
AMT adjustments		
Excess of MACRS over alternative depreciation on property placed in service after 1986	1,806,190	1,423,810
Gain on sale of asset (greater AMT basis than regular tax basis)	(44,000)	(27,000)
Long-term contracts	4,115,000	(4,205,000)
Tax preference items		
Appreciated property contributions	20,000	10,000
Excess accelerated depreciation on real property placed in service before 1987	320,000	280,000
Pre-book AMTI	$18,443,190	$20,717,810

Book income adjustment

	1988	
Adjusted net income	$23,234,000	
Pre-book AMTI	(18,443,190)	
Excess	$ 4,790,810	
	× 50%	2,395,405

	1989	
Adjusted net income	$20,645,311	
Pre-book AMTI	(20,717,810)	
Excess	—	
	× 50%	

	1988	1989
AMT exemption amount	—	—
AMTI	$20,838,595	$20,717,810
	× 20%	× 20%
TMT before AMT credits	$4,167,719	$4,143,562
AMT FTC	(90,000)	(114,000)
TMT	$4,077,719*	$4,029,562
Regular tax (after credits of $100,000 in 1988 and $134,000 in 1989)	(4,056,840)	$7,766,240
AMT	$ 20,879	

		1988	1989
Minimum tax credit			
AMT		$ 20,879	
Regular taxable income	$12,226,000		
Exclusion preferences	20,000		
Exemption	—		
	$12,246,000		
AMT rate	× 20%		
TMT before credits on exclusion preferences	$ 2,449,200		
Credits	(90,000)		
TMT	$ 2,359,200		
Regular tax (net)	(4,056,840)		
AMT on exclusion preferences		—	
MTC carryover		$ 20,879	
Less MTC			(20,879)**
Regular tax after MTC			$7,745,361*

*Tax liability actually paid.

**No limitation since the excess of the regular tax ($7,766,240) over the TMT ($4,029,562) is greater than the MTC carryover.

As presented here, the MTC for 1988 is equal to the AMT amount of $20,879, as there would be no AMT arising from the separate exclusion preference computation.

Note: There would be a $22,606 (($20,838,595 — $2,000,000) × 0.12%) environmental tax liability in 1988 and $22,461 in 1989 (($20,717,810 — $2,000,000) × 0.12%).

The 1988 AMT is comprised of, or can be determined by the following analysis:

		Tax
AMT adjustments and tax preferences		
Pre-book AMTI	$18,443,190	
Less regular taxable income	(12,226,000)	
Sum of AMT adjustments and tax preferences	$ 6,217,190	
AMT rate	× 20%	$ 1,243,438

		Tax

Book income adjustment

Excess of adjusted net income (book) over pre-book AMTI	$ 4,790,810	
Effective AMT rate (50% × 20%)	× 10%	479,081

Rate differential on regular taxable income

Regular taxable income	$12,226,000	
Rate differential (34% — 20%)	× 14%	(1,711,640)

Foreign tax credit difference

Regular tax offset	$ 100,000	
AMT offset	(90,000)	10,000
AMT		$ 20,879

Statement of Financial Accounting Standards No. 96 Accounting for Income Taxes

CONTENTS

This reprint does not include Appendices B, C, and D to FASB Statement of Financial Accounting Standards No. 96: Accounting for Income Taxes, December 1987. These appendices are an integral part of the document.

Statement of Financial Accounting Standards No. 96

Accounting for Income Taxes

December 1987

INTRODUCTION

1. This Statement addresses financial accounting and reporting for the effects of **income taxes**[1] that result from an enterprise's activities during the current and preceding years. **Income taxes currently payable**[2] for a year are determined by tax laws and regulations. **Taxable income** is multiplied by a specified tax rate (or rates), and the product is increased by tax surcharges or decreased by tax credits. Taxable income is the excess of taxable revenues over tax deductible expenses and exemptions for the year as defined by the governmental taxing authority. In some tax jurisdictions, there may be more than one method or system for determining the amount of taxes currently payable.

2. Income taxes currently payable for a particular year usually include the **tax consequences** of most **events** that are recognized in the financial statements for that year. However, because some significant exceptions exist, income taxes currently payable for a year:

a. May include the tax consequences of some events recognized in financial statements for an earlier or later year
b. May not include the tax consequences of some other events recognized in financial statements for the current year.

3. APB Opinion No. 11, *Accounting for Income Taxes,* was issued in 1967. Several accounting pronouncements amended, interpreted, or supplemented Opinion 11. Some people have supported those accounting and reporting requirements for income taxes. Others have criticized and questioned the underlying con-

---

[1]Words that appear in the glossary are set in **boldface type** the first time they appear.

[2]References in this Statement to income taxes currently payable and (total) **income tax expense** are intended to include also **income taxes currently refundable** and (total) **income tax benefit,** respectively.

cepts, the complexity of the requirements, and the meaningfulness of the results. Critics have not agreed on any single alternative. In 1982, the Board added a project to its agenda to reconsider accounting for income taxes. This Statement is the result of that project.

STANDARDS OF FINANCIAL ACCOUNTING AND REPORTING

Scope

4. This Statement establishes standards of financial accounting and reporting for income taxes that are currently payable and for the tax consequences of:

a. Revenues, expenses, gains, or losses that are included in taxable income of an earlier or later year than the year in which they are recognized in financial income
b. Other events that create differences between the tax bases of assets and liabilities and their amounts for financial reporting
c. Operating loss or tax credit carrybacks for refunds of taxes paid in prior years and carryforwards to reduce taxes payable in future years.

This Statement supersedes Opinion 11. It also supersedes or amends other accounting pronouncements listed in Appendix D.

5. The principles and requirements of this Statement are applicable to:

a. Domestic federal (national) income taxes (U.S. federal income taxes for U.S. enterprises) and foreign, state, and local (including franchise) taxes based on income
b. An enterprise's[3] domestic and foreign operations that are consolidated, combined, or accounted for by the equity method
c. Foreign enterprises in preparing financial statements in accordance with U.S. generally accepted accounting principles.

---

[3]The term *enterprise* is used throughout this Statement because accounting for income taxes is primarily an issue for business enterprises. However, the requirements of this Statement apply to a not-for-profit organization's activities that are subject to income taxes.

6. This Statement does not address:

a. The method of accounting for the U.S. federal investment tax credit (ITC) and for foreign, state, and local investment tax credits or grants (The deferral and flow-through methods as set forth in APB Opinions No. 2 and No. 4, *Accounting for the "Investment Credit,"* continue to be acceptable methods to account for the U.S. federal ITC.)
b. Discounting (Paragraph 6 of APB Opinion No. 10, *Omnibus Opinion—1966,* addresses that subject.)
c. Allocation of income taxes among components of a business enterprise (other than the disclosures required by this Statement)
d. Accounting for income taxes in interim periods (other than the effect of an enacted change in tax laws or rates). (APB Opinion No. 28, *Interim Financial Reporting,* and other accounting pronouncements address that subject.)

Basic Principles

7. The objective of accounting for income taxes is to recognize the amount of current and deferred taxes payable or refundable at the date of the financial statements (a) as a result of all events that have been recognized in the financial statements and (b) as measured by the provisions of enacted tax laws. To implement that objective, all of the following basic principles[4] are applied in accounting for income taxes at the date of the financial statements:

a. A current or **deferred tax liability or asset** is recognized for the current or deferred tax consequences of all events that have been recognized in the financial statements;
b. The current or deferred tax consequences of an event are measured based on provisions of the enacted tax law to determine the amount of taxes payable or refundable currently or in future years; and
c. The tax consequences of earning income or incurring losses or expenses in future years or the future enactment of a change in tax laws or rates are not anticipated for purposes of recognition and measurement of a deferred tax liability or asset.

---

[4]The only exceptions in applying those basic principles are identified in paragraph 8.

Generally accepted accounting principles specify the timing of recognition of events in financial statements, and the tax consequences of events[5] (as measured by the provisions of enacted tax laws) are recognized when the events are recognized in financial statements. Events that have not been recognized at the date of the financial statements under generally accepted accounting principles may affect the eventual tax consequences of other events that have been recognized at that date. However, those tax effects are recognized when the events that cause them are recognized under generally accepted accounting principles.

8. The only exceptions in applying those basic principles are that this Statement (a) does not amend the requirements for recognition of deferred taxes for the areas addressed by APB Opinion No. 23, *Accounting for Income Taxes—Special Areas,* (b) does not address recognition of deferred taxes for deposits in statutory reserve funds by U.S. steamship enterprises, (c) does not amend accounting for leveraged leases as required by FASB Statement No. 13, *Accounting for Leases,* and FASB Interpretation No. 21, *Accounting for Leases in a Business Combination,* and (d) prohibits recognition of a deferred tax liability or asset related to goodwill (paragraph 23).

Temporary Differences

9. The tax consequences of most events recognized in the current year's financial statements are included in determining income taxes currently payable. However, because tax laws and financial accounting standards differ in their recognition and measurement of assets, liabilities, equity, revenues, expenses, gains, and losses, differences arise between the following:

a. The amount of taxable income and pretax financial income for a year
b. The tax bases of assets or liabilities and their reported amounts in financial statements.

10. An assumption inherent in an enterprise's statement of financial position prepared in accordance with generally accepted accounting principles is that the reported amounts of assets and liabilities will be recovered and settled, respectively.[6]

---

[5]Some events do not have tax consequences. Certain revenues are exempt from taxation and certain expenses are not deductible. In the United States, for example, interest earned on certain municipal obligations is not taxable and fines are not deductible.

[6]References to **assumptions inherent in a statement of financial position prepared in accordance with generally accepted accounting principles** occur frequently in this Statement. That concept and its application have a significant effect on the accounting for the tax consequences of an event.

Because of that assumption, a difference between the tax basis of an asset or a liability and its reported amount in the statement of financial position will result in taxable or deductible amounts in some future year without regard to other future events. Examples follow:

a. *Revenues or gains that are taxable after they are recognized in financial income.* An asset (for example, a receivable from an installment sale) may be recognized for revenues or gains that will result in future taxable amounts when the asset is recovered.

b. *Expenses or losses that are deductible after they are recognized in financial income.* A liability (for example, a product warranty liability) may be recognized for expenses or losses that will result in future tax deductible amounts when the liability is settled.

c. *Revenues or gains that are taxable before they are recognized in financial income.* A liability (for example, subscriptions received in advance) may be recognized for an advance payment for goods or services to be provided in future years. For tax purposes, the advance payment is included in taxable income upon the receipt of cash. Future sacrifices to provide goods or services (or future refunds to those who cancel their orders) will result in future tax deductible amounts when the liability is settled.

d. *Expenses or losses that are deductible before they are recognized in financial income.* The cost of an asset (for example, depreciable personal property) may have been deducted for tax purposes faster than it was depreciated for financial reporting. Amounts received upon future recovery of the amount of the asset for financial reporting will exceed the remaining tax basis of the asset, and the excess will be taxable when the asset is recovered.

e. *A reduction in the tax basis of depreciable assets because of tax credits.*[7] Amounts received upon future recovery of the amount of the asset for financial reporting will exceed the remaining tax basis of the asset, and the excess will be taxable when the asset is recovered.

f. *ITC accounted for by the deferral method.* Under Opinion 2, ITC is viewed and accounted for as a reduction of the cost of the related asset (even though, for financial statement presentation, deferred ITC may be reported as deferred income). Amounts received upon future recovery of the reduced cost of the asset for financial reporting will be less than the tax basis of the asset, and the difference will be tax deductible when the asset is recovered.

---

[7]The Tax Equity and Fiscal Responsibility Act of 1982 provides taxpayers with the choice of either (a) taking the full amount of Accelerated Cost Recovery System (ACRS) deductions and a reduced tax credit (that is, investment tax credit and certain other tax credits) or (b) taking the full tax credit and a reduced amount of ACRS deductions.

g. *Foreign operations for which the reporting currency is the functional currency.*
Under FASB Statement No. 52, *Foreign Currency Translation,* certain assets
and liabilities are remeasured from the foreign currency into U.S. dollars using
historical exchange rates when the reporting currency is the functional currency.
After a change in exchange rates, there will be a difference between the foreign
tax basis and the foreign currency equivalent of the U.S. dollar historical cost of
those assets and liabilities. That difference will be taxable or deductible for foreign tax purposes when the reported amounts of the assets and liabilities are recovered and settled, respectively.

h. *An increase in the tax basis of assets because of indexing for inflation.* The tax
law for a particular tax jurisdiction might require adjustment of the tax basis of
a depreciable (or other) asset for the effects of inflation. The inflation-adjusted
tax basis of the asset would be used to compute future tax deductions for depreciation or to compute gain or loss on sale of the asset. Amounts received upon
future recovery of the amount of the asset for financial reporting will be less
than the remaining tax basis of the asset, and the difference will be tax deductible when the asset is recovered.

i. *Business combinations accounted for by the purchase method.* There may be
differences between the assigned values and the tax bases of the assets and liabilities recognized in a business combination accounted for as a purchase under
APB Opinion No. 16, *Business Combinations.* Those differences will result in
taxable or deductible amounts when the reported amounts of the assets and liabilities are recovered and settled, respectively.

The following example illustrates two of the above situations. The amount
of an enterprise's depreciable assets reported in its financial statements is
$1,500, and their tax basis is $900. The $600 difference might be attributable
to accelerated deductions for tax purposes or to an excess of assigned value if
the assets were acquired in a business combination accounted for by the purchase method. Future recovery of the $1,500 reported amount of the depre-
ciable assets will result in $600 of taxable amounts in future years because the
tax basis of those assets is only $900.

	Financial Reporting	Tax Return
Income before depreciation	$1,500	$1,500
Depreciation	1,500	900
Income before taxes (or taxable income)	$ —	$ 600

---

11. Examples (a)-(d) in paragraph 10 pertain to revenues, expenses, gains, or losses that are included in taxable income of an earlier or later year than the year in which they are recognized in financial income. Those differences between taxable income and pretax financial income also create differences (sometimes accumulating over more than one year) between the tax basis of an asset or liability and its reported amount in the financial statements. Examples (e)-(i) pertain to other events that create differences between the tax basis of an asset or liability and its reported amount in the financial statements. For all nine examples, the differences result in taxable or deductible amounts when the reported amount of an asset or liability in the financial statements is recovered or settled, respectively. This Statement refers collectively to the types of differences illustrated by those nine examples and to the ones described in paragraph 12 as **temporary differences.**[8]

12. Some temporary differences cannot be identified with a particular asset or liability for financial reporting. One example is a long-term contract that is accounted for by the percentage-of-completion method for financial reporting and by the completed-contract method for tax purposes. The temporary difference (income on the contract) is deferred income for tax purposes that becomes taxable when the contract is completed. Another example is organizational costs that are recognized as expenses when incurred for financial reporting if, for tax purposes, the costs are deferred and deducted in a later year. In both instances, there is no related, identifiable asset or liability for financial reporting but there is a temporary difference that results from an event that has been recognized in the financial statements, and based on provisions in the tax law, the temporary difference will result in taxable or deductible amounts in future years.

13. The amount actually recovered for a particular asset or paid to settle a particular liability in a subsequent year may be different from the amount recognized for financial reporting in the current year. If so, the tax consequences of recovering that asset or settling that liability may also be an amount that is different from the amount of tax consequences recognized in the current year. That change in the tax

---

[8]The meaning of *temporary differences* in this Statement is different from the meaning of *timing differences* in Opinion 11. By definition, timing differences are differences between the periods in which transactions affect taxable income and the periods in which they enter into the determination of pretax accounting income. As such, timing differences are limited to the situations illustrated in examples (a)-(d) in paragraph 10 and exclude other differences such as the situations in examples (e)-(i) in paragraph 10. Temporary differences include all existing differences that will result in taxable or deductible amounts in future years.

consequences (a) would be the result of a gain or loss from future recovery or settlement (or adjustment) of that asset or liability and (b) would be recognized when that gain or loss is recognized.

Recognition and Measurement

14. A liability or asset shall be recognized for the **deferred tax consequences** of all[9] temporary differences, that is, the amount of taxes payable or refundable in future years as a result of the deferred tax consequences (as measured by the provisions of enacted tax laws) of events recognized in financial statements in the current or preceding years. The recognition and measurement of a deferred tax liability or asset shall not assume any taxable or deductible amounts in future years as a result of events that have not been recognized in the financial statements at the end of the current year.

15. Incurring losses or generating profits in future years are future events that are not recognized in financial statements for the current year and are not inherently assumed in financial statements for the current year. Those future events shall not be anticipated, regardless of probability, for purposes of recognizing and measuring a deferred tax liability or asset in the current year. The tax consequences of those future events shall be recognized and reported in financial statements in future years when the events occur.

16. **Deferred tax expense or benefit** shall be recognized for the net change during the year in an enterprise's deferred tax liability or asset.[10] That amount together with income taxes currently payable or refundable is the total amount of income tax expense or benefit for the year. Income tax expense or benefit for the year shall be allocated among continuing operations, discontinued operations, extraordinary items, the cumulative effect of accounting changes, prior period adjustments, **gains and losses included in comprehensive income but excluded from net income,** and capital transactions.

---

[9]Refer to paragraph 8. A deferred tax liability shall be recognized for the temporary differences addressed by Opinion 23 in accordance with the requirements of that Opinion, as amended. The indefinite reversal criteria of that Opinion apply only to the temporary differences addressed by Opinion 23 and to deposits in statutory reserve funds by U.S. steamship enterprises and shall not be applied to analogous types of temporary differences.

[10]Paragraph 44 addresses the manner of reporting the transaction gain or loss that is included in the net change in a deferred foreign tax liability or asset when the reporting currency is the functional currency.

Annual Computation of a Deferred Tax Liability or Asset

17. In concept, this Statement requires determination of the amount of taxes payable or refundable in each future year as if a tax return were prepared for the net amount of temporary differences that will result in taxable or deductible amounts in each of those years. That concept is illustrated by the following procedures. If alternative tax systems exist, those procedures are applied in a manner consistent with the tax law. The procedures are applied separately for each tax jurisdiction.

a. Estimate the particular future years in which temporary differences will result in taxable or deductible amounts.
b. Determine the *net* taxable or deductible amount in each future year.
c. Deduct **operating loss carryforwards for tax purposes** (as permitted or required by tax law) from net taxable amounts that are scheduled to occur in the future years included in the loss carryforward period.
d. Carry back or carry forward (as permitted or required by law) net deductible amounts occurring in particular years to offset net taxable amounts that are scheduled to occur in prior or subsequent years.

Deferred Tax Assets

e. Recognize a deferred tax asset for the tax benefit of net deductible amounts that could be realized by loss carryback from future years (1) to reduce a current deferred tax liability and (2) to reduce taxes paid in the current or a prior year. (No asset is recognized for any additional net deductible amounts in future years.)

Deferred Tax Liabilities

f. Calculate the amount of tax for the remaining net taxable amounts that are scheduled to occur in each future year by applying presently enacted tax rates and laws for each of those years to the type and amount of net taxable amounts scheduled for those years.
g. Deduct **tax credit carryforwards for tax purposes** (as permitted or required by law) from the amount of tax (calculated above) for future years that are included in the carryforward periods. (No asset is recognized for any additional amount of tax credit carryforward.)
h. Recognize a deferred tax liability for the remaining amount of taxes payable for each future year.

Tax-Planning Strategies

i. **Tax-planning strategies** that meet certain criteria (paragraph 19) are used for purposes of *estimating the years* in which temporary differences will result in taxable or deductible amounts (step (a) above). By applying such a strategy:

(1) Amounts may become deductible in a different year and thereby provide a tax benefit by offsetting (step (d)) or by loss carryback (step (e)).
(2) Amounts may become taxable in a different year before a loss or tax credit carryforward expires (steps (c) and (g)) or in a particular year that maximizes the benefit of tax credits, for example, foreign tax credits (steps (f) or (g)).

18. In practice, the following approach sometimes may reduce the extent of scheduling and the detailed calculations described above for some tax jurisdictions.

a. Identify the type and nature of an enterprise's temporary differences.
b. For each type of temporary difference, determine whether the tax law precludes or effectively precludes tax-planning strategies that would change the particular future years in which temporary differences will result in taxable or deductible amounts.
c. For types of temporary differences for which the tax law precludes or effectively precludes tax-planning strategies, scheduling or other procedures may be necessary to determine whether deductible amounts in future years offset taxable amounts.
d. For all other types of temporary differences, determine whether there is a tax-planning strategy that meets the criteria of paragraph 19, and if there is, those temporary differences may be offset for deferred tax calculations.

Criteria for Tax-Planning Strategies

19. Measurement of a deferred tax liability or asset shall take into account tax-planning strategies that would change the particular future years in which temporary differences result in taxable or deductible amounts. Tax-planning strategies either reduce the recognized amount of taxes payable for net taxable amounts in future years or increase the recognized amount of tax benefits for net deductible amounts in future years. A tax-planning strategy (including elections for tax purposes that are required or permitted by the tax law) shall meet both of the following criteria:

a. It must be a prudent and feasible strategy over which management has discretion and control. Management must have both the ability and the intent to implement the strategy, if necessary, to reduce taxes.
b. It cannot involve significant cost to the enterprise, that is, significant expenses to implement the underlying transaction or significant losses as a result of changing the particular future years in which an asset is recovered or a liability is settled. The tax benefit derived from the strategy shall not be viewed as a

reduction of the cost of the strategy for the purpose of determining whether that strategy gives rise to a significant cost.

An Enacted Change in Tax Laws or Rates

20. A deferred tax liability or asset shall be adjusted for the effect of a change in tax law or rates. The effect shall be included in income from continuing operations for the period that includes the enactment date.

A Change in the Tax Status of an Enterprise

21. An enterprise's tax status may change from nontaxable to taxable. An example is a change from a partnership to a corporation. Temporary differences may be created or eliminated at the date of the change in tax status. A deferred tax liability shall be recognized for temporary differences in accordance with the requirements of this Statement at the date that a nontaxable enterprise becomes a taxable enterprise. A deferred tax liability or asset shall be eliminated at the date an enterprise ceases to be a taxable enterprise. The effect of recognizing or eliminating the deferred tax liability or asset shall be included in income from continuing operations.

Regulated Enterprises

22. Regulated enterprises that meet the criteria for application of FASB Statement No. 71, *Accounting for the Effects of Certain Types of Regulation,* are not exempt from the requirements of this Statement. Specifically, this Statement:

a. Prohibits net-of-tax accounting and reporting
b. Requires recognition of a deferred tax liability (1) for tax benefits that are flowed through to customers when temporary differences originate and (2) for the equity component of the allowance for funds used during construction
c. Requires adjustment of a deferred tax liability or asset for an enacted change in tax laws or rates.

If it is probable that the future increase or decrease in taxes payable for items (b) and (c) above will be recovered from or returned to customers through future rates, an asset or liability shall be recognized for that probable future revenue or reduction in future revenue pursuant to paragraphs 9-11 of Statement 71. That asset or liability also is a temporary difference, and a deferred tax liability or asset shall be recognized for the deferred tax consequences of that temporary difference.

Business Combinations

23. A deferred tax liability or asset shall be recognized in accordance with the requirements of this Statement for differences between the assigned values and the tax bases of the assets and liabilities (except goodwill, unallocated "negative goodwill," and leveraged leases) recognized in a purchase business combination. If not recognized at the acquisition date, the tax benefits of an acquired **operating loss or tax credit carryforward for financial reporting** that are recognized in financial statements after the acquisition date shall (a) first be applied to reduce to zero any goodwill and other noncurrent intangible assets related to the acquisition and (b) next be recognized as a reduction of income tax expense.

Financial Statement Presentation and Disclosure

24. A deferred tax liability or asset shall be classified in two categories—the current amount and the noncurrent amount—in a classified statement of financial position. The current amount of a deferred tax liability or asset shall be the net deferred tax consequences of:

a. Temporary differences that will result in net taxable or deductible amounts during the next year
b. Temporary differences related to an asset or liability that is classified for financial reporting as current because of an operating cycle that is longer than one year
c. Temporary differences for which there is no related, identifiable asset or liability for financial reporting (paragraph 12) whenever *other* related assets and liabilities are classified as current because of an operating cycle that is longer than one year.

Deferred tax liabilities and assets attributable to different tax jurisdictions shall not be offset. The types of temporary differences that give rise to significant portions of a deferred tax liability or asset shall be disclosed. A **public enterprise** that is not subject to income taxes because its income is taxed directly to its owners shall disclose that fact and the net difference between the tax bases and the reported amounts of the enterprise's assets and liabilities.

25. The following information shall be disclosed whenever a deferred tax liability is not recognized for any of the areas addressed by Opinion 23 or for deposits in statutory reserve funds by U.S. steamship enterprises:

a. A description of the types of temporary differences for which a deferred tax liability has not been recognized and the types of events that would cause those temporary differences to become taxable

b. The cumulative amount of each type of temporary difference

c. The amount of the unrecognized deferred tax liability for any unremitted earnings if determination of that liability is practicable or a statement that determination is not practicable and the amount of withholding taxes that would be payable upon remittance of those earnings

d. The amount of the unrecognized deferred tax liability for temporary differences other than unremitted earnings (that is, the bad debt reserve of a stock or mutual savings and loan association or a mutual savings bank, the policyholders' surplus of a life insurance enterprise, and the statutory reserve funds of a U.S. steamship enterprise).

26. The amount of income tax expense or benefit allocated to continuing operations, discontinued operations, extraordinary items, the cumulative effect of accounting changes, prior period adjustments, gains and losses included in comprehensive income but excluded from net income, and capital transactions shall be disclosed for each year for which those items are presented.

27. The significant components of income tax expense attributable to continuing operations for each year presented shall be disclosed in the financial statements or notes thereto. Those components would include, for example:

a. **Current tax expense[11] or benefit**

b. Deferred tax expense or benefit, exclusive of (f) below

c. Investment tax credits

d. Government grants (to the extent recognized as a reduction of income tax expense)

e. The benefits of operating loss carryforwards

f. Adjustments of a deferred tax liability or asset for enacted changes in tax laws or rates or a change in the tax status of an enterprise.

---

[11] Interest and penalties assessed on income tax deficiencies (underpayment or improper computation) shall not be reported as income tax expense.

28. The reported amount of income tax expense attributable to continuing operations for the year shall be reconciled (using percentages or dollar amounts) to the amount of income tax expense that would result from applying domestic federal statutory tax rates to pretax income from continuing operations. The "statutory" tax rates shall be the regular tax rates if there are alternative tax systems. The estimated amount and the nature of each significant reconciling item shall be disclosed. A **nonpublic enterprise** shall disclose the nature of significant reconciling items but may omit a numerical reconciliation.

29. The amounts and expiration dates (or a reasonable aggregation of expiration dates) of operating loss and tax credit carryforwards for financial reporting (that is, amounts not already recognized as reductions of a deferred tax liability) and for tax purposes (that is, amounts available to reduce taxes payable on tax returns in future years) shall be disclosed. An operating loss carryforward for financial reporting includes the amount of future tax deductions (temporary differences) for which a tax benefit has not been recognized in the financial statements. If significant, the amount of net operating loss or tax credit carryforwards for which any tax benefits will be applied to reduce goodwill and other noncurrent intangible assets (of an acquired enterprise) shall be disclosed separately.

30. An enterprise that is part of a group that files a consolidated tax return shall disclose in its separately issued financial statements:

a. The amount of current and deferred tax expense for each statement of earnings presented and the amount of any tax-related balances due to or from affiliates as of the date of each statement of financial position presented
b. The principal provisions of the method by which the consolidated amount[12] of current and deferred tax expense is allocated to members of the group and the nature and effect of any changes in that method (and in determining related balances to or from affiliates) during the years for which the disclosures in (a) above are presented.

---

[12]The *consolidated amount* is the amount of current and deferred taxes reported in the consolidated financial statements for the group, or the amount that would be reported if such financial statements were prepared. The sum of the amounts allocated to members of the group (net of consolidation eliminations) shall equal the consolidated amount.

Application of the Standards to Specific Aspects of Accounting for Income Taxes

31. Appendix A provides additional discussion and illustrations of how the provisions of this Statement shall be applied to specific aspects of accounting for income taxes. Appendix A constitutes an integral part of the requirements of this Statement.

Effective Date and Transition

32. This Statement shall be effective for fiscal years beginning after December 15, 1988. Earlier application is encouraged. Financial statements for fiscal years before the effective date may be restated to conform to the provisions of this Statement. Initial application of this Statement shall be as of the beginning of an enterprise's fiscal year.

33. For the earliest year restated or for the year this Statement is first adopted if no prior year is restated, the effect of applying this Statement on the amount of deferred tax charges or credits at the beginning of the fiscal year shall be reported as the effect of a change in accounting principle in a manner similar to the cumulative effect of a change in accounting principle as described in paragraph 20 of APB Opinion No. 20, *Accounting Changes,* except for any effects of the type required by this Statement to be excluded from net income (for example, refer to paragraph 54 for the manner of reporting certain tax benefits subsequent to a quasi reorganization). Those latter effects shall be recognized in a manner consistent with the reporting requirements of this Statement. If the earliest year restated is not presented in the financial statements, the beginning balance of retained earnings (and, if necessary, any other components of stockholders' equity) for the earliest year presented shall be adjusted for the effect of the restatement as of that date. Pro forma effects of retroactive application (Opinion 20, paragraph 21) are not required if statements of earnings presented for prior years are not restated.

34. When initially presented, the financial statements for the year this Statement is first adopted shall disclose:

a. The effect of adopting this Statement on income from continuing operations, income before extraordinary items, and on net income (and on related per share amounts) for the year of adoption if restated financial statements for the prior year are not presented
b. The effect of any restatement on income from continuing operations, income before extraordinary items, and on net income (and on related per share amounts) for each year presented.

35. If financial statements for prior years are restated, all purchase business combinations that were consummated in those prior years shall be remeasured in accordance with the requirements of this Statement. A purchase business combination consummated prior to the beginning of the earliest year restated or prior to the year for which this Statement is first applied (if no prior year is restated) shall not be remeasured, and the remaining balances of any assets and liabilities recognized in that purchase business combination shall not be adjusted to pretax amounts (that is, any remaining amounts that were originally assigned on a net-of-tax basis pursuant to paragraph 89 of Opinion 16 shall not be adjusted). Except for leveraged leases, any differences between those remaining balances and their tax bases are temporary differences, and a deferred tax liability or asset shall be recognized for those temporary differences pursuant to the requirements of this Statement as of the beginning of the year for which this Statement is first applied. The effect of that adjustment shall be included in the effect of initially applying this Statement and reported in accordance with the provisions of paragraph 33.

36. Some regulated enterprises that meet the criteria for application of Statement 71 have accounted for construction in progress on a net-of-tax or after-tax basis. Upon initial application of this Statement, those enterprises shall adjust the reported amount of construction in progress to the amount that would have resulted from applying the requirements of this Statement to that construction in progress in all prior years. The reported amount of plant in service at the beginning of the earliest year restated or at the beginning of the year for which this Statement is first applied (if no prior year is restated) shall not be adjusted. Any difference between the reported amount and the tax basis of that plant in service is a temporary difference, and a deferred tax liability shall be recognized for that temporary difference. If it is probable that amounts required for settlement of that deferred tax liability will be recovered from customers through future rates, an asset and the related deferred tax liability for that additional temporary difference shall be recognized for that probable future revenue. Any net effect of applying the provisions of this paragraph shall be included in the effect of initially applying this Statement and reported in accordance with the provisions of paragraph 33.

**The provisions of this Statement need
not be applied to immaterial items.**

Appendix A

APPLICATION OF THE STANDARDS TO SPECIFIC ASPECTS OF ACCOUNTING FOR INCOME TAXES

CONTENTS

Appendix A

APPLICATION OF THE STANDARDS TO SPECIFIC ASPECTS OF ACCOUNTING FOR INCOME TAXES

Introduction

37. This appendix provides additional discussion and examples that illustrate application of the standards to specific aspects of accounting for income taxes. This appendix constitutes an integral part of the requirements of this Statement.

Recognition of a Deferred Tax Liability or Asset

Deferred Tax Liability

38. A liability is recognized for the deferred tax consequences of temporary differences that will result in *net* taxable amounts in future years. Provisions in the tax law may permit or require that net deductions in a particular year offset net taxable amounts in certain earlier or later years.[13] On that basis, determination of the net taxable or deductible amount in each future year is as follows:

a. Deductible amounts in future years offset amounts that become taxable in the same future years.
b. Loss carryback of net deductions for a particular future year offsets net taxable amounts in certain preceding years.
c. Loss carryforward of net deductions for a particular future year offsets net taxable amounts in certain succeeding years.

A deferred tax liability is recognized for the aggregate amount of income taxes payable on net taxable amounts in each future year.

---

[13]The discussion and examples in this appendix assume that the tax law requires offsetting net deductions in a particular year against net taxable amounts in the 3 preceding years and then in the 15 succeeding years. Assumptions in this appendix regarding the tax law are for illustrative purposes only. The enacted tax law for a particular tax jurisdiction should be used for recognition and measurement of a deferred tax liability or asset.

The following example illustrates offsetting. At the end of year 1, the reported amount of an enterprise's installment receivables is $3,300, and the tax basis of those receivables is $1,800. An assumption inherent in the enterprise's statement of financial position for year 1 is that the $3,300 reported amount of installment receivables will be recovered in future years. Future recovery of the $3,300 reported amount will result in $1,500 ($3,300 − $1,800) of taxable amounts ($300 per year in years 2-6). In addition, at the end of year 1, a $1,300 liability for estimated expenses has been recognized in the financial statements, and those expenses will be deductible for tax purposes in year 5 when the liability is expected to be paid. Those two temporary differences are estimated to result in taxable or deductible amounts in future years as presented below.

	Year 2	Year 3	Year 4	Year 5	Year 6
Taxable amounts	$300	$300	$300	$ 300	$300
Deductible amount	—	—	—	(1,300)	—
	300	300	300	(1,000)	300
Loss carryback	(300)	(300)	(300)	900	—
Loss carryforward	—	—	—	100	(100)
Net taxable amount	$ —	$ —	$ —	$ —	$200

The $1,300 deductible amount in year 5:

a. Offsets the $300 that becomes taxable in year 5
b. Offsets (by loss carryback) the $900 that becomes taxable in years 2-4
c. Offsets (by loss carryforward) $100 of the $300 that becomes taxable in year 6.

Assuming a 40 percent tax rate, a net deferred tax liability for $80 ($200 at 40 percent) is recognized at the end of year 1.

Deferred Tax Asset

39. Tax deductions provide a tax benefit only by offsetting amounts that are taxable. Temporary differences sometimes will result in deductible amounts that either exceed or cannot offset (based on loss carryback and carryforward provisions in the tax law) taxable amounts in past or future years. A net deferred tax asset is rec-

ognized for the deferred tax consequences of net deductible amounts in future years only to the extent that a tax benefit could be realized (based on loss carryback provisions in the tax law) by refund of taxes paid in the current or a prior year. Any additional net deductible amounts in future years are, in substance, the same as operating loss carryforwards.

The following example illustrates recognition of a net deferred tax asset for temporary differences. Year 1, the current year, is an enterprise's first year of operations. The enterprise has a pretax financial loss and taxable income for year 1. The reconciliation between those two amounts is as follows:

Pretax financial loss	$ (100)
Estimated expenses that will be deductible for tax purposes when paid	2,000
Installment sale gain taxable when the receivables are collected	(1,200)
Taxable income	$ 700

At the end of year 1, the reported amount of the enterprise's installment receivables in the financial statements is $3,000, and the tax basis of those receivables is $1,800. Future recovery of the reported amount of the installment receivables will result in $1,200 of taxable amounts ($300 per year in years 2-5). Also, a $2,000 liability for estimated expenses has been recognized in the financial statements in year 1, and those expenses will be deductible in year 4 when the liability is expected to be paid.

Those two temporary differences are estimated to result in taxable or deductible amounts in future years (years 2-5) as presented below.

	Current Year	Year 2	Year 3	Year 4	Year 5
Taxable income	$700	$ —	$ —	$ —	$ —
Taxable amounts	—	300	300	300	300
Deductible amount	—	—	—	(2,000)	—
	700	300	300	(1,700)	300
Loss carryback	(700)	(300)	(300)	1,300	—
Loss carryforward	—	—	—	300	(300)
Net operating loss carryforward	$ —	$ —	$ —	$ (100)	$ —

The $2,000 deductible amount in year 4:

a. Offsets (by loss carryback and carryforward) the $1,200 of taxable amounts ($300 per year) in years 2-5
b. Offsets (by loss carryback) the $700 of taxable income in the current year
c. Gives rise to a $100 net deductible amount in year 4 that does not offset taxable amounts in any year.

At the end of year 1, the enterprise:

a. Recognizes taxes currently payable for $700 of taxable income in year 1
b. Recognizes a net deferred tax asset for the deferred tax benefit of $700 of deductions in year 4 that offset (by loss carryback procedures) taxable income for the current year
c. Does not recognize a tax benefit for the $100 net deductible amount (in year 4) that, in substance, is the same as an operating loss carryforward.

Offset of Taxable and Deductible Amounts

40. The tax law determines whether temporary differences that will result in taxable and deductible amounts in future years may be offset against each other. For example, if the tax law provides that capital losses are deductible only to the extent of capital gains, temporary differences that will result in future deductions in the

form of capital losses cannot be offset against temporary differences that will result in future ordinary income for purposes of determining net taxable amounts in future years.

Pattern of Taxable or Deductible Amounts

41. The particular years in which most temporary differences will result in taxable or deductible amounts is determined by reference to the timing of the recovery of the related asset or settlement of the related liability and may require estimates. An example is an estimated liability for product warranties that is settled over a period of several years. The annual amount of tax deductions resulting from settlement of that liability during each of those years has to be estimated. A second example is a temporary difference between the tax basis and the reported amount of inventory for which cost for financial reporting is determined on a last-in, first-out (LIFO) basis. A LIFO inventory difference will result in taxable or deductible amounts when the reported amount of that inventory is recovered. Future recovery of the reported amount of inventory is a future event that is inherently assumed in the statement of financial position for the current year—future purchases or production of inventory are not. The reported amount of LIFO inventory would be recoverable next year if inventory is estimated to "turn over" at least once a year. If so, a temporary difference for LIFO inventory would be considered to be taxable or deductible next year. The temporary difference for the excess of cash surrender value of life insurance over premiums paid is a third example.

42. For some assets or liabilities, temporary differences may accumulate over several years and then eliminate over several years. That pattern is common for depreciable assets. Future temporary differences for existing depreciable assets (in use at the end of the current year) are considered in determining the future years in which existing temporary differences result in *net* taxable or deductible amounts. Consideration of future originating differences may affect:

a. Measurement of deferred taxes when enacted tax rates differ for different years
b. Recognition of a tax benefit for other temporary differences that will result in deductible amounts in future years
c. Classification of deferred tax liabilities or assets in a statement of financial position.

The following example illustrates those effects. The assumptions are as follows:

a. Year 1, the current year, is an enterprise's first year of operations.
b. The enacted tax rates are 40 percent for year 1, 35 percent for year 2, and 30 percent for year 3 and thereafter.
c. For the current year, the enterprise has pretax financial income of $700, taxable income of $500, and taxes currently payable of $200 ($500 at 40 percent).
d. Temporary differences at the end of the current year are as follows:

Installment sale difference (taxable in year 2)	$300
Depreciation difference	100
Estimated expenses (deductible in year 7)	(200)
Net temporary difference	$200

e. Future recovery of the enterprise's depreciable assets (in assumed annual amounts equal to depreciation expense for financial reporting) is estimated to result in the following pattern of temporary differences: $900 of deductible amounts in year 2, and taxable amounts of $600 in year 3 and $400 in year 4.

Accrual of deferred taxes for the existing temporary differences is as follows:

	Current Year	Future Years			
		Year 2	Year 3	Year 4	Year 7
Taxable income	$ 500	$ —	$ —	$ —	$ —
Temporary differences:					
Installment sale	—	300	—	—	—
Depreciation	—	(900)	600	400	—
Estimated expenses	—	—	—	—	(200)
	$ 500	(600)	600	400	(200)
Loss carryback	(500)	500	—	(200)	200
Loss carryforward	—	100	(100)	—	—
	$(500)	$ —	$500	$200	$ —
Enacted tax rate	40%	35%	30%	30%	30%
Deferred tax liability (asset):					
Current	$(200)				
Noncurrent			$150	$ 60	

The enterprise's total tax expense for the current year is $210 (current tax expense of $200 plus deferred tax expense of $10), that is, 30 percent of the enterprise's $700 of pretax income.

Temporary Differences for Foreign Assets and Liabilities

43. After a change in exchange rates, temporary differences attributable to an enterprise's foreign assets and liabilities result from two sources. One source is temporary differences between the foreign currency carrying amount and the foreign currency tax basis of those assets and liabilities. The other source is temporary differences that arise when the reporting currency (not the foreign currency) is the functional currency and certain assets and liabilities are remeasured from the foreign currency into the reporting currency using historical exchange rates. After a change in exchange rates, there will be a temporary difference between (a) the current foreign currency equivalent of the historical cost as measured in the reporting currency and (b) the foreign currency tax basis of those assets and liabilities. Those temporary differences (regardless of source) will result in taxable or deductible amounts on the foreign tax return in future years.

The following example illustrates temporary differences attributable to foreign depreciable assets when the U.S. dollar is the functional currency. The assumptions are as follows:

a. A foreign subsidiary purchases depreciable assets for FC1,000 at the beginning of year 1 when FC1 = $1.
b. The foreign currency unamortized historical cost of those assets is FC900 and FC800 at the end of years 1 and 2, respectively. Remeasured at the historical exchange rate of FC1 = $1, the U.S. dollar unamortized historical cost of those assets is $900 and $800 at the end of years 1 and 2, respectively. Future recovery of the U.S. dollar unamortized historical cost is assumed.
c. Depreciation of those assets is accelerated for foreign tax purposes, and the foreign tax basis of those assets is FC700 and FC400 at the end of years 1 and 2, respectively.
d. The exchange rate is FC1 = $1.20 and FC1 = $1.40 at the end of years 1 and 2, respectively.
e. The foreign income tax rate is 40 percent for all years.
f. There are no other temporary differences.

	End of Year 1		End of Year 2	
	FC	**$**	**FC**	**$**
U.S. dollar unamortized historical cost of assets		900		800
Foreign currency revenues necessary to recover U.S. dollar cost*	750		571	
Foreign tax basis	700		400	
Foreign temporary difference	50		171	
Deferred foreign tax liability	20		68	
U.S. dollar equivalent of the deferred foreign tax liability[†]		24		95

*$900 ÷ $1.20, and $800 ÷ $1.40, respectively

[†]FC20 × $1.20, and FC68 × $1.40, respectively

44. When the reporting currency (not the foreign currency) is the functional currency, remeasurement of an enterprise's deferred foreign tax liability or asset after a change in the exchange rate will result in a transaction gain or loss that is recognized currently in determining net income. When the foreign currency is the functional currency, translation of an enterprise's foreign assets and liabilities will result in a translation adjustment that is not included currently in determining net income. Statement 52 requires disclosure of the aggregate transaction gain or loss included in determining net income but does not specify how to display that transaction gain or loss (or its components) for financial reporting. Accordingly, a transaction gain or loss that results from remeasuring a deferred foreign tax liability or asset may be included in the reported amount of deferred tax benefit or expense if that presentation is considered to be more useful. If reported in that manner, that transaction gain or loss is still included in the aggregate transaction gain or loss for the period to be disclosed as required by Statement 52.

In the example following paragraph 43, one alternative for financial reporting in year 2 is to report $71 of deferred tax expense for the net change ($95 − $24) in the U.S. dollar equivalent of the deferred foreign tax liability. The other alternative for financial reporting is to exclude the transaction loss from the amount reported as deferred tax expense. Computation of the two components of the $71 net change in the U.S. dollar equivalent of the deferred foreign tax liability is as follows:

Deferred tax expense:
   The net change (FC48) in the deferred foreign tax
   liability multiplied by the average exchange rate
   (assumed to be FC1 = $1.30) $62

Transaction loss:
   Beginning balance of the deferred foreign tax liability
   (FC20) multiplied by the change ($.20) in the
   exchange rate during the year (from $1.20 to $1.40) $4
   The net change (FC48) in the deferred foreign tax
   liability multiplied by the difference ($.10)
   between the average and ending exchange rate
   ($1.30 and $1.40, respectively)   5   9

                                               $71

Measurement of a Deferred Tax Liability or Asset

45. A deferred tax liability or asset is computed at the date of the financial statements by applying the provisions in the tax law to measure the deferred tax consequences of temporary differences that will result in net taxable or deductible amounts in each future year. Measurements are based on elections that are expected to be made for tax purposes in future years. Enacted changes in tax laws and rates that are scheduled for a particular future year (or years) are used to measure a liability for the deferred tax consequences of net taxable amounts that will arise in that year (or years). Tax laws and rates for the current year are used if no changes have been enacted for future years. An asset for the deferred tax consequences of net deductible amounts in future years is measured using tax laws and rates for the current or a prior year, that is, the year for which a refund could be realized based on loss carryback provisions in the tax law.

The following example illustrates measurement of the amount of taxes payable in each future year as the result of the deferred tax consequences of temporary differences. At the end of year 1, future recovery of the reported amount of an enterprise's installment receivables will result in taxable amounts totaling $240,000 in years 2-4. Also, a $20,000 liability for estimated expenses has been recognized in the financial statements in year 1, and those expenses will be deductible for tax purposes in year 4 when the liability is expected to be paid. Those temporary differences are estimated to result in net taxable amounts in future years as presented below.

	Year 2	Year 3	Year 4
Taxable amounts	$70,000	$110,000	$60,000
Deductible amount	—	—	(20,000)
Net taxable amounts	$70,000	$110,000	$40,000

This example assumes that the enacted tax rates for years 2-4 are 20 percent for the first $50,000 of taxable income, 30 percent for the next $50,000, and 40 percent for taxable income over $100,000. The liability for deferred tax consequences is measured as follows:

	Year 2	Year 3	Year 4
20 percent tax on first $50,000	$10,000	$10,000	$8,000
30 percent tax on next $50,000	6,000	15,000	—
40 percent tax on over $100,000	—	4,000	—
	$16,000	$29,000	$8,000

A deferred tax liability is recognized for $53,000 (the total of the taxes payable for years 2-4) at the end of year 1. (Paragraph 63 discusses factors and circumstances that would permit a single calculation using an estimated average tax rate.)

---

46. A deferred tax liability is measured using tax rates applicable to capital gains, ordinary income, and so forth, based on the expected type of net taxable amounts in future years. For example, evidence based on all facts and circumstances should determine whether a liability for the tax consequences of the equity in the earnings

of an investee should be measured as a capital gain or as a dividend. Another example is measurement of a liability for differences between the reported amount and tax basis of depreciable assets. The deferred tax consequences are measured at a capital gains rate if it is expected that the assets will be sold and that the temporary differences will result in amounts taxed as a capital gain. The tax rate for ordinary income is used if recovery will be by use of the assets. A consistent policy of selling a particular type of asset midway through its economic life, together with an accounting policy that estimates salvage values and determines depreciation on the same basis, would provide the basis for an estimate that recovery will be by sale.

Comprehensive Alternative Tax Systems

47. A tax law may require that more than one comprehensive method or system be used to determine an enterprise's potential tax liability, with the higher (or possibly, lower) outcome of the calculations determining the actual tax liability. For example, the current U.S. Internal Revenue Code requires a corporation to calculate its potential federal income tax liability using both the "regular tax" system and an "alternative minimum tax" (AMT) system, with the corporation's actual income tax liability for the year being the greater of the two. If alternative systems exist, they should be used to measure an enterprise's deferred tax asset or liability in a manner consistent with the tax law. After giving consideration to any interaction between the two systems, such as the U.S. alternative minimum tax credit, that enterprise's deferred tax asset or liability is recognized based on the results of the two calculations for each future year. Accordingly, under existing U.S. tax law, a U.S. enterprise uses both the regular tax system and the alternative minimum tax system for each future period to determine the deferred tax consequences of its current and past activities.

48. Because of different recognition or measurement provisions, existing temporary differences may be recognized or measured differently under each of the two tax systems, or a temporary difference may exist for only one system. The pattern (timing and amount) in which an existing temporary difference will result in a future taxable or deductible amount may also be different. However, in applying each system, the same assumptions or tax strategies are used to measure or recognize the deferred tax consequences of temporary differences that exist under both systems. For example, if it is assumed that an asset will be sold in two years, that same assumption is used for each system.

The following example illustrates measurement of the amount of deferred taxes payable in each future year for an enterprise when two comprehensive tax systems must be used to determine the enterprise's tax liability. For purposes of this example, it is assumed that the enterprise is a U.S. enterprise and that the tax liability is determined based on the Tax Reform Act of 1986. However, for ease of illustration, a 35 percent tax rate for regular taxable income is assumed for all years. Additional assumptions are as follows:

a. Year 1, the current year, is the enterprise's first year of operations.
b. The enterprise has tax exempt income of $1,300 from municipal bonds (nonpreference) in the current year.
c. U.S. tax law provides that the book income adjustment, a feature of the alternative minimum tax system, will be replaced by an adjustment for "adjusted current earnings" (ACE), and that change is assumed to occur in year 5.
d. Depreciable assets that cost $1,000 were acquired in the middle of the current year and will be depreciated as follows:

	Financial Reporting	Regular Tax	AMT	ACE
Year 1	$ 100	$ 200	$ 150	$
Year 2	200	320	255	
Year 3	200	192	178	
Year 4	200	115	167	
Year 5	200	115	167	125
Year 6	100	58	83	125
	$1,000	$1,000	$1,000	$250

e. Financial income and income taxes currently payable for the current year are as follows:

Regular tax calculation:

Pretax financial income	$2,000
Municipal bond income	(1,300)
Depreciation difference	(100)
Regular taxable income	$ 600
Regular tax (35 percent)	$ 210

AMT calculation:

Regular taxable income	$ 600
Depreciation adjustment	50
Tentative AMT income (tentative AMTI)	650
Book income adjustment	
[50 percent of ($2,000 − $650)][14]	675
AMT income (AMTI)	$1,325
Tentative minimum tax (TMT) (20 percent)	$ 265
Income taxes currently payable	$ 265

The enterprise's current tax liability will be $265, the higher of the regular tax and the AMT calculations. Within certain limitations, the tax law permits the excess of the TMT over the regular tax ($55 in this example) to be carried forward and used as a credit against the regular tax in future years. However, the AMT credit can only be carried forward and cannot be used to reduce a future year's regular tax below the TMT for that future year.

At the end of the current year (year 1), a liability for the deferred tax consequences of depreciation differences is calculated as follows (amounts are rounded to the nearest dollar):

	Carryback to Year 1	Year 2	Year 3	Year 4	Year 5	Year 6
Regular tax calculation:						
Taxable (deductible)						
amounts	$ —	$(120)	$ 8	$85	$85	$42
Loss carryback	(120)	120	—	—	—	—
Regular taxable						
amounts	$(120)	$ —	$ 8	$85	$85	$42
Regular tax (35 percent)	$ (42)	$ —	$ 3	$30	$30	$15

---

[14]The book income adjustment is equal to one-half of the amount by which pretax financial income exceeds tentative AMTI. No book income adjustment is made in years in which tentative AMTI exceeds pretax financial income.

	Carryback to Year 1	Year 2	Year 3	Year 4	Year 5	Year 6
AMT calculation:						
Regular taxable amounts before loss carryback and carryforward	$ —	$(120)	$ 8	$85	$85	$42
AMT depreciation adjustment	—	65	14	(52)	(52)	(25)
Tentative AMTI	—	(55)	22	33	33	17
Book income adjustment	—	28	—	—		
ACE adjustment[15]					32	(32)
AMTI before loss carryback	—	(27)	22	33	65	(15)
Loss carryback	(27)	27	(15)	—	—	15
AMTI	$ (27)	$ —	$ 7	$33	$65	$—
TMT (20 percent)	$ (5)	$ —	$ 1	$ 7	$13	$—
Higher of regular tax or AMT	$ (5)	$ —	$ 3	$30	$30	$15
AMT credit carry-forward applied	—	—	2	23	17	15
Deferred tax liability of $16	$ (5)	$ —	$ 1	$ 7	$13	$—
AMT credit carryforward:						
Beginning of year	$ 55	$ 92	$92	$90	$67	$50
Add (deduct)	37	—	(2)	(23)	(17)	(15)
End of year	$ 92	$ 92	$90	$67	$50	$35

---

[15]The ACE adjustment is equal to 75 percent of the difference between tentative AMTI and ACE. Unlike the book income adjustment, the ACE adjustment, subject to certain limitations, can result in deductible or taxable amounts. For purposes of this example, it is assumed that depreciation is the only reason for differences between pretax financial income, regular taxable income, tentative AMTI, and ACE.

The ACE adjustments for years 5 and 6 are calculated as follows:

	Year 5	Year 6
Regular taxable amounts	$85	$ 42
ACE depreciation adjustment	(10)	(67)
ACE	75	(25)
Tentative AMTI	33	17
ACE less tentative AMTI	$42	$(42)
75 percent of difference	$32	$(32)

Loss carryback to year 1 results in a $42 reduction in regular tax, a $5 reduction in TMT, and a $37 increase ($42 − $5) in AMT credit carryforward so that the carryforward amount becomes $92 at the end of year 1.

The enterprise's total tax expense for the current year will be $281 (current tax expense of $265 plus deferred tax expense of $16).

Operating Loss and Tax Credit Carryforwards and Carrybacks

Recognition of a Tax Benefit for Carrybacks

49. An operating loss (and certain deductible items that are subject to limitations) and some tax credits arising but not utilized in the current year may be carried back for refund of taxes paid in prior years or carried forward to reduce taxes payable in future years. An asset is recognized for the amount of taxes paid in prior years that is refundable by carryback of an operating loss or unused tax credits of the current year.

Recognition of a Tax Benefit for Carryforwards

50. An operating loss or tax credit carryforward is recognized as a reduction of a deferred tax liability for temporary differences that will result in taxable amounts during the operating loss or tax credit[16] carryforward period. Carryforward amounts from prior years are available (subject to limitations in the tax law) to reduce a deferred tax liability for temporary differences that arise in the current year. Provisions in the tax law that limit utilization of an operating loss or tax credits are applied in determining the amount by which a deferred tax liability is reduced. The tax benefit of an operating loss or tax credit carryforward that cannot be recognized as a reduction of a deferred tax liability is not recognized as an asset regardless of the probability that the enterprise will generate taxable financial income in future years.

---

[16]This requirement pertains to all ITC carryforwards regardless of whether the flow-through or deferral method is used to account for ITC.

The following example illustrates recognition of the tax benefit of an operating loss in the loss year and in subsequent carryforward years. The assumptions are as follows:

a. An operating loss occurs in year 5, and the enacted tax rate is 40 percent for all years.
b. The only difference between financial and taxable income results from use of accelerated depreciation for tax purposes. Differences that arise between the reported amount and the tax basis of depreciable assets in years 1-7 will result in taxable amounts before the end of the loss carryforward period from year 5.
c. Financial income, taxable income, and taxes currently payable or refundable are as follows:

	Year 1	Years 2-4	Year 5	Year 6	Year 7
Pretax financial income	$2,000	$5,000	$(8,000)	$ 2,000	$7,000
Depreciation differences	(800)	(2,200)	(600)	(800)	(600)
Loss carryback	—	—	2,800	—	—
Loss carryforward	—	—	—	(5,800)	(4,600)
Taxable income (loss)	$1,200	$2,800	$(5,800)	$(4,600)	$1,800
Taxes payable (refundable)	$ 480	$1,120	$(1,120)	$ —	$ 720

A liability for the deferred tax consequences that will result in taxable amounts in future years is calculated as follows:

	Year 1	Years 2-4	Year 5	Year 6	Year 7
Unreversed differences:					
Beginning amount	$ —	$ 800	$ 3,000	$3,600	$4,400
Additional amount	800	2,200	600	800	600
Total	800	3,000	3,600	4,400	5,000
Tax loss carryforward	—	—	(5,800)	(4,600)	—
Net taxable amount	$800	$3,000	$ —	$ —	$5,000

	Year 1	Years 2-4	Year 5	Year 6	Year 7
Deferred tax liability (40 percent):					
At end of period	$320	$1,200	$ —	$ —	$2,000
At beginning of period	—	320	1,200	—	—
Deferred tax expense (benefit)	$320	$ 880	$(1,200)	$ —	$2,000

Total tax expense for each period is as follows:

	Year 1	Years 2-4	Year 5	Year 6	Year 7
Tax expense:					
Payable	$480	$1,120	$(1,120)	$ —	$ 720
Deferred	320	880	(1,200)	$ —	2,000
Total	$800	$2,000	$(2,320)	$ —	$2,720

In year 5, $2,800 of the loss is carried back to reduce taxable income in years 2-4, and $1,120 of taxes paid for those years is refunded. The $5,800 loss carryforward exceeds the $3,600 of temporary differences that will result in taxable amounts in future years. Therefore, the $1,200 deferred tax liability at the beginning of year 5 is eliminated.

In year 6, a portion of the loss carryforward is used to offset taxable income earned in year 6. The remaining $4,600 of loss carryforward at the end of year 6 exceeds the $4,400 of temporary differences, and there is no deferred tax liability.

In year 7, the loss carryforward is used up, and $720 of taxes are payable on net taxable income of $1,800. No loss carryforward offsets the $5,000 of temporary differences that will result in taxable amounts in future years, and a $2,000 deferred tax liability is recognized.

---

51. An operating loss or tax credit carryforward from a prior year may sometimes reduce taxable income and taxes payable that are attributable to certain revenues or gains that the tax law requires be included in taxable income for the year that cash

is received. For financial reporting, however, there may have been no revenue or gain and a liability is recognized for the cash received. Future sacrifices to settle the liability will result in deductible amounts in future years. Under those circumstances, a tax benefit is not recognized for the reduction in taxable income and taxes payable from utilization of the operating loss or tax credit carryforward. In effect, the operating loss or tax credit carryforward has been replaced by temporary differences that will result in deductible amounts when a liability is settled in future years. The requirements for recognition of a tax benefit for those future tax deductions and for operating loss carryforwards are the same.

The following example illustrates the interaction of loss carryforwards and temporary differences that will result in net deductible amounts in future years. The assumptions are as follows:

a. The financial loss and the loss reported on the tax return for an enterprise's first year of operations are the same.
b. In year 2, a gain of $2,500 from a transaction that is a sale for tax purposes but a sale and leaseback for financial reporting is the only difference between pretax financial income and taxable income.

	Financial Income	Taxable Income
Year 1: Income (loss) from operations	$(4,000)	$(4,000)
Year 2: Income (loss) from operations	$ —	$ —
Taxable gain on sale		2,500
Taxable income before loss carryforward		2,500
Loss carryforward from year 1		(4,000)
Taxable income		$ —

The $4,000 operating loss carryforward at the end of year 1 is reduced to $1,500 at the end of year 2 since $2,500 of it is utilized to reduce taxable income. The $2,500 reduction in the loss carryforward becomes $2,500 of future tax deductions that will occur when lease payments are made. The enterprise has no deferred tax liability to be offset by those future tax deductions, and the future tax deductions cannot be realized by loss carryback because no taxes have been paid. A tax asset is not recognized at the end of year 2 for either the $2,500 of future tax deductions or the remaining $1,500 of operating loss carryforward.

Reporting the Tax Benefit of Operating Loss Carryforwards or Carrybacks

52. Except as noted in paragraphs 23 and 54, the manner of reporting the tax benefit of an operating loss carryforward or carryback is determined by the source of the income or loss in the current year and not by the source of the operating loss carryforward or taxes paid in a prior year. Thus, for example, the tax benefit of an operating loss carryforward reduces income tax expense from continuing operations if realization of the tax benefit results from income from continuing operations. Likewise, that tax benefit is reported as an extraordinary item if realization of the tax benefit results from an extraordinary gain.

Carryforwards for Tax Purposes and for Financial Reporting

53. An operating loss carryforward for tax purposes is an excess of tax deductions over gross income during a year that may be carried forward to reduce taxable income in future years. If there is an operating loss carryforward for tax purposes, an operating loss carryforward for financial reporting is the amount for tax purposes (a) reduced by the amount that offsets temporary differences that will result in net taxable amounts during the carryforward period and (b) increased by the amount of temporary differences that will result in net tax deductions for which a tax benefit has not been recognized in the financial statements. If there is no operating loss carryforward for tax purposes, an operating loss carryforward for financial reporting is the amount of temporary differences that will result in net tax deductions for which a tax benefit has not been recognized in the financial statements.

The following example illustrates an operating loss carryforward for financial reporting when a tax loss carryforward is reduced by temporary differences that will result in taxable amounts during the carryforward period. Year 1 is the first year of operations. The enterprise's only temporary differences are depreciation differences.

	Years 1-3	Year 4
Pretax financial income (loss)	$400	$(600)
Depreciation differences	(80)	(20)
Taxable income (loss)	320	(620)
Loss carryback for tax purposes	(320)	320
Loss carryforward for tax purposes	$ —	$(300)
Loss carryforward for tax purposes		$(300)
Loss applied to offset depreciation differences ($80 + $20)		100
Loss carryforward for financial reporting		$(200)

The following example illustrates an operating loss carryforward for financial reporting when a tax loss carryforward is increased by temporary differences that will result in net tax deductions for which a tax benefit has not been recognized in the financial statements. Year 1 is the first year of operations. The enterprise's only temporary differences are warranty expense differences that will result in deductible amounts in future years.

	Years 1-3	Year 4
Pretax financial income (loss)	$400	$(800)
Warranty expense differences	80	20
Taxable income (loss)	480	(780)
Loss carryback for tax purposes	(480)	480
Loss carryforward for tax purposes	$ —	$(300)
Loss carryforward for tax purposes		$(300)
Warranty expense differences ($80 + $20)		(100)
Loss carryforward for financial reporting		$(400)

The following example illustrates an operating loss carryforward for financial reporting when there is no operating loss carryforward for tax purposes. Year 1 is the first year of operations. At the end of year 3, a $1,000 liability for estimated expenses has been recognized in the financial statements, and those expenses will be deductible for tax purposes in year 4 when the liability is expected to be paid. That temporary difference is the enterprise's only temporary difference.

	Years 1-2	Year 3
Pretax financial income (loss)	$400	$ (800)
Estimated expenses	—	1,000
Taxable income	$400	$ 200
Total temporary differences		$(1,000)
Temporary differences for which a tax benefit is recognized based on recoverability by loss carryback		600
Loss carryforward for financial reporting		$ (400)

Quasi Reorganizations

54. The tax benefit of an operating loss or tax credit carryforward for financial reporting as of the date of a quasi reorganization as defined and contemplated (involving write-offs directly to contributed capital) in ARB No. 43, Chapter 7, "Capital Accounts," is reported as a direct addition to contributed capital if the tax benefits are recognized in subsequent years. Some quasi reorganizations involve only the elimination of a deficit in retained earnings by a concurrent reduction in contributed capital. For that type of reorganization, subsequent recognition of the tax benefit of a prior operating loss or tax credit carryforward for financial reporting is reported as required by paragraph 52 and then reclassified from retained earnings to contributed capital. Regardless of whether the reorganization is labeled as a quasi reorganization, if prior losses were charged directly to contributed capital, the subsequent recognition of a tax benefit for a prior operating loss or tax credit carryforward for financial reporting is reported as a direct addition to contributed capital.

Tax-Planning Strategies

55. The basic principles underlying the requirements of this Statement distinguish between two types of future events. One type of future event results in taxable or deductible amounts (in future years) that are attributable to temporary differences existing at the end of the current year. The deferred tax consequences of temporary differences are recognized in the current year as described in paragraph 14. The other type of future event results in taxable or deductible amounts that are attributable to generating profits or incurring losses that will be reported in financial statements in future years. The future tax consequences of generating profits or incurring losses in future years are not recognized in the current year (paragraph 15).

56. Tax-planning strategies, as that term is used in this Statement, apply exclusively to the first type of future event, that is, recovery of assets and settlement of liabilities in future years. Tax-planning strategies that anticipate the tax consequences of earning income or incurring losses in future years are prohibited for purposes of recognition or measurement of a tax liability or asset under the requirements of this Statement.

57. The deferred tax consequences of temporary differences sometimes will be affected by the particular future years in which those temporary differences result in taxable or deductible amounts. For example, an operating loss carryforward that expires in year 10 will offset taxable amounts arising from collections of an installment sale receivable through year 10, but not in year 11 or later. Tax-planning strategies for purposes of the recognition and measurement requirements of this Statement apply to actions that the management of an enterprise would take, if necessary, to affect the particular years in which temporary differences result in taxable or deductible amounts so as to minimize taxes. Those actions would accelerate or delay the recovery of an asset or the settlement of a liability.

58. Tax-planning strategies cannot disregard assumptions that are critical to determining the reported amount of an asset or liability. For example, assume that there is a temporary difference related to land. Also assume that the current market value of that land is significantly less than its reported amount in the financial statements. The reported amount of that land might not be reduced if the enterprise intends to hold the land for at least five years and if the market value of that land is expected to at least equal its reported amount by the end of five years. If the reported amount of that land is not reduced, a tax-planning strategy related to the temporary difference to sell that land in two years would not meet the criteria of this Statement if the sale of that land after only two years would result in a significant loss.

59. Tax-planning strategies may be relevant for recognizing a tax benefit for an operating loss or tax credit carryforward. A tax benefit for a carryforward is recognized only to the extent that a deferred tax liability is reduced. A carryforward amount does not reduce a deferred tax liability for temporary differences that will result in taxable amounts in years beyond the carryforward period. A tax-planning strategy, however, might be to accelerate taxable amounts to years before the carryforward period expires. Examples that might meet the criteria (paragraph 19) of this Statement include:

a. A sale and leaseback of plant or equipment would accelerate taxable amounts for a difference between the tax basis and the reported amount of the plant or equipment. (The sales price is assumed to equal the remaining balance of the reported amount of the plant or equipment at the sale date and, on that basis, would result in a taxable amount that is equal to the remaining balance of the temporary difference at that date.)

b. A sale of installment sale receivables would accelerate taxable amounts for the gains on the installment sales. (The sales price is assumed to equal the remaining balance of the reported amount of the receivables at the sale date and, on that basis, would result in a taxable amount equal to the remaining balance of the temporary difference at that date.)

60. Tax-planning strategies may be relevant for recognizing a tax benefit for temporary differences that will result in net deductible amounts in future years. A tax benefit is recognized only to the extent that those net deductible amounts offset taxable amounts in other years based on loss carryback and carryforward provisions in the tax law. Carryback of net deductible amounts cannot offset taxable amounts for years prior to the carryback period. A tax-planning strategy, however, might be to accelerate the deductible amounts to an earlier future year. Examples that might meet the criteria (paragraph 19) of this Statement include:

a. An annual payment that is larger than an enterprise's usual annual payment to reduce a long-term pension obligation (recognized as a liability in the financial statements) might accelerate a tax deduction for pension expense to an earlier year than would otherwise have occurred.

b. Disposal of obsolete inventory that is reported at net realizable value in the financial statements would accelerate a tax deduction for the amount by which the tax basis exceeds the net realizable value of the inventory.

c. Sale of loans at their reported amount (that is, net of an allowance for bad debts) might accelerate a tax deduction for the allowance for bad debts.

61. Consideration of tax-planning strategies is not elective. Strategies that meet the two criteria (paragraph 19) for tax-planning strategies are to be reflected in the recognition and measurement of a deferred tax liability or asset.

Aggregate Calculation of a Deferred Tax Liability or Asset

62. Calculation of the deferred tax consequences of temporary differences will require information about the particular future years in which temporary differences will result in taxable or deductible amounts because of:

a. The requirements for offsetting and for recognition of an asset for the deferred tax benefit of net deductible amounts in future years
b. The requirements for recognition of a tax benefit for operating loss and tax credit carryforwards
c. The requirement for measurements based on enacted tax rates or laws for each future year whenever (1) enacted changes in the tax law or rate will be phased in over more than one year or (2) graduated tax rates based on the amount of taxable income in a particular year are a significant factor
d. Classification of deferred tax assets and liabilities as current or noncurrent in a statement of financial position.

For (a)-(c) above, overall estimates for time spans of several years or calculations on an exception basis are permitted if an enterprise can:

a. Identify any significantly large net deductible amounts that do not qualify for recognition of a tax benefit based on the recognition requirements of this Statement
b. Determine whether net taxable amounts are at least sufficient to utilize an operating loss or tax credit carryforward before the carryforward period expires
c. Estimate the net taxable or deductible amounts arising in the years of a phased-in change in tax law or rate. (The tax accrual for all taxable or deductible amounts arising in years after the phase-in is based on the new law or rate.)

63. A deferred tax liability is measured as if net taxable amounts arising from temporary differences will be the only net taxable amounts in future years. If tax rates are graduated according to the amount of taxable income, those graduated tax rates are used to measure the amount of income taxes payable in each future year. For some enterprises, the deferred tax liability may be so large that there will be no significant difference if it is computed by applying the highest tax rate to the aggregate net taxable amount that will arise in all future years. For other enterprises, the net amounts that will become taxable in individual future years may seldom or never exceed the level of income subject to tax at the maximum rate. Those enterprises are permitted

to make aggregate calculations using an estimated average tax rate at which the aggregate net taxable amount would be subject to taxation in various future years provided that care and judgment are applied to identify and deal with unusual situations, for example, an unusually large amount that will become taxable in a single future year.

Regulated Enterprises

64. Paragraph 9 of Statement 71 requires a regulated enterprise that applies Statement 71 to capitalize an incurred cost that would otherwise be charged to expense if the following criteria are met:

a. It is probable that future revenue in an amount at least equal to the capitalized cost will result from inclusion of that cost in allowable costs for rate-making purposes.
b. Based on available evidence, the future revenue will be provided to permit recovery of the previously incurred cost rather than to provide for expected levels of similar future costs.

If the income taxes that result from recording a deferred tax liability in accordance with this Statement meet those criteria, an asset is recognized for those income taxes when the deferred tax liability is recognized. That asset and the deferred tax liability are not offset for general-purpose financial reporting; rather, each is displayed separately.

The following example illustrates recognition of an asset for the probable future revenue to recover future income taxes related to the deferred tax liability for the equity component of the allowance for funds used during construction (AFUDC). The assumptions are as follows:

a. During year 1, the first year of operations, total construction costs for financial reporting and tax purposes are $400,000 (exclusive of AFUDC).
b. The enacted tax rate is 34 percent for all future years.
c. AFUDC (consisting entirely of the equity component) is $26,000. The asset for probable future revenue to recover the related income taxes is calculated as follows:

> 34 percent of ($26,000 + A) = A (where A equals the asset for probable future revenue)
>
> A = $13,394

At the end of year 1, the related accounts are as follows:

Construction in progress	$426,000
Probable future revenue	$ 13,394
Deferred tax liability [34 percent of ($26,000 + $13,394)]	$ 13,394

The following example illustrates adjustment of a deferred tax liability for an enacted change in tax rates. The assumptions are the same as for the example above except that a change in the tax rate from 34 percent to 30 percent is enacted on the first day of year 2. As of the first day of year 2, the related accounts are adjusted so that the balances are as follows:

Construction in progress	$426,000
Probable future revenue	$ 11,143
Deferred tax liability [30 percent of ($26,000 + $11,143)]	$ 11,143

The following example illustrates adjustment of a deferred tax liability for an enacted change in tax rates when that deferred tax liability represents amounts already collected from customers for the future payment of income taxes. In that case, there would be no asset for "probable future revenue." The assumptions are as follows:

a. Amounts at the end of year 1, the current year, are as follows:

Construction in progress for financial reporting	$400,000
Tax basis of construction in progress	$300,000
Deferred tax liability (34 percent of $100,000)	$ 34,000

b. A change in the tax rate from 34 percent to 30 percent is enacted on the first day of year 2. As a result of the reduction in tax rates, it is probable that $4,000 of the $34,000 (previously collected from customers for the future payment of income taxes) will be refunded to customers, together with the tax benefit of that refund, through a future rate reduction. The liability for the future rate reduction to refund a portion of the deferred taxes previously collected from customers is calculated as follows:

$4,000 + 30 percent of L = L (where L equals the probable future reduction in revenue)

L = $5,714

As of the first day of year 2, the related accounts are adjusted so that the balances are as follows:

Construction in progress	$400,000
Probable reduction in future revenue	$ 5,714
Deferred tax liability [30 percent of ($100,000 − $5,714)]	$ 28,286

Leveraged Leases

65. This Statement does not change (a) the pattern of recognition for the after-tax income for leveraged leases as required by Statement 13 or (b) the allocation of the purchase price in a purchase business combination to acquired leveraged leases as required by Interpretation 21. Deferred tax credits attributable to a leveraged lease are reduced for both the tax benefits of (a) other temporary differences that will result in net deductible amounts and (b) operating loss and tax credit carryforwards that offset taxable amounts (paragraph 38) from future recovery of the net investment in the leveraged lease. However, to the extent that the amount of deferred tax credits for a leveraged lease as determined by Statement 13 differs from the amount of the deferred tax liability related to the leveraged lease that would otherwise result from applying the requirements of this Statement, that difference is preserved and is not offset by the deferred tax consequences of other temporary differences or by the tax benefit of operating loss or tax credit carryforwards. Interpretation 21 requires that the tax effect of any difference between the assigned value and the tax basis of a leveraged lease at the date of a business combination not be accounted for as a deferred tax credit. This Statement does not change that requirement. Any tax effects included in unearned and deferred income as required by Interpretation 21 are not offset by the deferred tax consequences of other temporary differences or by the tax benefit of operating loss or tax credit carryforwards. However, deferred tax credits that arise after the date of a business combination are accounted for in the same manner as described above for leveraged leases that were not acquired in a purchase business combination.

The following example illustrates integration of the results of income tax accounting for leveraged leases with the other results of accounting for income taxes as required by this Statement.

a. At the end of year 1, the current year, an enterprise has two temporary differences. One temporary difference is for a $120,000 estimated liability for warranty expense that will result in a tax deduction in year 5 when the liability is expected to be paid. The enterprise has no operating loss or tax credit carryforwards.

b. The other temporary difference is for a leveraged lease that was entered into in a prior year. During year 1, the enacted tax rate for year 2 and thereafter changed from 40 percent to 35 percent. After adjusting for the change in estimated total net income from the lease as a result of the change in tax rates as required by Statement 13, the components of the investment in the leveraged lease at the end of year 1 are as follows:

Net rentals receivable plus residual value less unearned pretax income		$150,000
Reduced by:		
Deferred ITC	$ 9,000	
Deferred tax credits	39,000	48,000
Net investment in leveraged lease for financial reporting		$102,000

c. The tax basis of the investment in the leveraged lease at the end of year 1 is $41,000. The amount of the deferred tax liability for that leveraged lease that would otherwise result from the requirements of this Statement is determined as follows:

Net rentals receivable plus residual value less unearned pretax income	$150,000
Temporary difference for deferred ITC	9,000
	141,000
Tax basis of leveraged lease	41,000
Temporary difference	$100,000
Deferred tax liability (35 percent)	$ 35,000

d. Loss carryback (to year 2) and loss carryforward (to year 20) of the $120,000 tax deduction for warranty expense in year 5 would offset the $100,000 of taxable amounts resulting from future recovery of the net investment in the leveraged lease over the remainder of the lease term.

e. At the end of year 1, a $35,000 deferred tax benefit is recognized for the reduction in deferred tax credits attributable to the leveraged lease from $39,000 (the amount determined as required by Statement 13) to $4,000 (the difference, not available for offset, between the $39,000 of deferred tax credits as determined by Statement 13 and the $35,000 deferred tax liability as determined by this Statement) as a result of the $120,000 temporary difference for accrued warranty expense.

Business Combinations

Nontaxable Business Combinations

66. This Statement requires that a liability or asset be recognized for the deferred tax consequences of differences between the assigned values and the tax bases of the assets and liabilities recognized in a business combination accounted for as a purchase under Opinion 16. A deferred tax liability or asset is not recognized for a difference between the reported amount and the tax basis of goodwill, unallocated "negative" goodwill, and leveraged leases (paragraph 65).

The following example illustrates recognition and measurement of a deferred tax liability in a nontaxable business combination. The assumptions are as follows:

a. The enacted tax rate is 40 percent for all future years.
b. An enterprise is acquired for $20,000, and the enterprise has no leveraged leases.
c. The tax basis of the net assets acquired is $5,000, and the assigned value (other than goodwill) is $12,000. Future recovery of the assets and settlement of the liabilities at their assigned values will result in taxable and deductible amounts that can be offset against each other.

The amounts recorded to account for the purchase transaction would be as follows:

Assigned value of the net assets (other than goodwill) acquired	$12,000
Liability for deferred tax consequences [40 percent of the $7,000 net taxable amounts ($12,000 − $5,000) that will arise upon recovery of the assigned value of those net assets]	(2,800)
Goodwill	10,800
Purchase price of the acquired enterprise	$20,000

Taxable Business Combinations

67. In a taxable business combination, the purchase price is assigned to the assets and liabilities recognized for tax purposes as well as for financial reporting. However, the amounts assigned to particular assets and liabilities may differ for financial reporting and tax purposes. A liability or asset is recognized for the deferred tax consequences of those temporary differences in accordance with the recognition and measurement requirements of this Statement. For example, a portion of the amount of goodwill for financial reporting may be allocated to some other asset for tax purposes, and amortization of that other asset may be deductible for tax purposes. Recognized benefits for those tax deductions should be applied to reduce to zero any goodwill and other noncurrent intangible assets related to the acquisition, after which any additional recognized benefits for those tax deductions should be applied to reduce income tax expense.

The following example illustrates recognition and measurement of the deferred tax consequences of temporary differences in a taxable business combination. The assumptions are as follows:

a. The enacted tax rate is 40 percent for all future years.
b. An enterprise is acquired for $20,000, and the enterprise has no leveraged leases.
c. The net assets (other than goodwill) acquired have a tax basis of $20,000 and an assigned value of $12,000, that is, there are $8,000 of temporary differences that will result in deductible amounts in future years.
d. As of the acquisition date (1) the acquiring enterprise has a liability for the deferred tax consequences of temporary differences that will result in $30,000 of net taxable amounts in future years and (2) the acquired $8,000 of temporary differences ($20,000 − $12,000) will result in deductible amounts in the same future years.

The amounts recorded to account for the purchase transaction are as follows:

Assigned value of the net assets (other than goodwill) acquired	$12,000
Reduction of acquiring enterprise's deferred tax liability (40 percent of $8,000)	3,200
Goodwill	4,800
Purchase price of the acquired enterprise	$20,000

Carryforwards—Purchase Method

68. Accounting for a business combination should reflect any provisions in the tax law that permit or restrict the use of either of the combining enterprises' operating loss or tax credit carryforwards to reduce taxable income or taxes payable attributable to the other enterprise subsequent to the business combination. If permitted by tax law or by tax elections (for example, the election to file a consolidated tax return) that are expected to be adopted by the combined enterprise,[17] an operating loss or tax credit carryforward for financial reporting of either combining enterprise is recognized as a reduction of a deferred tax liability of the other as of the acquisition date, thereby either reducing goodwill or noncurrent assets (except long-term investments in marketable securities) of the acquired enterprise or creating or increasing negative goodwill.

The following example illustrates recognition of a loss carryforward in a nontaxable business combination. The assumptions are as follows:

a. The enacted tax rate is 40 percent for all future years.
b. The purchase price is $20,000. The tax basis of the identified net assets acquired is $5,000, and the assigned value is $12,000, that is, there are $7,000 of temporary differences that will result in taxable amounts in future years. The acquired enterprise also has a $16,000 operating loss carryforward which, under the tax law, may be used by the acquiring enterprise in the consolidated tax return.
c. The acquiring enterprise has a liability for the deferred tax consequences of temporary differences that will result in $30,000 of net taxable amounts in future years.
d. All temporary differences of the acquired and acquiring enterprises will result in taxable amounts before the end of the acquired enterprise's loss carryforward period.

The $16,000 operating loss carryforward will offset:

a. The $7,000 of net taxable amounts that will result from future recovery of the assigned value of the acquired net assets
b. Another $9,000 of net taxable amounts attributable to the acquiring enterprise's deferred tax liability.

---

[17] If separate tax returns are expected to be filed, the accounting set forth in this paragraph and in paragraph 69 ordinarily would not apply. However, if a strategy to file consolidated tax returns for later years meets the criteria in paragraph 19, the effect of the strategy would be recognized in applying the accounting set forth in this paragraph and that in paragraph 69.

The amounts recorded to account for the purchase transaction are as follows:

Assigned value of the identified net assets acquired	$12,000
Reduction of acquiring enterprise's deferred tax liability (40 percent of $9,000)	3,600
Goodwill	4,400
Purchase price of the acquired enterprise	$20,000

Carryforwards—Pooling-of-Interests Method

69. The separate financial statements of combining enterprises for prior periods are restated on a combined basis when a business combination is accounted for by the pooling-of-interests method. For restatement of periods prior to the combination date, a combining enterprise's operating loss carryforward does not offset the other enterprise's taxable income because consolidated tax returns cannot be filed for those periods. If consolidated tax returns are expected to be filed (refer to footnote 17) subsequent to the combination date, however, one combining enterprise's operating loss carryforward in a prior period reduces the other enterprise's deferred tax liability in the loss and subsequent periods to the extent that (a) the temporary differences will result in taxable amounts subsequent to the combination date and (b) the loss carryforward can reduce those taxable amounts based on provisions of the tax law. That tax benefit is recognized as part of the adjustment to restate financial statements on a combined basis for prior periods. The same requirements apply to tax credit carryforwards and to temporary differences that will result in net deductible amounts in future years.

70. A taxable business combination may sometimes be accounted for by the pooling-of-interests method. The increase in the tax basis of the net assets acquired results in temporary differences. A deferred tax liability or asset is recognized and measured for those temporary differences the same as for other temporary differences. As of the combination date, recognizable tax benefits attributable to the increase in tax basis are allocated to contributed capital. Tax benefits attributable to the increase in tax basis that become recognizable after the combination date are reported as a reduction of income tax expense.

Subsequent Recognition of Carryforward Benefits

71. If not recognized at the acquisition date, the tax benefits of an acquired enterprise's operating loss or tax credit carryforward for financial reporting are recog-

nized in financial statements for the subsequent year(s) when those carryforward amounts reduce either a deferred tax liability or taxes payable on the tax return (except as noted in paragraph 51). The recognized benefit is:

a. First applied to reduce to zero any goodwill and other noncurrent intangible assets related to the acquisition
b. Next recognized as a reduction of income tax expense.

Additional amounts of operating loss or tax credit carryforward for financial reporting may arise after the acquisition date and before recognition of the tax benefit of amounts existing at the acquisition date. Tax benefits are recognized in later years as follows:

a. The tax benefit of amounts existing at the acquisition date is first applied to reduce goodwill and other noncurrent intangible assets to zero. Any additional tax benefit reduces income tax expense.
b. The tax benefit of amounts arising after the acquisition date is recognized as a reduction of income tax expense.

Whether a tax benefit recognized in later years is attributable to an amount (for example, an operating loss carryforward) existing at or arising after the acquisition date is determined for financial reporting by provisions in the tax law that identify the sequence in which those amounts are utilized for tax purposes. If not determinable by provisions in the tax law, a tax benefit recognized for financial reporting is prorated between a reduction of (a) goodwill and other noncurrent intangible assets and (b) income tax expense.

The following example illustrates recognition of tax benefits subsequent to a business combination. The assumptions are as follows:

a. A nontaxable business combination occurs on the first day of year 1, and the purchase transaction is accounted for as follows:

	Assigned Values	Tax Basis
Net assets acquired	$5,000	$6,000
Goodwill*	1,500	
Purchase price	$6,500	

*There are no other noncurrent intangible assets.

b. The $1,000 excess of tax basis over the assigned value of identified net assets acquired does not meet the criteria for recognition of a deferred tax asset.

c. The only difference between pretax financial and taxable income (amortization of goodwill is disregarded for this example) for years 1-2 is a $1,000 loss for tax purposes from disposal of the acquired identified net assets at amounts equal to their $5,000 assigned value on the acquisition date.

	Financial Income	Taxable Income
Year 1: Loss from operations	$(3,000)	$(3,000)
Disposal of acquired identified net assets		(1,000)
Loss carryforward (no taxes paid in prior years)		$(4,000)
Year 2: Income from operations	$ 2,500	$ 2,500
Loss carryforward		(4,000)
Taxable income		$ —

Assuming a 40 percent tax rate, the consolidated statement of earnings would include the following amounts attributable to the acquired enterprise:

	Year 1	Year 2
Pretax income (loss)	$(3,000)	$2,500
Income tax expense	—	250
Net income (loss)	$(3,000)	$2,250

The $4,000 loss carryforward at the end of year 1 has two components. One component (25 percent) is $1,000 attributable to the excess of tax basis over the assigned value of the identified net assets acquired at the date of the business combination. The other component (75 percent) is $3,000 attributable to losses occurring after the business combination. Provisions in the tax law do not distinguish between those two components, and the component that is utilized first for tax purposes is indeterminable. In year 2, therefore, the $1,000 tax benefit ($2,500 at 40 percent) is prorated so that goodwill is reduced $250 (25 percent of $1,000) and tax expense is reduced $750 (75 percent of $1,000). Because $250 of the tax benefit reduces goodwill, $250 of tax expense is reported in year 2.

Financial and taxable income for year 3 are as follows:

	Financial Income	Taxable Income
Income from operations	$1,500	$1,500
Loss carryforward		(1,500)
Taxable income		$ —

The consolidated statement of earnings would be as follows:

Pretax income	$1,500
Income tax expense	150
Net income	$1,350

The $600 benefit of the operating loss carryforward ($1,500 at 40 percent) is prorated so that goodwill is reduced $150 (25 percent of $600) and tax expense is reduced $450 (75 percent of $600). Because $150 of the tax benefit reduces goodwill, $150 of tax expense is reported in year 3.

The Tax Basis of the Stock of an Acquired Enterprise

72. An acquiring enterprise's tax basis of the stock of an acquired enterprise may exceed the tax basis of the net assets of the acquired enterprise. That excess will result in a deductible amount in a future year if the acquired enterprise is sold or liquidated. Prior to sale or liquidation, that potential tax benefit does not meet the recognition requirements of this Statement whenever a deferred tax liability is not recognized for that acquired enterprise's Opinion 23 differences or deposits in statutory reserve funds by U.S. steamship enterprises. (In those circumstances, that potential tax benefit is included in the computation of the unrecognized deferred tax liability that is disclosed for those items.) Otherwise, the recognition requirements would be met to the extent that the deductible amount reduces a deferred tax liability for temporary differences that do not result in taxable amounts until the acquired enterprise is sold or liquidated. For example, it would reduce the acquiring enterprise's deferred tax liability for the temporary difference related to a gain recognized after the acquisition date as a result of the acquired enterprise's sale of stock (a minority interest) to a third party at a price per share that exceeds the per share carrying amount (prior to the sale) of the acquiring enterprise's investment in the acquired enterprise.

Classification in a Statement of Financial Position

73. A deferred tax liability or asset is classified in two categories—the current amount and the noncurrent amount—in a classified statement of financial position.

The following example illustrates classification in a statement of financial position at the end of year 1 if temporary differences will result in a net deductible amount in year 2. The enterprise has no taxable income for year 1, the first year of operations. Therefore, the net deductible amount does not provide a realizable tax benefit in year 2. Instead, it provides a recognizable tax benefit based on loss carryforward to reduce a noncurrent deferred tax liability. The tax rate is 40 percent for all years.

	Temporary Differences	Future Years Year 2	Year 3
Liability for warranties	$(500)	$(500)	$ —
Installment receivables	800	—	800
	$ 300	$(500)	$800
Classification:			
Current deferred tax asset	$ —		
Noncurrent deferred tax liability			
($300 at 40 percent)	120		
	$ 120		

The following example illustrates classification in a statement of financial position at the end of year 1 if temporary differences will result in a net deductible amount in year 3 and a tax benefit for those differences is recognizable based on loss carryback to offset a net taxable amount for other temporary differences in year 2. The enterprise has no taxable income for year 1, the first year of operations. The tax rate is 40 percent for all years.

	Temporary Differences	Future Years Year 2	Year 3
Liability for warranties	$(500)	$ —	$(500)
Installment receivables	800	800	—
	$ 300	$800	$(500)

Classification:
Current deferred tax liability
($800 at 40 percent) .... $ 320
Noncurrent deferred tax asset
($500 at 40 percent) .... (200)
$ 120

The following example illustrates classification in a statement of financial position at the end of year 1 if one type of an enterprise's temporary differences is attributable to an asset (for example, a liquor inventory) that is classified as current based on a three-year operating cycle and the types of temporary differences addressed in paragraph 42 are not present. The enterprise has no taxable income for year 1, the first year of operations. The tax rate is 40 percent for all years.

	Temporary Differences	Future Years Year 2	Year 3	Year 4
Liability for warranties	$ (500)	$(500)	$ —	$ —
Installment receivables	800	—	800	—
Liquor inventory	700	—	—	700
	$1,000	$(500)	$800	$700

Classification:
Current deferred tax liability
($700 at 40 percent) .... $ 280
Noncurrent deferred tax liability
($300 at 40 percent) 120
$ 400

Allocation of Income Tax Expense between Pretax Income from Continuing Operations and Other Items

74. The amount of income tax expense or benefit allocated to continuing operations (in addition to adjustments for changes in tax status and tax laws or rates) is the tax consequences of the pretax income or loss from continuing operations exclusive of any other category of items (for example, extraordinary items) that occurred during the year. The amount allocated to a category of items other than continuing operations is the incremental effect on income taxes that results from that category of items. When allocated to two or more categories of items other than continuing operations, the sum of the incremental tax effects of each category of items sometimes may not equal the incremental tax effect of all categories of items because of, for example, a **statutory limitation** on the utilization of tax credits. In those circumstances, the procedures to allocate the incremental tax effects to categories of items other than continuing operations are as follows:

a. Determine the incremental tax benefit of the total net loss for all net loss categories

b. Apportion that incremental tax benefit ratably to each net loss category

c. Apportion ratably to each net gain category the difference between (1) the incremental tax effect of all categories other than continuing operations and (2) the incremental tax benefit of the total net loss for all net loss categories.

The procedure for allocating income taxes to each item within each category of items is similar to the procedure described above.

The following example illustrates allocation of income tax expense if there is only one item other than income from continuing operations. The assumptions are as follows:

a. The enterprise's pretax financial income and taxable income are the same.

b. The enterprise's loss from continuing operations is $500, and a loss carryback would give rise to a $100 refund of taxes paid on the $250 of taxable income during the carryback years.

c. The enterprise also has an extraordinary gain of $900.

d. The tax rate is 40 percent, and income taxes currently payable are $160 on $400 of taxable income.

Income tax expense is allocated between the pretax loss from operations and the extraordinary gain as follows:

Total income tax expense	$160
Tax consequences associated with the loss from operations	(100)
Incremental tax consequences attributable to the extraordinary gain	$260

The following example illustrates allocation of income tax expense if there is more than one category of items other than income from continuing operations. The assumptions are as follows:

a. The tax rate is 34 percent.
b. The enterprise has $300 of tax credits available subject to a limitation of 90 percent of taxes payable. There are no temporary differences.
c. Pretax financial income for the year comprises:

Income from continuing operations	$600
Discontinued operations	(100)
Extraordinary items	500
Cumulative effect of an accounting change	(200)
Total pretax financial income	$800

d. Income tax expense attributable to continuing operations and total income tax expense are determined below.

	Continuing Operations	Total
Pretax financial income	$600	$800
Tax at 34 percent	$204	$272
Tax credits (90 percent limitation)	184	245
Tax expense	$ 20	$ 27

The incremental effect on income taxes that results from all categories of items other than continuing operations is $7 ($27 − $20). For the year, the enterprise has two net loss categories: discontinued operations (loss category #1) and the cumulative effect of an accounting change (loss category #2).

The incremental tax effect of (a) the sum of all net loss categories and (b) each net loss category is determined below.

	Sum of Loss Categories	Loss Category #1	Loss Category #2
Taxable income	$ 800	$800	$ 800
Loss category	(300)	(100)	(200)
Taxable income without the loss category	$1,100	$900	$1,000
Tax at 34 percent	$ 374	$306	$ 340
Tax credits (90 percent limitation)	300	275	300
Tax without the loss category	$ 74	$ 31	$ 40
Total tax expense for the year	27	27	27
Incremental tax effect	$ 47	$ 4	$ 13

A $47 tax benefit is allocated to the sum of the net loss categories. That tax benefit is apportioned ratably to each net loss category based on the incremental tax benefit of each net loss category.

	Each Loss Category		Apportioned Amounts
	Amount	Percent	
Loss category #1	$ 4	24	$11
Loss category #2	13	76	36
	$17	100%	$47

The $54 of tax expense allocated to the single net-gain category is the difference between the $7 of tax expense for all items other than income from continuing operations and the $47 of tax benefit for both net loss categories.

Total tax expense is allocated as follows:

	Pretax Income	**Tax Expense**
Income from continuing operations	$600	$20
Discontinued operations	(100)	(11)
Extraordinary items	500	54
Change in accounting	(200)	(36)
	$800	$27

The example above assumes that each category of items comprises a single item. If any category has more than one item, a procedure similar to that illustrated in this example would be used to allocate the total tax effect of that category to its components.

---

75. Stockholders' equity is charged or credited for the income tax effects of (a) adjustments of the opening balance of retained earnings for a change in accounting principles or correction of an error, (b) gains and losses recognized in comprehensive income but excluded from net income, (c) an increase or decrease in contributed capital (for example, expenditures reported as a reduction of the proceeds from issuing capital stock), and (d) expenses for employee stock options recognized differently for financial reporting and tax purposes (refer to paragraph 17 of APB Opinion No. 25, *Accounting for Stock Issued to Employees*). An income tax benefit for the tax deductibility of dividends paid to stockholders is recognized as a reduction of income tax expense and is not credited directly to stockholders' equity.

The following example illustrates the allocation of income taxes directly to stockholders' equity.

a. A foreign subsidiary has earnings of FC600 for year 2. Its net assets (and unremitted earnings) are FC1,000 and FC1,600 at the end of years 1 and 2, respectively.
b. The foreign currency is the functional currency. For year 2, translated amounts are as follows:

	Foreign Currency	Exchange Rate	Dollars
Unremitted earnings, beginning of year	1,000	FC1 = $1.20	1,200
Earnings for the year	600	FC1 = $1.10	660
Unremitted earnings, end of year	1,600	FC1 = $1.00	1,600

c. A $260 translation adjustment ($1,200 + $660 − $1,600) is charged to the cumulative translation adjustment account in stockholders' equity for year 2.
d. The U.S. parent expects that all of the foreign subsidiary's unremitted earnings will be remitted in the foreseeable future, and under Opinion 23, a deferred U.S. tax liability is recognized for those unremitted earnings.
e. The U.S. parent accrues the deferred tax liability at a 20 percent tax rate (that is, net of foreign tax credits, foreign tax credit carryforwards, and so forth). An analysis of the net investment in the foreign subsidiary and the related deferred tax liability for year 2 is as follows:

	Net Investment	Deferred Tax Liability
Balances, beginning of year	$1,200	$240
Earnings and related taxes	660	132
Translation adjustment and related taxes	(260)	(52)
Balances, end of year	$1,600	$320

f. For year 2, $132 of deferred taxes are charged against earnings, and $52 of deferred taxes are credited directly to the cumulative translation adjustment account in stockholders' equity.

Appendix E

GLOSSARY

206. This appendix contains definitions of certain terms or phrases used in this Statement.

Assumptions inherent in a statement of financial position prepared in accordance with generally accepted accounting principles

An assumption inherent in an enterprise's statement of financial position prepared in accordance with generally accepted accounting principles is that the reported amounts of assets and liabilities will be recovered and settled, respectively.

Current tax expense or benefit

The amount of income taxes paid or payable (or refundable) for a year as determined by applying the provisions of the tax law to the taxable income or excess of deductions over revenues for that year.

Deferred tax asset

The amount of deferred tax consequences attributable to temporary differences that will result in net tax deductions in future years that could be recovered (based on loss carryback provisions in the tax law) by refund of taxes paid in the current or a prior year. Recognition and measurement of a deferred tax asset does not anticipate the tax consequences of financial income that might be earned in future years.

Deferred tax consequences

The future effects on income taxes as measured by the provisions of enacted tax laws resulting from temporary differences at the end of the current year without regard to the effects of events not yet recognized or inherently assumed in the financial statements.

Deferred tax expense or benefit

The net change during the year in an enterprise's deferred tax liability or asset.

Deferred tax liability

The amount of deferred tax consequences attributable to temporary differences that will result in net taxable amounts in future years. The liability is the amount of taxes that would be payable on those net taxable amounts in future years based on the provisions of the tax law. Recognition and measurement of a deferred tax liability does not anticipate the tax consequences of losses or expenses that might be incurred in future years.

Event

A happening of consequence to an enterprise. The term encompasses both transactions and other events affecting an enterprise.

Gains and losses included in comprehensive income but excluded from net income

Under present practice, this category includes certain changes in market values of investments in marketable equity securities classified as noncurrent assets, certain changes in market values of investments in industries having specialized accounting practices for marketable securities, adjustments from recognizing certain additional pension liabilities, and foreign currency translation adjustments. Future changes to generally accepted accounting principles may change what is included in this category.

Income taxes

Domestic and foreign federal (national), state, and local (including franchise) taxes based on income.

Income taxes currently payable (refundable)

Refer to **Current tax expense or benefit.**

Income tax expense (benefit)

The sum of current tax expense (benefit) and deferred tax expense (benefit).

Nonpublic enterprise

An enterprise other than one (a) whose debt or equity securities are traded in a public market, including those traded on a stock exchange or in the over-the-counter market (including securities quoted only locally or regionally), or (b) whose financial statements are filed with a regulatory agency in preparation for the sale of any class of securities.

Operating loss carryback or carryforward for tax purposes

An excess of tax deductions over gross income during a year that may be carried back or forward to reduce taxable income in other years. Different tax jurisdictions have different rules about whether an operating loss may be carried back or forward and the length of the carryback or carryforward period. The discussion and examples in this Statement assume that the tax law requires that an operating loss first be carried back for up to 3 years and then be carried forward for up to 15 years. As used in this Statement, this term is intended to also include carrybacks or carryforwards for individual deductions that exceed statutory limitations.

Operating loss carryforward for financial reporting

The amount of an operating loss carryforward for tax purposes (a) reduced by the amount that offsets temporary differences that will result in net taxable amounts during the carryforward period and (b) increased by the amount of temporary differences that will result in net tax deductions for which a tax benefit has not been recognized in the financial statements.

Public enterprise

An enterprise (a) whose debt or equity securities are traded in a public market, including those traded on a stock exchange or in the over-the-counter market (including securities quoted only locally or regionally), or (b) whose financial statements are filed with a regulatory agency in preparation for the sale of any class of securities.

Statutory limitations

Provisions in the tax law that limit the amount by which certain deductions or tax credits are applied to reduce taxable income or income taxes payable.

Taxable income

The excess of taxable revenues over tax deductible expenses and exemptions for the year as defined by the governmental taxing authority.

Tax consequences

The effects on income taxes—current or deferred—of an event.

Tax credit carryback or carryforward for tax purposes

Tax credits that exceed statutory limitations that may be carried back or forward to reduce taxes payable in other years. Different tax jurisdictions have different rules regarding whether a tax credit may be carried back or forward and the length of the carryback or carryforward period.

Tax credit carryforward for financial reporting

The amount of a tax credit carryforward for tax purposes reduced by the amount recognized as a reduction of a deferred tax liability for temporary differences that will result in net taxable amounts during the tax credit carryforward period.

Tax-planning strategy

A transaction or series of transactions that meet certain criteria (paragraph 19) and that, if implemented, would affect the particular future years in which temporary differences result in taxable or deductible amounts. A tax-planning strategy (including elections for tax purposes that are required or permitted by the tax law) either reduces the amount of a deferred tax liability or increases the amount of a deferred tax asset that would otherwise be recognized.

Temporary difference

A difference between the tax basis of an asset or liability and its reported amount in the financial statements that will result in taxable or deductible amounts in future years when the reported amount of the asset or liability is recovered or settled, respectively. Paragraph 10 cites nine examples of temporary differences. Some temporary differences cannot be identified with a particular asset or liability for financial reporting (paragraph 12), but those temporary differences (a) result from events that have been recognized in the financial statements and (b) will result in taxable or deductible amounts in future years based on provisions in the tax law. Some events recognized in financial statements do not have tax consequences. Certain revenues are exempt from taxation and certain expenses are not deductible. Events that do not have tax consequences do not give rise to temporary differences.